New Maricón Cinema

New Maricón Cinema

OUTING LATIN AMERICAN FILM

Vinodh Venkatesh

University of Texas Press *Austin*

Printed in the United States of America
First edition, 2016

Requests for permission to reproduce material from this work should be sent to:

Permissions
University of Texas Press
P.O. Box 7819
Austin, TX 78713-7819
http://utpress.utexas.edu/index.php/rp-form

♾ The paper used in this book meets the minimum requirements of ANSI/NISO Z39.48-1992 (R1997) (Permanence of Paper).

LIBRARY OF CONGRESS CATALOGING-IN-PUBLICATION DATA

Venkatesh, Vinodh, author.
New Maricón cinema : outing Latin American film / Vinodh Venkatesh. — First edition.
pages cm
Includes bibliographical references and index.
ISBN 978-1-4773-1014-4 (cloth : alk. paper)
ISBN 978-1-4773-1015-1 (pbk. : alk. paper)
ISBN 978-1-4773-1016-8 (library e-book)
ISBN 978-1-4773-1017-5 (non-library e-book)
1. Homosexuality in motion pictures. 2. Gay men in motion pictures. 3. Motion pictures—Latin America. 4. Masculinity in popular culture—Latin America. I. Title.
PN1995.9.H55V46 2016
791.43′653—dc23
2015035741
doi:10.7560/310144

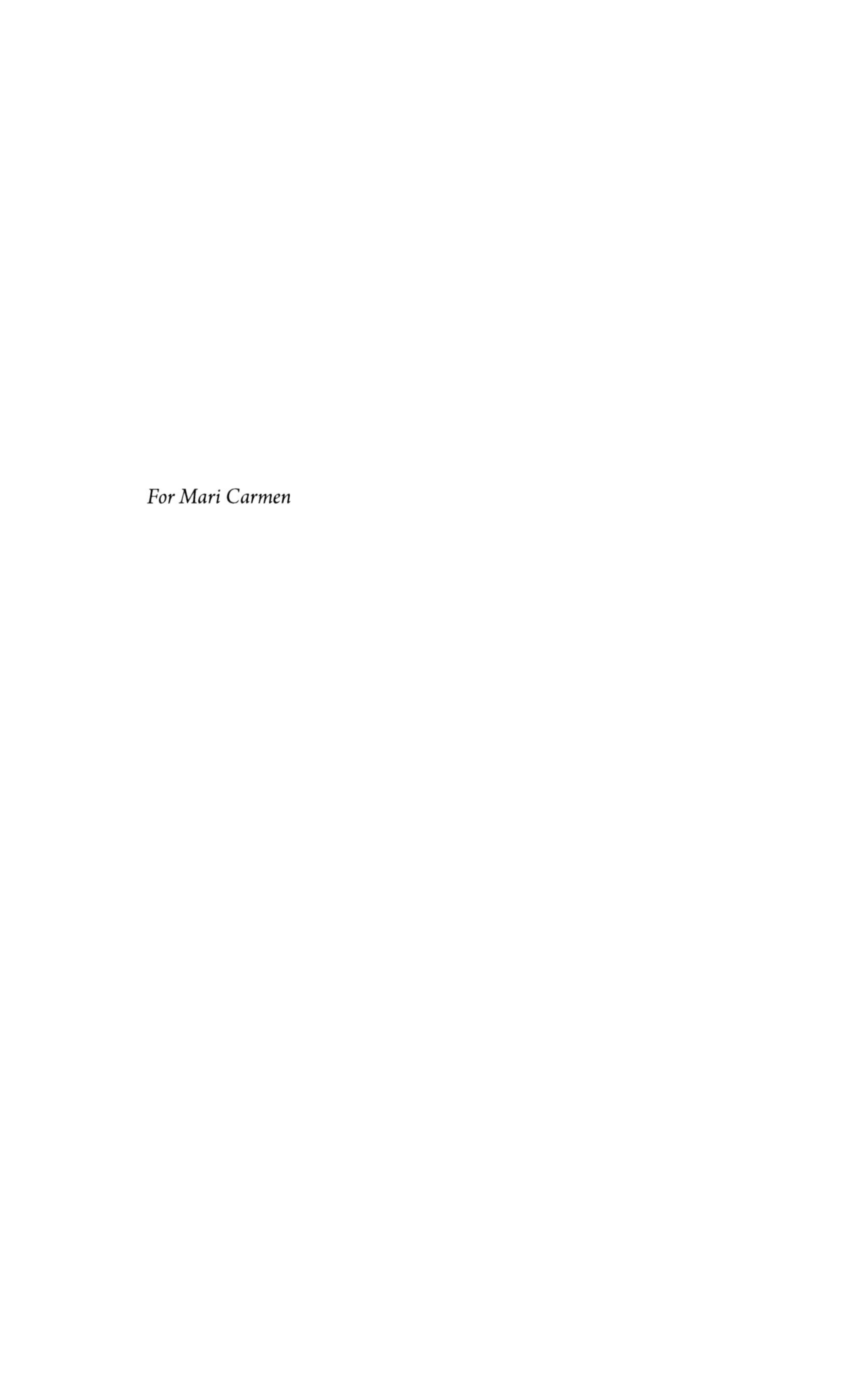

For Mari Carmen

Contents

Preface

THE PRINCIPAL IDEAS FOR THIS BOOK WERE QUICKLY jotted down on a now-lost notepad on Tuesday, September 25, 2012, when, minutes before the screening of Javier Fuentes-León's *Contracorriente*—the second movie in the first Hispanic Film Series at Virginia Tech—my co-organizer, Mari Carmen Caña Jiménez, and I realized that we would need introductory remarks to prepare our audience of mostly undergraduate students for the film. Jogging my memory back to the secondary area of my doctoral qualifying exams, I loosely traced some points of contact and difference between the film and others belonging to the corpus that David William Foster so expertly outlines and analyzes in *Queer Issues in Contemporary Latin American Cinema*.

That chicken scratch then made its way to a more structured outline, which then became the basis for an article on the film. At the outset, my main purpose was to explore the affective strategies behind Fuentes-León's film and to somehow understand the faces, gestures, and tears that flowed from the audience on that fateful Tuesday. Working with theories of phenomenological film analysis, I realized that this facet of the moving image had yet to be explored in the research on nonnormative gender and sex in Latin American cinema. Reading through the literature on a global queer cinema, I also realized that the films produced in the region had largely gone unnoticed by wider scholarship. What I initially intended as an article to work through the affective dimensions of *Contracorriente* soon took on a more ambitious scope; I pushed the boundaries of the journal's word limit by briefly outlining at the end my thoughts concerning a Maricón and a New Maricón cinema and how we might understand the proliferation of films such as XXY, *El último verano de la Boyita*, and *Plan B*. More important, and here I am indebted to Foster's work, I was interested in undertaking an archaeology of the subject on the Latin American screen.

While several of the films mentioned above can be and have been included in a global queer cinema (an identification I very much agree with), the principal focus of this book is to find context and to understand difference through specific sociocultural formations and milieus; after all, we continue to see films made in Latin America that have very little to do with a Queer ethos. Here I am indebted to the critical angles forwarded by José Quiroga and Ben Sifuentes-Jáuregui. As such, this book does not aim to disassociate recent Latin American films from a global discussion but, rather, to home in on and better contextualize a particular genealogy of cinema.

New Maricón Cinema: Outing Latin American Film is an initial step in this process. It provides broad outlines of how we may view these two distinct swaths of films that deal with sex-gender difference through an analysis of style, technique, and thematics. It is by no means an exhaustive study; in fact, readers will quickly note that several key films are mentioned but not fully examined. This project is also very much one that comes in medias res of current cinematic production where both genres are being made and commented on simultaneously. This, I maintain, is a key concept in *New Maricón Cinema*: we cannot view these films as distinct or diachronic phenomena; we must view them as coexisting genres that simply speak to the complexity of talking about a "Latin American" cinema. The films I have focused on, then, are arguably representative of the dichotomy that I maintain is at the core of understanding both the region's filmic production and its location in broader critical circles.

Acknowledgments

THIS BOOK IS THE PRODUCT OF AN ON-AND-OFF AFFAIR I have maintained with cinema studies over the years. First and foremost, I must recognize Rich Cante at the University of North Carolina—Chapel Hill for taking me under his wing and encouraging my interest in film during the early years of the Interdisciplinary Program in Cinema. Lectures by Rich and José Manuel Polo de Bernabé on Spanish film first introduced me, someone trained in literary studies, to the language and intricacies of film analysis.

My interest in cinema has matured at Virginia Tech. I am deeply indebted to Mari Carmen Caña Jiménez for being the driving force behind the annual Hispanic Film Series that we co-organize. The series began in 2012, and I am grateful to the students, faculty, and members of the community who have made it a point to come to the Fralin Auditorium every Tuesday in September to see what new surprise the series has concocted. The series is made possible through a grant by Pragda and the government of Spain. I am thankful for having been given the opportunity to teach cinema courses at the undergraduate and graduate levels and appreciate my students for being ready and creative interlocutors.

Several scholars and colleagues either gave me feedback or provided advance copies of their research as I was writing this book. I am indebted to Ignacio Sánchez Prado and Deborah Shaw for their acute readings and for making suggestions that have very much improved the final manuscript. David William Foster initially green-lighted the article on *Contracorriente*, which got the ball rolling. Gustavo Subero and Carolyn Pedwell graciously shared their work with me, as did Dierdra Reber. I also thank Debra Castillo for discussing her anthology, coedited with Andrés Lema-Hincapié, *Despite All Adversaries: Spanish-American Queer Cinema*. A special thanks goes out to Paco Brignole, Esteban A. Brignole, and Pablo Martín for helping with the identification of locations in Buenos Aires. Some of the films discussed here were almost impossible to source; I must thank Diego Araujo for giving me special screening privileges to watch *Feriado* in Blacksburg.

I also want to give thanks to my family for their unwavering support, kindness, and love. To my siblings, Sabitha and Vishnu, you enrich my life in so many ways. My cinematic consciousness is and always will be shaped by conversations with Vish, who somehow manages to curate one of the most eclectic libraries of film I know. To my in-laws, *cuñados, cuñadas,* Yaya, Blanca, and Julia, thank you for your spirit and joy. Most important, I am thankful for having two wonderful parents, Narayini and Venkatesh, who have been role models and sounding boards for everything. They first encouraged my love for cinema through countless viewings of films starring Rajinikanth, Kamal Haasan, Sathyaraj, and Arvind Swamy, among others. They also put up with Vishnu and my reenactments of the many fight scenes in these films. For this and more, I love you.

I have also counted on the support of many both here in Blacksburg and in Chapel Hill who provided moments of laughter and friendship. I want to give particular thanks to Oswaldo Estrada, Juan Carlos González Espitia, Cristina Carrasco, and Birgitte Bonning for their unwavering conversation, support, and friendship. Thank you all.

I am also grateful to my colleagues in Foreign Languages and Literatures at Virginia Tech, who create a great work environment. Much gratitude is also given to the members of the Women's and Gender Studies Program at Virginia Tech for allowing me to present my work and for important and invaluable theoretical feedback on the early drafts as I moved from the article to the completed book manuscript.

My biggest thanks go to Mari Carmen, who has been my pillar in every sense of the word. This book would not have been possible without her love, kindness, joy, and curiosity. You make me a better person every day, and make everything in this life worthwhile. I love you.

I want to thank my editor, Jim Burr, at the University of Texas Press for all that he has done to get this project on firm footing. He stood behind this manuscript from the very beginning and has been indispensable throughout the process. Many thanks as well to Sarah McGavick, Nancy Bryan, and Robert Kimzey at the University of Texas Press, in addition to my copyeditor, Kathy Bork.

An early version of chapter 4 originally appeared in the *Journal of Popular Romance Studies*; I am grateful to the editors for giving me permission to use a version of that chapter here.

New Maricón Cinema

Introduction

TWO ROOMMATES SHARE A FEW BEERS ALONE IN AN apartment after a night out. Javier (Ariel Levy) drowns his sorrows after another misstep with his love interest, Sofía (Lucy Cominetti), while Walter (Nicolás Martínez), a bartender, tries to cheer him up with a game of *esconderlo en la boca*, a game he once played with other inmates to quell the physical aloneness of incarceration. When Javier rejects his increasingly persistent advances, Walter chides him: "Lower your pants. Don't be a faggot" [Bájate los pantalones. No seas maricón].[1]

I watched this comical scene play out in Nicolás López' *Qué pena tu vida* [Fuck my life] (2010), a Chilean film rightfully massacred by critics that did, however, go on to great commercial success, spawning two sequels that were widely distributed in Latin America and abroad.[2] The film lacks narrative and aesthetic depth and is, if anything, a calque of countless similar features produced in Hollywood that cater to a particular socioeconomic and ideological class of viewer.[3] What struck me, though, in this scene was the almost casual insertion of same-sex relations. Not unlike what happens in earlier Latin American films, homosexual actions are ostracized and become the target of the narrative and the audience's mockery in *Qué pena tu vida*. Javier's desperate flight from Walter is meant to make us laugh, but then we may ask, at what? Perhaps it is the surprise of seeing the otherwise burly barkeep propose oral sex. Perhaps it is the flight from the sticky tentacles of homoeroticism that merits nervous laughter. Or perhaps it is the very incongruence of Walter telling Javier to not be a maricón, when his advances would suggest that *he* is the homosexual and not the comically pathetic protagonist.

In the film's first sequel, *Qué pena tu boda* [Fuck my wedding] (2011), Javier serendipitously runs into Walter in an American-style diner in one of the many shopping malls that dot the landscape of Sanhattan and its peripheries.[4] Walter,

0.1. The homosocial quickly becomes homoerotic, Qué pena tu vida. *Copyright Sin perdón de Dios.*

now a waiter at the diner, effusively affirms that he "has changed a lot" [ha cambiado muchísimo]; he is no longer a man of "the night and darkness" [la noche y la oscuridad] but is in a committed relationship with Jesús.

López again uses comedic prompts and situational cues to introduce the issue of same-sex relations. The implication is that Walter is now an evangelical Christian, though we soon find out that Jesús is his boyfriend: to Javier's (and our) surprise, Walter seemingly is now *out*. Javier expresses his disbelief by declaring: "You've finally accepted . . . that you're gay" [Por fin te asumiste . . . que eres *gay*]. Walter reacts angrily and argues, with the support of Jesús, that he is more virile and macho after having taken a male lover. Jesús explains that *he* is gay but that Walter is *not* and that "there are people with closed minds in this country" [hay gente de mente cerrada en este país].

What jars a viewer familiar with gay liberation and LGBTQ movements and discourses, in both Anglo and Pan-Hispanic contexts, is Walter's seeming evasiveness about his identity. His leaving the "oscuridad" would suggest coming out, akin to politico-ethical movement into and from the closet. His reaction, however, at being *called* gay is almost counterintuitive: if not gay, then what is he? What is this outside space or condition if not analogous to the Anglo embracing of sexuality as identity? More baffling perhaps is Jesús' pronouncement of being gay as a natural complement to Walter's macho virility. Yet perhaps most thought provoking is Javier's (and the audience's) need to find labels for sexuality, assuming that genital interactions and libidinal charges somehow define or lend categories to the human condition.

All in all, this short sequence reminds us of Ben Sifuentes-Jáuregui's assertion that the "refusal to claim and assume a 'gay' or 'lesbian' identity should not be simply read as a marker of indifference . . . but rather this refusal may be phrased more strongly as a postcolonial affront to the imposition of identities and categories that do not (cor)respond to the experiences and needs of a particular cultural context" (*The Avowal of Difference*, 1–2).

This early scene, short and with no real narratological importance, underlines the tacit discussion of Latin American sexual difference and plurality usually observed and analyzed in art house and more aesthetically challenging features. Sex and gender are not only discussed but also problematized through matrices that refuse to accept simple overlays.

My surprise, then, in watching this interplay mature in the *Qué pena* series was an epiphany. I asked myself when homosexual desire—and, more accurately, the muddling of practice and identity—had entered the realm of pop cinema acceptability? At which point in the genealogical tracing of Latin American films did same-sex relations gain the complicity of auteurs and audiences to the extent that they could be casually discussed over French fries, burgers, and milkshakes?[5]

The physical setting of Jesús and Walter's explanation (or complication, depending on one's perspective) in *Qué pena tu boda* is thought provoking in that López situates the complexity of desire in a spatial agglomeration of Anglo influences (fast food, mass production, consumerism, etc.), including those that run in the identitarian vein of sex and gender.

This contact zone is a microcosm of a greater cultural contact zone wherein local expressions and subjectivities interact with and often challenge hegemonizing and/or imported notions, such as gay identity, that Sifuentes-Jáuregui

0.2. Moving beyond identity and the closet, Qué pena tu boda. *Copyright Sobras Producciones.*

challenges in *The Avowal of Difference*. My interest in these films thus follows his exploration of how sex and gender are discussed, which inevitably brings up José Quiroga's contention that "in spite of what U.S. gay and lesbian leaders seem to imply in most of their discursive statements, to 'be' gay or lesbian is not a universal given. The word 'gay,' accepted as an Anglicism in many other parts of the world, is consumed, cannibalized, digested, and reworked" (*Tropics*, 201).[6] Does performing fellatio make Walter a homosexual? Is Javier's rejection of this service thus emasculating?

While López' feature is trifling and superficial (and here I am being kind compared to some of the critiques the film has received in both Chile and abroad), it does call our attention to the problematics—if we may call it that—of Latin American sexuality studies. Though some may write off *Qué pena tu boda* as symptomatic of the neoliberal turn—an aesthetic deficiency that poses no sustained inquiry into broader thematics—I am more inclined to view Javier's and Walter's (and Jesús', for that matter) grappling with divergent erotics as a symptom of a wider shift in Latin American cinema, wherein the representations and existence of sexual difference are no longer confined to "the dark side of compulsory heterosexuality in the bleak terrain created by hypocrisy" (Foster, *Queer Issues*, 109).

In a discussion of homosexuality in Latin American cinema, Jorge Ruffinelli rightfully notes that "at the end of the 20th century and at the start of the 21st, almost as a personification of this change of epoch, Latin American cinema multiplied its references, characters, and themes of sexual difference" [al terminar el siglo XX e iniciarse el XXI, como uno de los avatares del traspaso a otra época, el cine latinoamericano multiplicó sus referencias, personajes, temas de la diferencia sexual] ("Dime tu sexo," 67).[7] In previous decades same-sex and queer desires and bodies were scarce in the cinema produced in Latin America—note Foster's distinction between queer issues and an actual global queer cinema in *Queer Issues in Contemporary Latin American Cinema*, or the lack of any films from Latin America in studies of New Queer Cinema. This lack is palpable even in the Latin American section of Thomas Waugh's comprehensive study of global queer cinema, *The Fruit Machine*, where he discusses, instead, films that deal with homosexuality though never through a complex and nuanced perspective of difference. Viewers of Latin American film, however, will note (and Ruffinelli does so as well) that there have been representations of sex/gender difference on the Latin American screen, though often solely through the prism of the stereotype. Even in these cases, the sightings of these bodies have been few and far between. This perhaps explains the only very recent appearance of Debra Castillo and Andrés Lema-Hincapié's *Despite All Adversities: Spanish-American Queer Cinema* (2015).

Given these critical and cultural gaps, recent films in the oeuvre of Lucía

Puenzo, Javier Fuentes-León, Marco Berger, and Gustavo Loza, to name a few, and their resounding cultural and critical substrates may be seen as anomalous, almost foreign to the Latin American cinematic ecosystem.[8] Testaments to this boom, if we can call it that, are the many awards won at festivals both in Latin America and abroad, including the Teddy Award at the Berlinale for films by Berger, Julián Hernández, and Santiago Otheguy, and the 2014 Goya for Best Latin American Film for Miguel Ferrari's *Azul y no tan rosa* [My straight son] (2012). Audiences and critics are now privy to an ever-burgeoning corpus of films, characters, tropes, and bodies that decenter any sanctity previously afforded to the normative.[9] If anything, López' *Qué pena* series is only a popular manifestation of an in-place and already evolving lineage of films that, at the turn of the century, placed sexual and gender difference at the core of its aesthetic and ethical treatise.[10]

I want to draw us back to the issue of circulation, of both the films and the emotions and affects that they generate. Writing on homosexuality in Hollywood, Vito Russo underlines that "gay visibility has never really been an issue in the movies. Gays have always been visible. It's *how* they have been visible that has remained offensive" (*The Celluloid Closet*, 325). Russo's emphasis on how homosexuality is portrayed is a strategic entry into the corpus of films that Foster and others have studied, that is, films prior to the boom that Ruffinelli highlights.

In Latin America, there are two considerations to keep in mind when we classify this *how*. First, like early Hollywood, which presented homosexuals as suggestions or sideshows, Latin American cinema followed a similar trajectory. From the *fichera* films that Sergio de la Mora examines to Arturo Ripstein's *El lugar sin límites* [Hell without limits] (1978) and Jaime Humberto Hermosillo's body of work, Latin American depictions of difference have originated in the planting of stereotypes that were countertypical to the iconic male, a body that was coded for discourses of normativity, modernity, and nation-building.[11] This, however, did evolve to an extent in later films such as *No se lo digas a nadie* [Don't tell anyone] (1998) or the ever-popular *Fresa y chocolate* [Strawberry and chocolate] (1993), where the principal homosexual character is rounder, so to speak, and nuanced in his representation of same-sex desire.

In terms of how gayness was represented in early Latin American films, it is imperative to note that these films and their aesthetics and techniques always maintained sexual and gender difference at a polite distance from the viewer. Herein we observe the second consideration: whether through voyeuristic angles or placements that disoriented (in empathic and framing terms) the audience from the subject, these maricón films—as same-sex desiring bodies are catalogued as such, evoked no doubt by Walter's warning to the uncooperative Javier—maintained a scopic regime wherein the visual, both as narrative and image, encouraged a detachment from the territory and bodies of difference. By "scopic" I mean an emphasis on visuality or seeing, where the image and apparatus create specific lines of sight that guide how we look at the moving image. Scopic films tend to use the visual as a path into the narrative; that is, the nonvisual characteristics of the image and how it is framed lie in the background to the mise-en-scène. We are encouraged to look at and to read the image as we would a printed page, guided by the lens to focus on particular actions and speech over any other consideration that the moving image may engender.

What do I mean by a Maricón cinema? It is, after all, a term, like many others from Latin America, such as "*loca*," that resists facile translation.[12] The term is stylistic, as it accounts for how homosexuality is portrayed in film, yet it is also an ethical designator. "Maricón" here is not used as a *description* of sexual practice on the screen (though in many instances it is used to label effeminate men), but rather as a *designator* of power, schematically separating the enunciator from the object. In other words, the term emphasizes difference as a position of subalternity. It is a politico-ethical indicator of difference, and even queer subjects may use it to establish themselves over normative counterparts. A simple example can be seen in how the title character in *Antes que anochezca* [Before night falls] chides a straight man uninterested in his advances as a "maricón."

I use the term, then, not as one of identity but as an affirmation of power based on nonnormativity. Maricón cinema is culturally significant in that it, for the first time, allows for the discussion and appearance of plural sexualities and genders, yet establishes and maintains an ethico-aesthetic boundary between the nonnormative and the viewer. As such, viewing these films is an almost impersonal process: the audience is shackled into a passive role, allowed entry into the narrative through the lens and the scope behind it but never permitted to align or orient itself with difference.

What changed in the turn-of-the-century boom in Latin America, populated by such works as XXY, *Contracorriente* [Undertow], *Plan B*, *Feriado* [Holiday], *El niño pez* [The fish child], *El cuarto de Leo* [Leo's room], and *Pelo malo* [Bad hair], among many others? These films, after all, may be included in a globalized discussion of queer cinema, a position that many have and will follow. Rosalind Galt, for example, argues that features not unlike those I use above as examples may be included in a "nonwestern queer sensibility" or "mode of queer worldliness" ("Default Cinema," 62). Working through ideas posed by David Eng, Teresa de Lauretis, and Hok-Sze Leung, Galt suggests that a global queer mode can be defined by a cinematic challenge to narrativity, in terms of both content and form. In other words, a queer cinema moves away from the purely visual (in its multiple facets) toward a cinema of sensation.

While Galt's teasing out of a queer mode is fruitful in bringing films by recent directors included in Ruffinelli's boom to the forefront of a transnational exchange of ideas, it does not explain the boom of other gay-themed films (that are decidedly not queer, such as *Azul y no tan rosa*) in Latin America, nor does it adequately contextualize these films within a regional or national genealogy or trajectory, a move that Sifuentes-Jáuregui sees as imperative in "moving away from imposition toward something that resembles more a dialogue" (*The Avowal of Difference*, 11). These films, after all, have not emerged from nor are they viewed in a (specific sociocultural) vacuum.

Keeping with this gesture, in this book I further several theories that together underline how we can not only explain, but also trace the emergence of a boom in films that radically shift the terrain of Latin American sexualities. In this archaeological exercise, I propose the core tenets of a distinct genre of film and its specific structure of feeling.[13] First, there is a conscious and progressive break with the scopic regime through a series of films that I trace in the interstitial space between what I term Maricón cinema and New Maricón cinema. In such films the viewer encounters a self-conscious moviemaking that explicitly addresses and then breaks with the ethical distance established in earlier films between the image and the viewer. Then, replacing the stylistics and epistemics of Maricón film, we see in New Maricón features a preference for an affective schema, that is, a milieu of techniques, images, sounds, textures, and surfaces that engender a polysensorial, haptic interaction with the moving image. We see what Dierdra Reber calls "the tendency toward emotional narrative" [la tendencia hacia una narrativa emocional] where "the images and sounds of the sensitive body occupy the space traditionally reserved for dialogue and background information that orients the viewer" [las imágenes y sonidos del cuerpo sensible ocupan el espacio tradicional reservado para el diálogo y la información de trasfondo que orienta el espectador] ("La afectividad," 93). In this relationship, the viewer is no longer privy to the ethical comfort or distance afforded by the scopic but is instead oriented to and actively encouraged to feel (through the five senses) and partake in the (sometimes lateral) exploration of difference. The viewing experience, unlike that of the Maricón genre, is intimate, defined more by varying affective flows and perceptions than by any sustained thesis. These New Maricón films transmit and relay affective intensities that align the viewer with sex and gender difference, producing a contagion that is individual and communal. In essence, New Maricón cinema asks us to explicitly "interrogate the ways in which affect shapes narrative itself" (Reber, "Headless Capitalism," 67). We no longer simply *see* difference, we are invited to actively touch, caress, and participate in the sensuality of libidinal urges, body identifications, and often-multidirectional orientations that engender new structures of feeling vis-à-vis bodies and desires.[14] New Maricón cinema is rooted in a viewership experience that is embodied; we feel these films, narratives, and characters in ways that surpass any traditional "reading" of the moving image. Instead, the relationship between the image and spectator is an intimate one that, at times, is underlined in prelinguistic sensations and somatic reactions.

The viewer comes into contact with and emerges with the film and difference, partaking transiently in the decentering of the normal. Intrinsic to this affective outing—which is both ethical and libidinal—is a spatial movement or outing toward textures and planes that, across the corpus of movies studied here, establish inter- and intrapersonal relationships between the moving image and the body of the viewer. It is not so much viewers "losing" themselves in the films as it is their moving past the skin of the film and the subject and occupying the ephemeral, protolinguistic sensations that an affective cinema provokes. Such a shift is both dynamic, in the sense of viewership, and constitutive, in that the impressions left and provoked by the cinema dematerialize the viewer only to rematerialize in a new configuration that, if only for a moment, viscerally occupies the position of difference. Such a shift is both personal, in that reconfigured structures of feeling are imposed over antiquated regimes, and plural, in that individual reorientations further a change of directionality and feeling in the group. New Maricón cinema is a personal experience that then engenders a communal experience. The affective economies, to borrow Sara Ahmed's terminology, created in and around these films then shape the very surfaces of the bodies (again, both individual and communal), markets, and production channels for Latin American cinema.

But such a process cannot be conceived of as taking place in a vacuum. Cinema, after all, is, as Steven Shaviro understands it, a "productive" medium, as it does "not *represent* social processes, so much as [it] participate[s] actively in these processes, and help[s] constitute them" (*Post Cinematic Affect*, 2). We are, as we know, living in an age during which Latin America is moving toward according same-sex couples the same civil rights afforded by the institution of marriage. Countries such as Argentina, Brazil, Colombia, Mexico, and Uruguay have established legislative frameworks that uphold the civil rights of their citizens irrespective of sexual and gender identification. Such moves have coincided with the boom in New Maricón cinema, part and parcel, I argue, of the symbolic and real contouring engendered by the affective economies that come into existence as a result of their production, emission, and reception. In this "productive" ecosystem, the aesthetic and technical qualities of a more haptic (and less scopic) cinema put in motion affective and, as a result, emotional circulations that cyclically and countercyclically shape communal surfaces, attitudes, and orientations.

Working with and through theories of affect in Hispanic cinema is a relatively new phenomenon. Laura Podalsky's *The Politics of Affect and Emotion in*

Contemporary Latin American Cinema is a useful point of departure.[15] Podalsky undertakes a careful examination of the intersection of affective transmissions and circulations in relation to politics in contemporary Latin American films, which many have dubbed as "apolitical and sensationalistic" (*The Politics of Affect*, 7); she offers "an alternate account . . . that inventories [Latin American cinema's] emergent sensorial dynamics and interrogates their significance to the political field" (7). What I find most useful in Podalsky's framework is a renegotiation of cinema as a "productive" medium. She argues that the visual is not always the only plane of expression and reception but that affect and its study merit a central place. She "situates affective work . . . in relation to a moment of epistemological crisis wherein the visual record is rendered insufficient to the task of registering past experiences and their influence on the present, as well as widespread uncertainties about the future" (*The Politics of Affect*, 19). Podalsky's analysis thus decenters the critical lens from the visual to the affective.

Though I follow this cue in *New Maricón Cinema*, I argue that the recent genre is self-reflexively conscious of the contours and intensities of affect vis-à-vis the cinema. That is, the scholar does not necessarily shed new light on critically exhausted films (or, equally, on films dismissed as political), but, rather, the cinema itself—as a compendium of images, sounds, textures, and so on—establishes and perpetuates an affective regime over the scopic. Such a shift moves us, then, into the practice of phenomenological film analysis as a strategy to unearth the polysemantic and cognitive interactions that lay bare the fallacies of the strictly scopic.

Michele Aaron summarizes the disjunction between an affective and scopic cinema and its accompanying critical tools when she notes that "a major problem with the classical model [of spectatorship and its critique] and its assertion of a hypothetical all-inclusive-spectator-subject, was its failure to address difference: how differences between spectators meant that there were different ways of experiencing film" (*Spectatorship*, 24).[16] Note the action of "experiencing" the image versus simply seeing the narrative unfold in a visual manner. Aaron positions herself in opposition to—or at least opens up an alternative to—objective critique, which takes as its fulcrum an asubjective position vis-à-vis the image. She follows in the footsteps of Vivian Sobchack's well-known development of Maurice Merleau-Ponty's phenomenological approach to cinema. In *Carnal Thoughts*, Sobchack furthers that "instead of seeking essences . . . a phenomenological approach seeks . . . the meaning of experience as it is embodied and lived in context—meaning and value emerging in the *synthesis* of the experience's *subjective* and *objective* aspects" (2, emphasis in the original). I find her interpellation of both the visual and the affective-sensorial useful here in going beyond analyzing cinema as imaged narrative. She argues that vision "informs our other senses in a dynamic structure that is not necessarily or always sensually hierarchical," and that "it is no longer metaphorical to say that we 'touch' a film or that we are 'touched' by it" (*Carnal Thoughts*, 80). For Sobchack and others following her (including me), the cinema is an experience, and its critique must take into account the dynamics of the visual *and* the sensorial, which is often relegated to the realm of the unaddressed in classical models.[17]

Sobchack's work has undoubtedly left its impression on subsequent perspectives that can be housed under the "affective turn" label in cinema studies. In Jennifer Barker's *The Tactile Eye*, for example, Sobchack's reading and positioning of Merleau-Ponty's musings inform the conceptualization of polysomatic and bodily contacts with the image. Building from both Sobchack and Sara Ahmed, Barker furthers that the individual is deconstructed into multiple organs, namely, the skin, musculature, and viscera, in the experience of cinema. She notes that this approach to film criticism "focuses neither solely on the formal or narrative features of the film itself, nor solely on the spectator's psychic identification with characters or cognitive interpretation of the film. Instead, phenomenological film analysis approaches the film and the viewer as acting together, correlationally, along an axis that would itself constitute the object of study" (*The Tactile Eye*, 18). Barker's perspective expands on a tactile relationship between the viewer and the image wherein the former "emerges" in the "contact between [the] body and the film's body" (19). For Barker, then, the cinema is an experience, and here we must underline the polysensoriality of the term, and not a purely visual or disaffected process.

The notion of tactility and, as well as in, the image and the emergence of a viewer is a critical characteristic of New Maricón films, where rich textures and sounds that move the viewer-subject into direct contact with the image are favored. We thus "emerge" from these films through our intimate and tactile contact with the erotics of the image, and not necessarily through a particular alignment with any one subject or character. Barker's reference to tactility and the moving image is no doubt built on Laura Marks's seminal work on haptic visuality, or the idea that one may touch a film through the eyes. Marks conceives of the film as a skin "that acknowledges the effect of a work's circulation among different audiences, all of which mark it with their presence"; film and video are to be "thought of as impressionable and conductive, like skin" (*The Skin*, xi). Here Barker, working with Ahmed, flips Marks's notion of the film as skin that can be imprinted by arguing that the film also marks the viewer by coming into contact with different layers of the body through specific affective modes. The relationship between the skin of the film and that of the viewer, then, is multilateral, in a constant touch-and-release that inevitably dynamizes another touch. For Barker, the skin of the film implies the existence and subsequent shaping of many epithelial layers in the viewer.

But what if we were to suggest that this relationship is not purely idiosyncratic to the experience of viewership? Since the delineations of the skin, musculature, and viscera are undoubtedly affirmations of subjectivity, perhaps Sobchack's signaling that it is "important not to confuse [the] process of subjectivity with individualism or particularity: subjectivity is a socially mediated process" (*Carnal Thoughts*, 6) merits further attention. Barker's notions of tactility and experience, while foundational to any affective critique, must be viewed contextually, that is, outside the layers that are loci of the parameters of the individuated subject. Herein we evidence the links I want to draw throughout *New Maricón Cinema* between an affective cinema, an affective critique, and the circulation of specific intensities that generate an economy of "productive" cinema vis-à-vis nonnormative sexualities. I rely on Sobchack's teasing out of the value of the phenomenological approach in going beyond facile subjective criticism. As she points out,

> although in historical and cultural existence particular experiences may be lived idiosyncratically, they are also, and in most cases, lived both generally and conventionally . . . a phenomenological description and interpretation, on the one hand, attempts to *adequate* the objective and subjective aspects of a given embodied experience and, on the other, also seeks to acknowledge their historical and cultural *asymmetries* . . . attending not only to the *content* and *form* of embodied experience but also to its *context*. (*Carnal Thoughts*, 5, emphasis in the original)

The notion of context is key and clarifying in unearthing the tensions and mechanisms behind Ruffinelli's observation, as what a phenomenological approach to New Maricón cinema provides is the tools for specifying and situating the aesthetics of a cinema that provokes affective circulations (in opposition to a purely disaffected regime). A phenomenological approach thus moves us to view subjectivity as a collective experience, taking up Martine Beugnet's suspicion that "there are crucial advantages in following the inkling one might have that a group of works, highly diverse yet bound by a related historical background and parallel aesthetic quests, have a comparable effect on us and raise similar questions of film form" (*Cinema*, 13). Such an inkling and, of course, such a group of works, inform the theorization of a new genre versus the old, one that, I argue, is reflective and productive of important social and legislative changes in Latin America in the twenty-first century.

This assertion is built largely around the possibility of a circulation of particular affective intensities and their accompanying emotions as a result of the experiencing (not solely *seeing*) of certain films (that favor a haptic visuality) that I map out in the theorization of a New Maricón cinema.[18] What I am posing, then, is that these films exhibit both a break from a praxis of disaffection in what I term "Maricón" film (part I) and a symbiotic politico-ethical compromise in the viewer (New Maricón cinema), leaving thus an impression in the community. In this affective economy, both at the local and the international levels (one cannot forget the different spheres of reception and distribution that contemporary Latin American cinema is marketed under), "emotions *do things*, and they align individuals with communities—or bodily space with social space—through the very intensity of their attachments" (Ahmed, "Affective Economies," 119). Ahmed discusses the potentials of emotion in suturing the individual to the community or, within the framework built around hapticity and phenomenology, the individual's skin is both always in contact with the community and, to an extent, constituted partly by communal cells. In biopolitical terms, then, the individual is never severed from the group but carries and is able to reformulate its collective DNA through contact with and emergence through the cinema, that is, through the transmission of affect and the generation of emotive sensations.[19] In this circulation, the impressions, that is, the real and symbolic signs of presence and contact left on (individual and communal) bodies, allow not only for a tracking of "how emotions circulate between bodies [but] how they 'stick' as well as move" (Ahmed, *The Cultural Politics*, 4).

Of note in the development of an affective economy, though, is the interchange that occurs between affect and emotion. In *The Cultural Politics of Emotion*, Ahmed underlines that emotions are tied primarily to bodily sensations, sensations, as I will argue throughout this book, that are intrinsic to the experience of this new aesthetic. Sensations lead to emotions, which then lead to (the potential for) action, or, as Margaret Wetherell notes: "a burst of affect involves not just major somatic changes in the body; it also has cognitive, motivational-behavioural and subjective-experiential components" (*Affect and Emotion*, 29). Ahmed furthers that "emotions are relational: they involve (re)action or relations of 'towardness' or 'awayness' in relation to such objects" (*The Cultural Politics*, 8), which are really orientations of the viewer toward the image. New Maricón cinema is defined by a relation of towardness, of the audience and individual and as a group in alignment with the body and desire of difference. It is in this relation of towardness that these films generate, through positive affective intensities, the emotional charge of empathy.

In Maricón films, for example, I (as a viewer) would *see* La Manuela, but the image would not engender a specific relationality or setting in motion of cognitive networks that oriented me toward her difference. In New Maricón films, however, specific techniques and audiovisual qualities (and not solely visual and narrative modes) move me toward difference through the generation of empathic feelings. This orientation is, as Barker reminds us, not

> simply a matter of the viewer sharing a character's physical location by means of point-of-view shots and first-person narration, for example. It is instead a kind of empathy between our own body and the film's body that happens even in a non-narrative film or one without actors, for example. Our bodies orient and dispose themselves toward the body of the film itself, because we and the film make sense of space by moving through it muscularly in similar ways and with similar attitudes. (*The Tactile Eye*, 75)

Of importance here is going beneath the surface of the skin, as in films like Javier Fuentes-León's *Contracorriente* and Lucía Puenzo's XXY. Our bodies move—muscularly and viscerally, though first engaged in "impressions" through dermal contact with the image—in rhythm with nonnormative (or queer) desires. Our feeling of empathy as emotion, which is then circulated and stuck to particular bodies, tropes, or images, is bent first on the transmission of affect that, microreferentially, moves through the viewer's multiple dermal and subcutaneous layers, engaging at a cellular level with our experience of the moving image.[20] Inherent in such a model is the notion that empathy is not defined as a simple emotion but as a complex mechanism and body in its own right. It is, as Carolyn Pedwell argues, "at once imaginative and sensorial, conscious and unwilled, personal and impersonal, cultural and biological, human and non-human" and "required to negotiate the affective intricacies of a transnational world in flux" (*Affective Relations*, 5).

There is, however, an econo-cultural facet to this transnational matrix that Ahmed hints at and that I consider primal in erecting an economy around the ecosystem of certain films: language.[21] Though I mention Brazil as being a key example of the juridico-ethical changes at the turn of the century, I am excluding its cinematic production from this study for two principal reasons, neither of which, however, necessarily removes Brazil or its accompanying cultural critique from the equation of Latin Americanness. First, for an affective economy to take shape, a distributive economy of democratic and popular consumption must be in place wherein market entry is not unnecessarily curtailed or controlled; that is, affective signs (the cinema, in this case) must be in free circulation and issues of language, as an example, not be inhibiting. On a trip to Costa Rica, for example, I was able to catch on Canal Golden the second half of Teresa Suárez' *Así del precipicio* [Like this from the edge] (2006) in my hotel room in San Pedro. The film—a clear example of the neoliberal turn and its accompanying structure of feeling (which I will touch on in the concluding chapter)—includes several plot lines centered on gender and sex difference amid the broader (flimsy) plot of how a group of young, rich female urban professionals manages the excesses of money, drugs, and rock and roll. One of the main characters harbors lesbian urges, while the cast of secondary characters includes a transsexual and an openly gay male. The film, then, may be seen as a portrait of neoliberal modernity (a term that I will not discuss in great detail), which includes bodies and attitudes in line with the civic changes in Latin America in relation to difference. The fact, though, that I was able to watch the film on a private Mexican channel, such as Golden, in Costa Rica is a small example of how cinematic artifacts and signs enter into circulation through the intersecting quality of language. With no need for subtitles or for dubbing technology, the film, its narrative lines, and its politics are open to circulation and movement, entering into contact with and molding a (Spanish-speaking) transnational public that may otherwise not be privy to such features—that same transnational public that is conveniently entered into the equation of a "Latin American" cinema. In the economy I am planting here around New Maricón film, there is a principal role attributed to language that democratizes (if one can say that still, and only to an extent) the distribution and access to films that foster an intimate connection with difference.[22]

New Maricón films provoke, participate in, and perpetuate a circulation—an affective economy—of positive emotions, namely, empathy, around gender and sex difference in Latin America. Caught up in viewing, writing about, and diffusing these films, we produce, as Lauren Berlant argues, "a calculus of public affect and emotion, usually without knowing it, and in a way that suggests massive analytic disrepair in our conceptualization of political attachments" ("Unfeeling Kerry," 2). We are thus not only on the cusp of an aesthetic renovation and uncharted circulations of nonnormative representations in the cinema, but also at a key moment (that is perhaps more global and less sutured to the Latin American condition) at which the politico-ethical discourses around same-sex and polysex and polygender desires and bodies are undergoing a recalibration, moving closer to the center of public acceptability.

New Maricón Cinema, then, is a tracing of *how* difference and nonnormativity have been represented and then evolved on the Latin American screen. Working through theories of affect and circulations, I employ phenomenological tools to examine the technical and sensory qualities of films and genres to explain how the recent boom appeals to the viewer through a shift to the sensory, which, in turn, makes possible the generation of an empathic economy around difference.[23]

There can be no discussion of a New without establishing a referent: as such, Part I tackles the construction of what I call a Maricón cinema in Latin America, a genre that negates productive drives in the moving image. I provide a definition of the genre, specify a loose collection of aesthetic and ethical qualities, and posit its relation to wider Latin American cinematic production. Chapter 1 builds on Sergio de la Mora's excellent mapping of the *fichera* genre and the presence of *jotos* (fags) in several films. I not only study the characterizational traits of these subjects of difference but also analyze, in technical terms, *how* they are represented and framed. I examine the scopic techniques employed in the *fichera* genre, focusing particularly on Carlos Vasallo's *El día del compadre* [The pal's day] (1983) to underline the relationality of the viewer to desire, wherein the former is placed strategically at a removed, almost omniscient, point of intake of the diegetic circulations of bodies and desires. The distance of the viewer, I argue, informs how Arturo Ripstein's La Manuela is framed in the iconic *El lugar sin límites*. I examine not only the technical montage of homosocial desires and bodies but also how the camera frames La Manuela in relation to Pancho's advances. Ripstein's film houses the possibilities of a productive image but falls into the trappings of the scopic, which, in turn, focuses instead on the narratological. The murder of La Manuela at the conclusion of the film is thus viewed as an example of homophobic violence and the matrices of restraint that keep the homosocial purely social, yet can equally be faulted for posing no strategic—whether didactic or affective—way out.

Chapter 2 builds on the dynamics of spectatorship in these films to examine several works that have entered the canon of homosexual-themed cinema in Latin America. I study the spatiality of narratives such as Jaime Humberto Hermosillo's *Doña Herlinda y su hijo* [Doña Herlinda and her son] (1985) and Francisco Lombardi's *No se lo digas a nadie* to further the notion that a Maricón cinema is also politically disaffected.

Chapter 3 offers some concluding notes on the description of the genre. I include several films that, I argue, place nonnormativity and difference as a secondary concern to a broader interrogative—a further subdescriptor of the genre. I conclude this chapter with an analysis of Hermosillo's *Amor libre* [Free love] (1978), a film that narratologically suggests feminine homosocial desire. My interest, though, is centered on how this desire is captured and framed and the relationality or experience of viewership that it engenders.

Part II, divided into four chapters, begins with a delineation of the parameters of a New Maricón cinema, which, I argue, is an aesthetic and praxis at the very core of the boom that Ruffinelli rightfully notes. I suggest that New Maricón cinema can be described by the following, though not exhaustive, list of characteristics: a qualitative focus on sex and gender difference that is not treated as a subset or subtheme of a broader debate; and the minting of varying aural and visual affective intensities—often engendered through an engineered hapticity of the viewing experience, and often through references to and visualizations of the aqueous—that stimulate an empathic viewership experience, placing the viewer in an osmotic cellular relationship with difference. We also see a technical dismembering of the body in that the subject of difference is no longer viewed as a "whole" character but instead in the vein of what Elena del Río calls "bits and pieces" of the body (*Deleuze and the Cinemas of Performance*, 95). New Maricón films also tend to use nonurban spaces, metaphors, and movements that shift the reference of the subject away from the gendered tautology of the city. The urban, after all, is the site par excellence of Maricón films, as it, counterintuitively (if we are to consider queer theories of metronormativity), is the principal space around which the scopic is constructed.

New films "out" narratives of difference from structured spaces of patriarchy; New films out the spectator from the telephoto lens of the scopic; New films out Latin American cinema to a global circulation of productive aesthetics. New films, furthermore, out the cinematic body image: it is no longer a visual representation or node of a particular subjectivity within the negotiations of a narrative, but a denatured assemblage that, in its parts, breathes affective transmissions and potentials into the moving image. I forward, through parts II and III, an examination of *how* and to what *effect* the body's framing, segmentation, and (possible) reconstitution impact the experience of viewership, and what implications this may then have on the cinema's reception and circulation.

In chapter 4, I specify the parameters by which the spatial contract of heteronormativity regiments difference and gender expression in Fuentes-León's *Contracorriente*. I argue that sexed/gendered bodies come into being through interpellation with specific spatial assemblages and sites that code for normativity.

Chapter 5 focuses on the trope of spatial outings from the urban to the rural in Julia Solomonoff's *El último verano de la Boyita* [The last summer of the Boyita]. My analysis develops theories of masculinity and how these dialogue with transness and puberty. I argue that it is only through an intimate relationship with the marine and the natural that the principal characters emerge as queer bodies.

Chapter 6 matures the postulates and positions introduced in the previous two chapters by examining homosexual desire in Lucía Puenzo's XXY and *El niño pez*. Relying again on the audile-tactile nature of several key scenes and shots, I argue that what really is at stake in the first movie is the male adolescent's grappling with same-sex desire, and that the film is more an exploration of how social norms regulate desire than a true treatise on intersexuality in Latin America. My analysis of *El niño pez* traces the geopolitical implications of movement and desire, a dialectic fundamental to the poetics of New Maricón film.

I develop throughout part II the importance of the aqueous both as metaphor and as haptic texture in stimulating an economy of empathy around these films. New Maricón cinema, I argue, is a political cinema if we are to follow Felicity Colman's assertion that "the political is to be found in screen media that depict [a] modal shift or break, moments where the ethics of choice are presented . . . This shift is demonstrated in a range of pivotal screen moments . . . where the political can be understood as a perspective on the position of something and its situation within the collective set of images" (*Deleuze and Cinema*, 151). I pay particular attention to the aqueous as narrative device, affective sign, and polystate substance in the establishing of a New cinema.

Chapter 7 ties together the principal characteristics and trajectories of New Maricón cinema but also proposes that the genre cannot be viewed as a definitive break with Maricón films; rather, it is a process. New films do not come into existence through a masterstroke or definitive film but, instead, as a practice that develops through "pivotal screen moments" that I identify in *Antes que anochezca*, *La mujer de mi hermano* [My brother's wife], and *Y tu mamá también* [And your mother too], which renegotiate the space and role of the spectator in relation to the ethics of the image. I draw attention to how these films mobilize the aqueous as a Deleuzian vector of difference and engage a haptic visuality to build affective ties between the viewer and the narrative—a fundamental step in the generation of an empathic economy around New Maricón films. I also call attention to the filmmakers' repeated cutting or severing of the gaze, an implicit manifesto away from the scopic in favor of polysensorial conditions of experiencing film.[24]

The epistemics of outing are central to New Maricón film but are not inclusive per se of a newer trend of urban films that bridge affective ties between subjects and difference. In part III, I focus on how several key films rematerialize the maricón in the urban space, in what can be considered a subset or evolution of the initial turn toward the New. Chapter 8 works through the oeuvre of Marco Berger, wherein I identify several key stylistic and aesthetic qualities of the moving image that intersect the tenets of the New within an urban cityspace. In a different but not separate trajectory, Berger's films engage a haptic visuality and affective poetics to participate in the circulatory dynamics of empathy already set in motion by New Maricón films.

Chapter 8 reintroduces the possibility of a spatial refraction of difference into the same sites that perpetuated the scopic, thereby positing a cinema that postulates an affective experience within the urban. Chapter 9 shifts the analytical lens onto commercial films—not unlike the *Qué pena* series—that deal with same-sex relations and nonnormative gender expressions. This is an altogether separate trajectory that benefits from circulations of empathy yet is not productive in that the audiovisual style is narrative based.

Chapter 9 specifically examines the trope of the child as a didactic mechanism and as an assemblage of complementary neoliberal discourses. In *La otra familia* and *Lokas*, acceptance and plurality become, under the neoliberal regime, signs of modernity and inclusion in a global order. Integral to this reading is a development of what Ignacio Sánchez Prado calls neoliberal structures of feeling, which place at an impasse specific structures of affect and the demographics of distribution and circulation.

Chapter 10 is a conclusion or a point of departure for future work in the field. I correlate recent films and trends within emerging trajectories that are too early to pinpoint.

On a final note, I must clarify a few points that guide the progression of chapters. First, I am interested not only in working through the most contemporary films but also in placing them within an aesthetic genealogy in Latin America. Any evaluation of the current affective regime must enter into a dialogue with the scopic—hence my insistence on not claiming a break with the old but in adding the modifier "New" to current itineraries.

Second, the division into distinct genres is not definitive or evolutionary. Maricón films continue to be made (such as *Azul y no tan rosa*) in the same "national" markets as New Maricón films (as is the case with Mariana Rondón's *Pelo malo*).

Third, I am interested not only in how criticism approaches this circulatory economy (and the impressions it may make) but also in explaining this boom in relation to and in the shaping of particular Latin American audiences and industries. The naming of a Latin American cinematic ecosystem must contend with difference from within. In general terms, we can talk of a dyadic division evidencing the tensile globalizing forces of cultural homogeneity and heterogeneity or, in spatial terms, such forces that are correlated but not necessarily mutually exclusive, of territorialization and deterritorialization. Both lines, however, are not exhaustive or definitive but allow for a general tracing of recent film.[25] The former dyad (homogeneity/territorialization) can be understood, for example in Claudia Llosa's or Pablo Larraín's filmographies, which are strongly localized, whereas the latter (heterogeneity/deterritorialization) is evident in Fuentes-León's *Contracorriente*. The film is explicitly heterogeneous, favoring identifiers of Latin Americanness over any one set of localized markers, and deterritorialized, as the visual topographies and topologies do not necessarily articulate the film within a (in this case) Peruvian landscape. Such cultural and spatial lack of specificity lies at the heart of any possibility of a circulatory economy produced by affect transmission, as by nature it appeals to the emotive capacity of a larger community. As the director explains:

> My intention was not to talk about the political context of Cabo Blanco, of a man in this particular town in Peru that deals with being gay or with a homosexual relationship. I don't even mention that it's Cabo Blanco—you see it on a few boats, some of them say Cabo Blanco, but I don't even say it's Peru. There was even a line that was taken out that talked about Lima, because I wanted it to be an archetype of a town,

> more than the political and social context of a specific town and country . . . I made this film for as many people as can get to see it, but I had the Latin American audience in mind, and I wanted to highlight the romance and the love between the two men, and be a little bit careful about how much to push that envelope. I didn't want to lose [the audience], especially because [scenes with Miguel and Santiago] come early in the movie. (Fuentes-León, "Interview," 8 February 2010)

The film, like others in the New genre, is thus engaged less in the micropolitics of the national in relation to sex and gender difference and more in creating an affective substrate and the circulation of particular signs that gain in value and intensity as they begin to move. This affective impulse, as Mabel Moraña understands it, "models the relationship between the community and its past, the ways of reading its present and its projection toward a possible future" [modela la relación de la comunidad con su pasado, las formas de lectura de su presente y la proyección hacia el futuro posible] ("Postscríptum," 315). The continuing boom in New Maricón films, then, is not occurring purely at the behest of favorable market structures and public and legislative sentiment; it is subject to the active shaping and participation of this "Latin American" audience in making the compendium of its images and affects a productive one.

Part I

MARICÓN CINEMA

David William Foster's *Queer Issues in Contemporary Latin American Cinema* provides a succinct and thoroughly researched discussion of homosexual-themed cinema in Latin America. While Foster focuses primarily on queer issues, what I want to undertake here is a tangential though not mutually exclusive interrogation into how queerness is portrayed and to what collective effect. I do not focus solely on narratological traits or plot turns; my perusal of some of these films that Foster and others identify as belonging to a homosexual-themed canon is, instead, preoccupied with the praxis and composition of representation and how these impact and shape our perception of gender and sexual difference.

Foster's meticulous study provides both a needed chronology of gay-themed contemporary cinema and an answer to Ramiro Cristóbal's ethical interrogation: Is it "fair to speak of homosexual cinema" [lícito hablar de cine homosexual] (*La homosexualidad*, 7)? Cristóbal problematizes the notion of gay cinema when he circumscribes the difference between a homosexual and a queer cinema (*La homosexualidad*, 13–29), posing that what we see produced in the contemporary Peninsular Spanish context is more aligned with Anglo notions of queerness, which can be understood as "everything that establishes a defiant stance to patriarchal heteronormativity . . . queerness can represent . . . a range of sexual practices between human beings that do not comply with the precepts of the Church and its projections onto the laws of the secular state" [todo aquello que instaura una postura desafiante a la heteronormatividad patriarcal . . . lo *queer* puede representar . . . toda una gama de prácticas del amor entre seres humanos que no cumplen con los preceptos de la Iglesia y sus proyecciones en las leyes y los códigos del estado laico] (Foster, *Ensayos* 197).

Latin American film, however, largely falls outside these parameters. Discussing a similar genealogy in Mexican cinema, Alfredo Martínez Expósito goes as far as to argue that "the very inexistence of a specifically homosexual cinema can be considered as symptomatic of the structural violence perpetrated against homosexuals" [la propia inexistencia de un cine específicamente homosexual se podría considerar como sintomático de la violencia estructural contra los homosexuales] ("El cine gay"), though I feel that his position is quite hyperbolic.

While I went over Foster's definition of the queer in earlier pages and, by default, had to contrast it with prevailing positions of queerness, it does provide a useful base from which to investigate films about sexual and gender difference produced in Latin America. The implication here, and I will clarify this further in the section on New Maricón Cinema, is that the bulk of homosexual-themed Latin American cinema is not really queer, but, instead, Maricón cinema, which does not enter into a queer unpacking of heteronormative politics and subjectivities. This is a broad statement and one that is likely to invite political and critical discord. But let me clarify: while queerness and a cinema of the queer on a global scale actively interrogate patriarchal demands and subjectivities, questioning and decentering the normative as a referential point, Maricón cinema is a localized and sociohistorically sensitive phenomenon that is primarily concerned with representing the (male) homosexual by bringing him into being and out of the shadows of innuendo and ostracism, though not necessarily out of the Anglo closet. Maricón films, which Foster rightfully calls homosexual-themed or lesbigay cinema, are an important first step in recognizing plural sexualities but fall short of any critical positioning vis-à-vis the normative. By nature, however, they are an ethical intervention (which I will attempt to elucidate in my analysis of several films below) but maintain the binary of homo versus hetero. More important, Maricón cinema is a scopic cinema that portrays the maricón but always maintains the viewer in a safely distant and voyeuristic space and plane of feeling.[1] We are never invited to engage in or feel the body of difference; Maricón cinema builds no lasting affective ties that "circulate" emotions of empathy.[2] It is a closed and ethically unaffected system of representation that implicates viewership, with no specific call to action or induced intrapersonal contact between the subject-body (of the viewer) and the object-image (of the film). The moving image and its components (sounds, montages, sequences, cuts, textures, etc.) do not engender a haptic relating or relationship but, instead, methodically foment an observational or commentarial position.[3] These films, as a result, are more about queer issues, as Foster correctly affirms, and less about queerness as praxis or ethics.[4] Latin American films in this vein are Maricón films, naming homosexuality yet maintaining it as an extraneous and othered condition that exists (by virtue of the visual and the explicitness of naming) yet is not assimilated into a wider social circulation or ethical sense of community.[5]

A Maricón genealogy can be traced from Arturo Ripstein's *El lugar sin límites* and Jaime Humberto Hermosillo's *Amor libre* and *Doña Herlinda y su hijo* to Francisco Lombardi's *No se lo digas a nadie.* In these films, homosexuality and homoeroticism "never exist in any other space than the dark side of compulsory heterosexuality in the bleak terrain created by hypocrisy" (Foster, *Queer Issues,* 109). These films expose and let live the homosexual subject without necessarily questioning structural and epistemological facets of heteronormativity. This divide is further noticed in critical approximations to the region's cinema: the Latin American section of Thomas Waugh's comprehensive study of global queer cinema, for example, is, unsurprisingly, titled "The Kiss of the Maricon," albeit without an accent (*The Fruit Machine,* 173).

This distinction between a queer and Maricón cinema is further exemplified by the exclusion of Latin American films from any critical discussion of New Queer cinema, a descriptive label for gay-themed films beginning in the 1990s that pushes forth an aesthetics and politics of defiance (Aaron, "New Queer Cinema," 3). This subgenre focuses on minority groups within the lesbian-gay-bisexual-transgender (LGBT) community, eschews positive imagery, defies the sanctity of the (homophobic) past, questions the fatality of death—particularly in relation to AIDS, and defies cinematic convention in terms of form, content, and genre (Aaron, "New Queer Cinema," 4–5). How can we expect Latin American films to even be a dialoguing agent when representations of difference are, more accurately, representations of deviance? The absence of Latin American cinema in Michele Aaron's anthology on New Queer cinema and its legacy in the twenty-first century is thought provoking, especially since the region has not been a stranger to homosexual-themed films. The absence is further felt in New Queer cinema–inspired Hispanic critical projects such as Leandro Palencia's *La pantalla visible,* where only three out of thirty-three movies are in Spanish. None of these, as might be expected, come from Latin America. This disconnect, on the one hand, may be explained by New Queer cinema's lack of concern with people of color or other cultures, as they tend to appear only haphazardly as token others. On the other hand, we can further the argument that Latin American gay-themed cinema is less queer and more Maricón, as the bulk of films do not effectively and affectively queer anything.

It is worthwhile at this juncture to return to Foster's genealogy of homosexual-themed, or Maricón, cinema in Latin America, as a thematic trend can be gleaned from his critical queer reading of each film. It is important to note that the critic does not insert these themes in a global queer movement, but rather provides a queer hermeneutic for understanding Maricón films. In establishing a corpus, Foster encounters films that superficially portray homosexual subjects and relationships without explicitly interrogating or mining them for their queer potential (*Queer Issues*, 25), and more complex films that problematize gender, but usually within a broader study of power systems.

Martínez Expósito argues for a similar division: a first phase composed of hackneyed stereotypes; a second grouping of films that problematize the ontology and phenomenology of gender difference, including the social tensions it evidences; and a third phase, where homosexual characters and plot lines are incorporated as secondary elements in films in which the main theme is quite broader, akin to Foster's second grouping.[6]

Of note in both groupings is a replacement of the negative sissy stereotype with rounder characters, though not always distinctively "positive" tropes.[7] The final group in both genealogies includes *La virgen de los sicarios* (Our lady of the assassins, 2000, the globalized drug trade), *En el paraíso no existe el dolor* (There is no pain in paradise, 1997, border studies), Cuban films on homosexuality during Castro's government, and *No se lo digas a nadie* (globalization and urbanity). Even Hermosillo's *Doña Herlinda y su hijo* can be read through the optics of nation-building and the role of popular culture in imagining the nation (Schulz-Cruz, *Imágenes gay*, 21–28). There is a critical disconnect in talking about a queer Latin American cinema, as what is often represented, studied, and problematized is a gay cinema. Bernard Schulz-Cruz, for example, uses the word "queer" interchangeably with "gay, homosexual, joto, loca" (*Imágenes gay*, 18). This is a dangerous practice, as criticism is confusing the queer (as a decentering position, practice, and epistemology) with the homosexual (which does not necessarily question heteronormative systems and structures).

Therein lies my choosing of Maricón as both a designator and a description of the practice of naming, identification, and distancing extant in these films. Within this theorization of a distinct Maricón cinema in juxtaposition to a global queer is an understanding of the role of space and spatiality in Latin American cultural production and film. A perusal of contemporary novels provides a strong textual basis for affirming that spatiality is intrinsic to gender subjectivities. The urban, the public, and the central forms the site of heteronormativity, where hegemonic masculinity (Connell, *Masculinities*, 81) reigns over feminine and queer positions. More recent texts such as Ana Clavel's *Cuerpo náufrago* (2005), Alberto Fuguet's *Mala onda* (1991), and Alfredo Bryce Echenique's *El huerto de mi amada* (2002) can be read in a long sequence of narratives dating back to colonial and independence-era literature that gender the center as urban. In fact, we can consider Luis Zapata's *El vampiro de la colonia Roma* (1978) to be most innovative not necessarily due to the writing of a queer figure, but because it queers the praxis of the masculine homosocial in the urban space.

The films Foster establishes in a Latin American homosexual-themed filmic canon similarly follow a spatial mapping of the subject vis-à-vis gendered topologies, as sexuality is negotiated within the urban and, microstructurally, within the domestic. Orlando Rojas's *Las noches de Constantinopla* (Nights in Constantinople, 2002), for example, clearly illustrates the spatiality of the domestic in maintaining and perpetuating heteronormative systems (Lewis, *Crossing Sex*, 90).

But this observation is banal or, at best, elementary; these films take place in the city. Who cares? Isn't cultural production, and here I really mean literary and filmic production, predominantly urban, especially in a place of such stark demogeographic reorganization in the twentieth century?

My focus on space is not simply thematic but also structural when we take into consideration the material and semiotic construction of such arrangements as the "domestic" and the "closet," which are both semantic conglomerations. They are, furthermore, real and virtual spatial planes that intersect subjectivity on the personal and fictive levels in the form of framing devices, real locations, and referential points in the construction of filmic characters. Maricón cinema is strongly urban and locates gender and sexual difference within the seeming anonymity of the large city, as sort of a metronormative trope, that is, that homosexual subjects gravitate toward the urban and away from the hard-to-hide-in openness of the rural.[8]

But what effect does this setting or placing of the narrative to be told have on perceptions and praxes of representation? In the films I analyze below, I argue that the geographies of the urban and its vertical and horizontal topographies (and their respective alleyways, nooks, windows, apartments, etc.) engender a scopic perception of the gendered subject that nullifies any act of orientation, alignment, or empathy. In its place we are left with a simple vision or flat image of the body—akin to the experience of the *flâneur*, who sees but never touches—which impacts both the ethics and the politics of making, viewing, and collocating these films as cultural artifacts of real sociocultural behaviors. While I will specify and analyze how spatiality frames and molds the subject in the following films, I will approach how a rupture of this motion can prompt a different sort of cinema only in the second section of this book, where the reader discussing a New Maricón cinema may find further definitions and descriptors of the originary Maricón genre.

On a final note, I am aware that my terminology may prove contentious, even offensive. Why use a noted gender slur when other, less charged, terminology is available? Shouldn't a simple descriptor like "homosexual-themed" cinema suffice? Doesn't the term itself imply a cultural hegemony of the South by a falsely universalizing Anglo appropriation of the term?[9] Doesn't this term exclude other nonheteronormative identities and practices from the moving image?

To begin with the final question, I want to emphasize that my usage of the male homosexual term "maricón" reflects the gender variance of the majority of these films, where female homosexualities or transgender and other plural configurations are often left unmentioned and untouched (this, we will see later, only becomes a narrative focus in later films that generate a different spectatorial relationship to the image). The word, furthermore, appears sporadically in the films I discuss below as a slur, directed by both heterosexist *and* homosexual characters toward instances or bodies of homoeroticism.[10] It is not a reference to actual practice, orientation, or identity but, instead, an affirmation of power relations between two subjects. The maricón is always at a safe distance, separated from the ontological center of power of the enunciator. It is an ethical and political positioning and not a description of actual sexual-gender dynamics.

In a connected fashion, I use the Spanish "maricón"—especially in New Maricón film—much in the vein of similar reappropriations that are politically charged yet are also ethically conducive of a broader emancipation of rights and identities. This use reflects Jorge Brioso and Óscar Montero's ruminations on the usage of the term in popular and literary circles:

> The need to appropriate in order to resemanticize, recycle, and "rework" certain concepts that were originally used as a means to isolate and condemn defines the dilemma faced by every minority group when confirming that the ideas that serve as cohesive elements are instead permeated by a knowledge based on exclusion and scorn. The absence of uncontaminated terminologies in the oppressive web of knowledge-power leads to the appropriation of certain terms that then become emblems of struggle and awareness.[11]

"Maricón" is a term that in more than one case has been defended and supported by lesbigay community groups in Latin America, not as a renewal of semantic oppression but as a political affront to this charge, much in the way that racial and ethnic minorities have renegotiated slurs as points of contestation.[12] I follow Jaime Manrique's resemanticization of the term, which equally acknowledges the word's historical and current derogatory use yet forges a renegotiating of authority, inflection, and enunciation along political lines.[13]

I use the word "maricón," then, in the spirit of the rhetoric of challenge that acknowledges the oppression and injustice meted out to sexual and gender minorities in and out of the cinema. At the same time, I contend that it is through these injustices, oversights, and examples of gross negligence that we can as a community move forward in gender and sex equality on a global scale. Forgetting or glossing over the historico-cultural semiotics of the "maricón" is not conducive to reconciliation or liberation. By excising the word "maricón" from an original sign system and reinscribing it within a new social syntactics, my usage is aware of the symbolic and real vestiges of the term but encourages the Manriquean resemanticization that renegotiates agency and power vis-à-vis sexuality.

CHAPTER ONE

Ficheras and Jotos in Mexican Cinema

WE JUST WANT TO BE SEEN!

OUR CURSORY OVERVIEW OF THE SCREENING OF NON-heteronormative sexualities begins with the popular Mexican *fichera* genre produced in the 1970s and 1980s. I use this as a starting point as it chronologically comes after an awakening or politicizing of LGBT issues in the South as a result of contact with the North, and because these films were popular all over Latin America because of their simple story lines, predictable comic interludes, and general (female) sexiness, which is always well exported. Sergio de la Mora uses these films to springboard a study on cinematic Mexican masculinity, focusing on the *fichera* genre in general and then transitioning to an analysis of Arturo Ripstein's *El lugar sin límites*. I find de la Mora's approximation and corpus to be useful and timely and thus follow a similar strategy in this chapter as I outline some of the principal characteristics of the Maricón genre. De la Mora focuses on the "queeny *jotos*" that populate these films and argues that they "function as minstrel figures and are a site of pleasure and celebration of sexual difference while at the same time registering homophobic and misogynistic anxieties about heterosexual masculinity" (*Cinemachismo*, 5).[1] Machismo, for de la Mora, needs its masculine other (the *joto*) to define and reproduce itself (*Cinemachismo*, 108).

Unlike de la Mora, who acutely inspects sexual subjects on the screen, I am more intent on examining the nuances of how these subjects are portrayed and what relationship they initiate with the viewer. That is, how does the *joto*'s coming into being impact the erotics and politics of the screen, and what effect does this have in generating positive and negative affective intensities?

The *fichera* genre proliferated in the 1970s and 1980s, with almost a third of the films made in Mexico in 1981 being categorized under this description.[2] They were commercially successful and easily exported, as their plot lines often were sociohistorically neutral and thereby easily assimilated into and received in other viewing venues of the Spanish-speaking Americas. The films revolve around the cabaret or brothel and the men, women, transvestites, and *jotos* who bring a certain picaresque flavor to the otherwise mundane excuses for slapstick humor and the baring of breasts and buttocks. The *joto* appears in these locales as a worker or as a reminder of libidinal excess; the brothel, after all, is a place of patriarchal becoming and order, given its private nature, but also a venting point for satisfying otherwise restricted desires. The *joto*, then, has a checks-and-balances function, a reminder that whatever the urge, male sexuality must adhere to a heterosexual practice and stance vis-à-vis femininity.[3] The trope functions in a similar fashion to George Mosse's countertype within the functional dynamics of the stereotype (*The Image of Man*).

Perhaps most important in this genre of film is the use of spectacle as a production point and as a schema of viewership. Connecting the proliferation of the genre with prevailing industry norms on censorship and *buen gusto* (good taste), Jorge Ayala Blanco underlines that these films represent a snapshot, or zeitgeist, of a particular working-class demographic that reacts to the sanitation of popular films by embracing cheap and belligerent nudity and innuendo, or what de la Mora calls "proto-pornographic" films (*Cinemachismo*, 111). They are held together by a blatant affirmation of heteronormativity as a glue that binds tensions in and outside the brothel space.

Looking, then, at the *fichera* genre, and in concert with de la Mora's thesis, we can safely pose that the *joto* exists merely as a cog in the construction of heterosexuality and hegemonic masculinities. Conversely, the *joto* is also "spectacularized" in the sense that he is to be viewed as a construct, didactically paraded before the hetero gaze to show how men are not supposed to be. Perhaps due to this, *fichera* films have often been left out of serious studies into a "queer" Latin American cinema. My inclusion, however, is not thematic or genealogical but, rather, archaeological, as I affirm that the genre provides a litmus test of erotic relationality that will influence later films that can be grouped under the loose umbrella of homosexual-themed cinema.[4] Not necessarily involved in a causal relationship, these films, however, underline a method of viewership and foster an association with the erotics of the moving image that will influence subsequent generations of Maricón films and moviemakers.

Before furthering this angle, let us pause at Carlos Vasallo's *El día del compadre* (1983), a useful example of how the relational construction of sexualities is conceived in *fichera* features.[5] Starring Jorge Rivero and Andrés García as muscular and virile men, the film begins with aerial shots of Mexico City, of buildings, housing complexes, and cars moving through its labyrinthine streets. The film emphasizes in a subtle and silent way that the urban is a complicit referent in the erotics of the diegesis.

The first narrative shot shows Susana Dosamantes (Bertha) dressed as a housewife in one of the living spaces glossed over by the moving aerial camera in the credits. Her husband, Pepe, played by Andrés García, is shown in a medium image in the shower that cuts just below his waist. She enters the bathroom and opens the shower curtain as the camera captures her downward gaze. The female character's eyes stay below the strategic visual cutoff that was previously established in the composition shot of the bathing male, provoking the viewer's imagination to go below the visual line. This detail, furthermore, suggests that what is below is equally as impressive (virile, macho, etc.) as what is above, establishing the male body as an erotic site of spectacle, seduction, and sexuality. More important, the visual dynamic created by the diegetic gaze and the unseen (to the audience) furthers this body as a site of interrogation to be questioned and probed. This latter action is almost tactile, as the cascading shower and almost mobile movement of Bertha's field of vision downward into the unseen provokes a viewer action that is cognitively similar; that is, we are encouraged to imagine the proportions of what lies below.

Their dialogue draws further attention to the deified point of his anatomy, as Bertha asks for sex and Pepe reaffirms that he cannot copulate every day, as he needs his energy for work. The farcical nature of the conversation between the sex-crazed wife and the denying husband evokes Ayala Blanco's description of the genre as a sort of venting point for frustrated (male) libidos during this period.

The camera's emphasis on the void left by our not seeing Pepe's penis is repeated in a subsequent shot in this scene when he goes to the bedroom to dry off. Strategically positioned between his groin and the viewer is a television set that again marks a line or area of invisibility on the male body. The usage of the television set permits two separate but connected readings of this image: first, that the television set and popular media are ingrained in the telos of everyday life and as such played a fundamental role in the visibility of gendered bodies (and others); and second, that the television set as a screen or surface of spectatorship can be transposed onto the male body and occupy the semantic areas left bare by the unseen penis and testicles. In this second reading, the body is, then, like the television set—something to be viewed, seemingly flat and two-dimensional, but ideologically representative and representational of a plurality of images, bodies, politics, and experiences. The masculine body *is* the screen, thereby placing the camera and viewer in a *mise en abyme* of the erotics of the film.

The relationship between the camera and the body is reiterated in the subsequent scene, after Pepe affirms that he has to work and provide for his family, unlike the *huevón* (idiot) Chema (played by the also muscular Jorge Rivero). The image cuts to the outside, and the camera takes Pepe's cue to zoom in on a particular window in an apartment building. The kinetics of the outside images suggest that the inside shots of the domestic are caveats or samplings of a greater societal practice and that the erotics of the particular couples and bodies shown in *El día del compadre* can be extrapolated to the outside space, that is, to wider Mexican society.

Inside Chema's apartment, we hear an off-frame female voice call him a *huevón*, thereby establishing continuity within the diegesis. Chema is shown scantily dressed and flexing his muscles while performing bicep curls in front of a wife who chastises him for not working (presumably, like Pepe). The camera first captures Chema above the chest then zooms out to show a greater section of his body. As in the visual play on the seen-unseen in Pepe's introduction, the camera highlights a praxis of viewership that centers the heterosexual male body as an axis of referentiality and desire for other diegetic bodies *and* the audience. Chema's wife, like Bertha, complains of the lack of sex in their daily life, to which Chema replies that coitus is a waste of bodily energy.

Unlike Pepe, who argues that work takes precedence over intercourse, Chema simply turns his wife's attention to another compadre, Mon, who is happy to provide a libidinal outlet for the desiring female. Played by the insatiable and nonmuscular (read: layman) Alfonso Zayas, a key figure in the development and popularity of the genre, Mon does what the other men refuse to do.

The camera repeats the spatial and technical characteristics of Chema's introduction as it zooms in on the window of a lower-level apartment where an aroused Mon is shown reading an imported pornographic magazine. Standing next to a window while his partner, Lupita, lies sensually on their bed, Mon asks her to disrobe. Drawing attention to the zooming camera that brought us into the domestic space, Lupita, played by Rossy Mendoza, comments that they will be *seen*.

Her facetious attempt at propriety draws attention to the act of viewing that the movement and placement of the camera in the previous two snapshots evoked, that sex and its bodies are the focal point of the voyeuristic experience of the *fichera* genre. Lupita, stripped naked as a randy Mon kisses and gropes her exaggerated curves, cuts her gaze outward, but to a different aerial angle, and zooms in on a different window.

When juxtaposed with the angle of Mon's introductory zoom, the second image can be located in a sort of shot-reverse shot relation to the first, as though this second apartment is immediately in front of the first. In this space we see a bespectacled man, Tito (Rafael Inclán) playing a string instrument. Dressed in a luxurious robe and wearing a tie, his mustachioed, slender features contrast vividly with the previous three imaginings of male virility. He is almost un-Mexican in demeanor and dress (following established stereotypes of the male aesthetic in the cinema and literature), a European dandy who contrasts with the unbridled machismo of his peers. He superficially does, however, emblemize the aesthetic of the statesman that was prevalent in early-twentieth-century discussions of modernity in the Mexican state, and perhaps harkens to this previous hegemonic model of masculinity.[6] His partner, Petra, played by Lucila Mariscal, draws his attention to the scandalous behavior of their naked neighbors (Mon and Lupita), who are apparently repeat offenders in the neighborhood. The image cuts to a point-of-view zoom on Mon's window, where the viewer (and Petra, much to her fancy) sees Mon and Lupita engaged in randy foreplay.

Integral to this image is the camera's usage of binocular outlines for a point-of-view shot that originates in Petra's apartment. The shot explicitly calls our attention to the action of seeing and establishes it as a praxis of viewership within and outside the constraints of the image; this allows an approximation to the erotics of the film. The image, furthermore, is a point of view from a point of acceptability: it is perfectly acceptable to view the performing male body from the position of the desiring female (or approving male, as in a later shot in which Chema is shown to be spying on Mon and his curvaceous prey). Mon directly acknowledges Petra's (and our) voyeurism by looking over at the window and yelling "¡Gerónimo!" before pouncing on the naked female.

These four erotic microcosms are presented in the first minutes of *El día del compadre* and impose a system onto the structures of heteronormativity that are inscribed and reinforced in the film. They, furthermore, institute a relationship between the lens and the male body, placing the latter in the crosshairs of viewership. Ideologically intrinsic in them is a definition of maleness that is dependent on corresponding yet exclusive definitions of nonmasculinities. Tito, the least virile and least physically powerful example of these different masculinities is later juxtaposed with Flor de lis (a typecast Roberto Cobo), a *joto* who entertains patrons in a brothel visited by Tito. While comparatively feminine (when played against Chema, Pepe, and Mon), Tito is emphatically the masculine referent in his game of *albures*, or sexual puns, with Flor.

As de la Mora specifies, the *joto* appears as a reminder of heterosexuality and as a sort of prop in the characterization of the masculine, even in cases where this masculine is decidedly nonhegemonic. This being said, my interest in these films, as demonstrated in my concentrating on the early images of *El día del compadre*, is centered on the binomial of camera and body that stimulates an erotics of voyeurism that maintains the body as a visual referent or idealization from a relational locus that reinscribes heteronormativity (whether it be the yearning woman or the approving man). Nonconforming bodies, sexualities, and desires are equally distributed along this relationship; that is, they are collocated as viewed objects that represent deviations from the idealized position. This detail is salient but truly relevant only in our discussion of Maricón and New Maricón films below. Integral to this process is a framing of the subject

1.1. The audience as voyeur, El día del compadre. *Copyright Alianza Cinematográfica Mexicana.*

1.2. The afeminado *on the outside,* El día del compadre. *Copyright Alianza Cinematográfica Mexicana.*

within strict visual and cognitive boundaries that do not permit an easy escape from normativity.

My brief discussion of framing and voyeurism brings us inevitably to the starting point of a genealogy of Maricón film: Arturo Ripstein's *El lugar sin límites* (1978).[7] De la Mora addresses the film within the discussion of the *fichera* genre, affirming that Ripstein's adaptation of José Donoso's novel of the same name is "the only instance in Mexican cinema in which a gay male is invested with such a degree of subversive power in terms of challenging the dominant gender and sexual system" (*Cinemachismo,* 116).[8] David William Foster similarly locates the film at a starting point on a spectrum of cinema that discusses the social semiotics of heterosexuality. Both critics, thus, consider *El lugar sin límites* as a primary denotatum in any discussion of plural sexualities in Latin American cinema, and I am largely in accord with this position, though my interest in the film is less in how it defines a social semiotic of normativity.

Divided into three parts, Ripstein's film chronicles the slow disintegration of a fictional town, El Olivo, as the economic structures of *caciquismo* lay bare the struggle of the worker class to thrive. The three sections of the film revolve around the brothel space and La Manuela, a homosexual transvestite who co-owns the locale, and her violent sexual relationship with Pancho, the son of a local peon who returns to El Olivo after squandering an investment by Don Alejo, the local cacique who controls and owns every part of the local town with the exception of the brothel. Previous studies have underlined the tensions between hetero and homo and the fine line that is walked by Pancho between these two poles, resulting inexorably in the murder of La Manuela at the hands of Pancho and his brother-in-law Octavio.[9]

While the final murder of the transvestite *joto* reflects a wider social rejection of faggotry (and this is a topic that merits its own study and ethical intervention), I want to bring the reader back to how specific gendered bodies are framed and situated vis-à-vis the lens, and what relationship their imaging portends for the viewer when read contextually with the voyeurism espoused by the *fichera* genre, though *El lugar sin límites* is, of course, not a *fichera* film per se.[10]

This relational system is evident in the first images of the film, where we see a rumbling truck make its way down a dirt road toward the camera. The brightness of its hue immediately draws our attention to the vehicle and its muscular contours, a foreshadowing of the subsequent cut to the muscled hands of the driver confidently holding the steering wheel. Like *El día del compadre,* which fetishizes the male body by making it an object of heterosexual and heteronormative desire, Ripstein's film opens with a similar visual semiotics that reflects a social order regimented by the powerful male aesthete. Within this scene, a separate shot captures the driver's forearms and tightly clothed biceps; by moving the camera slightly away from the subject, Ripstein emphasizes the commodification of the body, in this case, male, into a succinct locus of desire and power. Just as the *fichera* genre often focuses on the almost ridiculous buttocks of Alfonso Zayas pumping away at a topless vedette to evoke masculine power, Ripstein's film centers itself on the musculature of the male lead to underscore a semanticization of the body as it relates to the erotics of the narrative. Of note in the image of Pancho's muscled arms is the bordering of the pieces of the body, as the car window frames his muscles. This innocuous detail, however, places the male body in a *mise en abyme* of viewership; that is, Pancho's arms are erotically framed within the erotics of the already framed image, leading us to pay particular attention to their sinews and curves, akin to early sequences of *El día del compadre,* which emphasize spectatorship and voyeurism in regard to the male body and virility, both aesthetic and coital.[11]

The technical specifics of framing the image serve to outline a tangential point: that both our experiences of viewing and assimilating the erotics of the image and the very composition of this image (in terms of bodies, loci of desire, and interpersonal links that are visibly invisible) are regimented by the structures in place in patriarchy. Along the lines of the hetero gaze and what de la Mora and Foster identify as the compulsory nature of heterosexuality, the framing of the (parts of) the male body in *El lugar sin límites* visually reminds the viewer of the matrices and lattices of power that run concurrently in plural directions to keep the heteronormative web in place.

I want to draw the reader's attention to the ending sequences of the film, immediately prior to La Manuela's murder, when Octavio and Pancho come to the brothel in search of drink and flesh. Knowing the potential for violence that such an outing insinuates, La Manuela flees with her red dress and hides outside. This outdoor space is composed of chicken wire and wooden poles that evoke the standing structure of a livable space, although it lacks a roof or

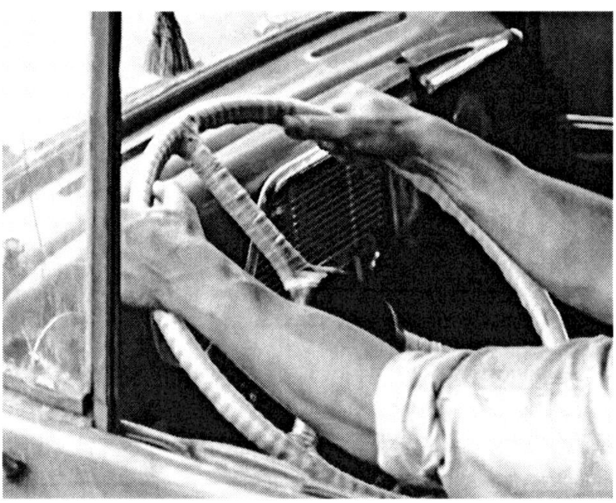

1.3. The body in frame, El lugar sin límites. *Copyright Conacite Dos.*

other proper groundings of domesticity. The point being alluded to here is that this outer refuge, a spatial escape from the homosociality and heterosexism of the brothel, is suggestive of the places of domesticity and patriarchy in this and other *fichera* films: one only has to go back to the beginning of *El día del compadre* to understand the spatial semiotics of desire and gender construction. By hiding in this vestigial/potential assemblage of the domestic, La Manuela signals her physical and symbolic exclusion and provokes a dimensional inquiry into gender and sexuality that will truly be critically interrogated only in New Maricón films. Within *El lugar sin límites,* La Manuela's spatial outing provides the vantage point for the repetition of the praxis of voyeurism that we noted in *El día del compadre*.

After she finds a hidden nook next to some fowl, the camera reverses to show her partially hidden body and face looking fearfully and inquisitively at the salon as the men enter the brothel. This is a striking image, due to both the visual impact produced by the bright red of her dress (evocative of the first scene with the truck in the film) and the framing of her gaze within an opening in the outdoor wooden structure. The latter emphasizes her positioning in relation to the lens and patriarchy, that is, as a body to be objectified (akin to Pancho when he is nothing more than muscle in the early sequence) and as a sexuality that is compartmentalized within the morphology of heteronormativity. This observation is reiterated in the reverse shot of the peering Manuela, when the camera captures the action inside the brothel through her point of view. We see through the lattices framing the windows the two men greeting prostitutes and getting comfortable. The shot emphasizes the transvestite's ex-

1.4. *La Manuela framed and peering in,* El lugar sin límites. *Copyright Conacite Dos.*

1.5. *Bodies and erotics placed at an ethico-political distance,* El lugar sin límites. *Copyright Conacite Dos.*

clusion and the segmentation of desire and bodies along carefully framed lines that maintain the patriarchal order in place.

The men proceed to pair up with women and dance, and Pancho propositions La Japonesita. The image quickly cuts to La Manuela (La Japonesita's father) making her way out of the hidden niche to get a closer look at the window and then cuts back to the dancing couples. The brief interpellation of the transvestite at the window reiterates the action and tensions of forbidden yet complicit viewership in the erotics of the film, which parallels Mon's performance of potent male virility by the window.

A second reverse angle foregrounds La Manuela spying on the couples through the window, though her expression has changed from one of fear to, arguably, one of longing and curiosity, perhaps posturing that she, too, despite her condition as a *joto,* should be allowed to openly dance with Pancho. Her gaze is explicitly marked by the window frame, making her a possible dialoguing agent within the *mise en abyme* of desire and objectification that is reiterated in the scene.

The image cuts to a point-of-view shot to reaffirm this reading, as we see Pancho lift La Japonesita off her feet in a sensual yet violent show of desire foregrounded by the wooden frame of the window, which establishes the positionality of the lens as analogous to the transvestite's gaze. The scene then briefly alternates between a close-up of La Manuela's face, which now is openly desirous of the erotic intensity generated by Pancho's musculature, and a point-of-view shot that shows the men drinking and groping the girls. This second image is repeated in a long take after Octavio leaves with a prostitute for one of the bedrooms and Pancho and La Japonesita engage in a dialogue that is erotically tense and suggestive of an impending violence between the powerful penetrating male and the curvaceous available female.

The sexual tensions between them climax when Pancho reveals the sado-dominant aspect of his desire and the film cuts to a now-worried La Manuela, who still bears the corporeal and psychological scars of masculine violence. Inside the brothel, we learn the true reason for Pancho's visit (and I use only Pancho here, as Octavio clearly comes only for alcohol and a willing partner): to see La Manuela dance. He brutishly grabs at La Japonesita's chest, coincidentally, an organic site of lacking in the *joto*-transvestite, and exclaims: "I came to *see* La Manuela! Go on and call her . . . tell her to come and dance. I want to *see* her!" [¡Vine a *ver* a La Manuela! Ándale vete a llamarla . . . dile que venga a bailar. ¡Que yo quiero *ver*la!] (my emphasis). Though only a naïve viewer would assume that Pancho's interests lie solely in *seeing* La Manuela, it bears emphasizing his words as a discursive inscription of the visual traits of a scene that is contingent on the ability to see—to occupy the subjective position of the voyeur in relation to the objects of desire within the frame, albeit one of wood that is symbolic of the camera's own framing of desire and acceptability.

La Manuela enters the brothel in full dress just as the interchange between Pancho and her daughter heats up; she is now reinscribed within the space of normativity as a feminine object of the male's libido, outfitted in a gaudy flamenco dress that emphasizes her lack of cleavage. The *joto*-transvestite is recalibrated along the erotic lines cleaved by the earlier act of voyeurism; she becomes the spied woman in relation to the violent masculinity of the male.

Reflecting on the dyad of the seer and the seen, Patrícia Vieira affirms that "the two elements of seeing are locked in a reciprocal exchange, a relation that betrays the ethical grounding of vision as commerce with alterity" and argues that "there is a latent potential for ethics in the specular dynamics between the eye and its object. . . . The power of what is beheld . . . hinges then on the fact that it determines the beholder, even as she or he attempts to define it" (*Seeing Politics Otherwise*, 8).[12] In the particular case of La Manuela first spying on and then acting in the developing erotics of the brothel, Vieira's argument vis-à-vis ethics and alterity can be reinscribed as a conversation between desire and alterity, this second relationship being intrinsic to La Manuela's actions and the film's representation of such, where difference becomes a pantomime of the hegemonic order.

What follows in Ripstein's film is the confluence of an anxiety inherent in homosociality on the part of Pancho and the incongruences of the libidinous urges that are prompted by the *joto*-transvestite: the two men kill La Manuela in the outskirts of El Olivo after chasing her down in the red muscle truck that reappears in an image perpendicular to the opening scene of the film. The climax of *El lugar sin límites* foregrounds a few critical axes in what is at this moment a nascent Maricón cinema: the structured use of space and spatiality as designators of homo and hetero bodies and desires; the insertion of the desire for the nonnormative body within a social semiotics of patriarchy; and, last but most important, a cinematic focus on viewing and viewership as the principal means of apprehending or coming into contact with the erotics of the image. This last characteristic is at the core of any ethical treatise in a Maricón cinema as it underlines de la Mora's affirmation that at least now the *joto* and other gender and sex minorities are allowed to be seen, even if only as minstrels, props, and countertypes to a domineering order.

The principal object and production site of desire, however, remain the muscled heterosexual male, who provides an organizational axis for the erotics of the film. In other words, and I cannot say this better, Michael Schuessler's evaluation of *El lugar sin límites* bears highlighting: "While I fully recognize Ripstein's (and, of course, Donoso's) important thematic innovations, I also believe that his movie is transitional in nature and, as such, serves as a touchstone for later films, such as *Doña Herlinda y su hijo* and others that, in time, will follow" ("*Vestidas*," 140).

CHAPTER TWO

The Maricón

ON CLOSETS AND SPECTACULAR BODIES

SCHUESSLER'S CONCLUDING EVALUATION OF RIPSTEIN'S film brings us to Jaime Humberto Hermosillo's *Doña Herlinda y su hijo* (1985) as the next step in identifying the primary traits and developments of a Maricón genre. The endgame, of course, is an explanatory exercise into the transition and what I argue to be a boom in homosexual-themed cinema that we can broadly categorize as New in the twenty-first century. A contemporary of Ripstein and others such as Jorge Fons, Hermosillo is "the first Mexican director to not treat male homosexuality as a problem" (de la Mora, *Cinemachismo*, 191). Martínez Expósito, among others, is unwavering in his praise of the film, highlighting how "the gay spectator finally had a symbolic referent in the cinema . . . This film, without a doubt, defends homosexuality, love, and gay couples" [el espectador gay por fin tuvo un apoyo simbólico en la gran pantalla . . . Sin lugar a dudas esta película reivindica la homosexualidad, el amor y la pareja gay] ("El cine gay mexicano").

While I agree with these critical interventions, which largely explain the film's inclusion in any sex- and gender-based genealogy of Latin American cinema, I want to draw our attention to several key scenes in the film that present an autopsy of how homosexuality is represented, that is, how the image is crafted and to what effect these characteristics and idiosyncrasies reflect on an ethics of representing difference.

Based on the novel of the same name by Jorge López Páez, the film shows the evolution of Hermosillo's treatment of homoerotic desire in previous films such as *Matinée* (1976) and *Las apariencias engañan* (Looks are deceiving, 1978).[1] Though produced and filmed in 1985, it was not until 1987 that the film was first commercially shown in Mexico after having enjoyed a successful run abroad at festivals in London, New York, and Paris, among other places.

Based around four principal characters in Guadalajara—a city known at the time for its provincialism and conservatism (Ruffinelli, "Dime tu sexo," 61)—the film chronicles the marriage of Rodolfo (an upper-class youth portrayed with "deliberate touches of the filmic image" of Jorge Negrete [Balderston, "Excluded Middle?" 192]) and Olga (an educated member of the same social class with aspirations of being more than a housewife) and the subsequent re-accommodation of his homosexual relationship with Ramón (a younger and poorer university student studying music). This triangle is amorphic and develops varying degrees and angles as we learn of Rodolfo's relationship with both partners. We also learn that Olga may be a lesbian (as strongly suggested by her donning pants and aesthetically reproducing, albeit in a female body, many of the structural and personality traits of Ramón) and that Ramón is not the *pasivo* (bottom) that the first scenes of the film would have us believe. In the one image of homoerotic penetration (though both bodies are shown only from the waist up), it is clear that Ramón is the *activo* (top).

Hermosillo's at times comic yet at other times tragic narrative is overseen by the matronly figure of Rodolfo's mother, Doña Herlinda, who seemingly plays along with the charade of homosociality while engineering a renovation of her household architecture to facilitate Rodolfo and Ramón's relationship, which is decidedly not one of pure *compadrismo* (brotherhood). We can, furthermore, see in the film "examples of cultural intertextuality" (Schuessler, "*Vestidas*," 141) as Hermosillo weaves into the images well-known persons from the budding Mexican homosexual scene and locales such as the bar Los Panchos, which is a principal gay space in urban Guadalajara.

While criticism has rightfully focused on issues of transgression and gender-structure reinscription in Hermosillo's film, I am particularly interested in Foster's and Martínez Expósito's readings of the film.[2] The former underlines the importance of public versus private spaces and their implications for gendered behavior (*Queer Issues*, 88), whereas the latter identifies the importance of moving sexual difference out of the brothel space ("El cine gay mexicano"). These interventions, when read in concordance with my genealogical effort, incisively place *Doña Herlinda* at a critical crux, where "outing" and "coming out" as examples of a social semiotics are assembled with the "closet" as a spatial designator. While *fichera* films and *El lugar sin límites* are acutely aware of the spatiality of heteronormativity, that is, that space is both gendered and genderizing, they do not probe or posit a critical evaluation of this thesis. They do, though, represent this relationship, which is in itself culturally and theoretically significant.

Hermosillo's film, however, places the issue of space at the principal axis of the questioning of patriarchal norms and the seemingly impermeable fabric that binds them together.[3] If anything, the film undertakes a micropolitical inquiry into how we can go about normativity. If *fichera* films were characterized by the use of aerial shots of the urban milieu to establish a topography of desire, and if *El lugar sin límites* equally explicated the gender dynamics of the brothel as still being held to the values of patriarchy, Hermosillo's film would have to be congratulated both for extricating difference from the sordid spaces of the night and for locating homoeroticism within the same spaces that previously paraded the antics of Mon, Chema, and Pepe in the city. Ramón, after all, is an example of the move to the city by sexual minorities, what Judith Halberstam calls "metronormativity," and he substitutes for the urban sexual character, though in a less picaresque fashion than Zayas's incarnations. As Luis Zapata does in his groundbreaking gender inversion of the urban picaresque novel, Hermosillo takes the streets, buildings, and heavily populated cities of the *fichera* genre as a characterizing plane of desire for the Rodolfo-Ramón-Olga triangle. This step is important, as we have a first example of "outing" that will develop only in later examples of a New Maricón cinema. *Doña Herlinda* is, in this regard, a touchstone or a development, if you will, of Schuessler's reading of *El lugar*, as an important first step for entries in the Maricón genre that will follow.

There is, however, also an "in-ing," because the homosexual relationship is constrained to the domestic compound as Doña Herlinda renovates the house to give Ramón his own wing. While critics may argue that this narrative gesture is conservative, I want to echo Foster's and Martínez Expósito's view that the film is less an ideological posture of gay liberation and more an exploration of how gayness, understood here in the most broadly culturally sensitive sense, can be inscribed onto extant structures. In fact, by bringing Ramón *into* the house, the film positions itself at a critical line of inquiry into how difference can be accepted and negotiated within a specific micropolitical topology. The domestic arena as bastion and coding of normativity, then, is challenged in Hermosillo's film, as Doña Herlinda takes it upon herself to recode what those domestic spaces are complicit in. Most important, the in-ing in the film is also an outing of the homosexual from the libidinous space of the brothel and into the everyday tactics and strategies of normativity.

Taking the film's spatiality as a starting point, I want to draw our attention to three scenes that merit consideration when apposed to this brief informal genealogy of Maricón film and the implications of seeing difference. Following a scene where Ramón and Rodolfo lie naked in bed (a first in Mexican cinema, and provocative for even an international audience), the film cuts to the two lovers working out by Doña Herlinda's swimming pool within the walled compound. The svelte Ramón is shown working his abdominals while a more bearish Rodolfo skips rope. Ramón's flexing body is centered in the shot, dividing the image with the pool on their right and a drying bed sheet to their left.[4]

Rodolfo comes to Ramón as the camera zooms in on the men and straddles him, kissing his lean and smooth pectorals and neck. Just as things are about to heat up, we spy Doña Herlinda making her way to poolside with a tray of orange juice for the budding athletes. The camera moves slightly to the left as the two men realize that they have been caught in flagrante, and Rodolfo begins to massage Ramón with karate chops, showing us just how easily the lines between homoeroticism and homosociality can be blurred.[5] Unperturbed by the obviously amorous actions between her son and his friend, Doña Herlinda casually walks over to the clothesline and checks the sheet for dryness. She then calmly and quietly walks away as Rodolfo leans in and kisses Ramón.

As others have thoroughly argued, she is the empowering entity within the sociogendered dynamics of the film, a potentially queer pivot that identifies, challenges, contradicts, and retunes spatiogendered norms within a patriarchal system. Of particular interest in this scene, however, is her brief tactile acknowledgment of the hanging sheet. First, her gesture draws attention to an apparent prop that, visually speaking, could easily divide the homoerotic and the homosocial into the clean lines of the visible and the invisible. Her action explicitly indicates to the men that they should be more careful when openly displaying affection and desire—a reference to the vestiges of the brothel and other spaces and praxes of invisibility that previously cloaked gayness on film. The gesture, furthermore, signals the camera's positioning and framing of the image of the two men exercising in relation to her *and* the viewer, as an alternate angle would not have so clearly contrasted an approaching Doña Herlinda and the hanging sheet. By touching it, the character draws our attention to the location of the lens as a privileging optic into the vicissitudes of desire within the domestic space and to the technical qualities of Hermosillo's framing privileging a (more) open cinematic discussion of subordinate sexualities. The viewer in this dynamic is positioned in a pseudo-omniscient angle to the action wherein he or she can map out the materiality of bodies (and the discourses they code for) within a specific social space.

A second scene merits special attention if we are to discuss *Doña Herlinda*'s critical antecedents and successors. While the films I discuss above focus on the spectatorial nature of desire and the spectacle of the homosexual, Hermosillo, following, in a sense, Vieira's treatise on ethics and seeing, asks us to critically consider how desire is exposed and projected onto bodies. While La Manuela was a sight to be consumed in all her glorious extravagance and artifice, a trope evolved from similar depictions in *Un macho en la cárcel de mujeres* (A man in the women's prison, 1986) and *Modisto de señoras* (The couturier, 1969). Hermosillo forces a reevaluation of this essentializing prototype through both the complications of penetration and its role in the various intimate scenes between the two men and a singular scene of foreplay that occurs immediately after Doña Herlinda accompanies Olga to the gynecologist following the couple's return from their honeymoon. It is, in fact, photos from the honeymoon that initiate

2.1. *Framing homoeroticism,* Doña Herlinda. *Copyright Clasa Films.*

this sequence, as Rodolfo almost mechanically goes over slides of their trip to Hawaii, performing the role of the male combing over the images of an event that defines for the public world his heterosexuality. In one long take, Ramón interrupts the viewing by standing directly in front of the projection screen. In other words, and through simple substitution, both visual and semiotic, his body is now the screen; the flat surface projected on also, though, arguably, conversely, a surface of reproduction. Ramón's torso is, thus, the surface onto which Hermosillo makes possible a rearrangement and resemanticization of allowable and public desire, as his full body comes into direct contact with the projected images that code for his lover's other (public) relationship.

This particular image, though illuminative in tracing an ideological positioning of homoerotic desire in the film, maintains the homosexual as a site of spectacle given that Ramón's body occupies the principal axis of seeing in the sequence, in both intranarrative and viewer-reception angles of analysis. He is still the object to be seen, the object that does not enter into a sustained affective relationship with the viewer, though the very act of seeing him (and what he represents) interjects an analytical inquiry into the erotics of the film. Like La Manuela, who garnered Pancho's and our attention in the final dance of seduction in *El lugar sin límites,* Ramón is the ethical and libidinal locus of the image and any critical ideology it may forward. But unlike Roberto Cobo's transvestite in Ripstein's film, Ramón is not a stereotyped *joto* or an archetypal *pasivo,* but an incongruous and pliant desiring-desired body that problematizes Rodolfo's attempts at passing or maintaining his homosexuality in the closet. Though one can argue that it is Doña Herlinda who actively subverts the patriarchal order

2.2. *The body as screen — screening the body,* Doña Herlinda. *Copyright Clasa Films.*

by building a (homoerotic) annex to her house, we cannot discount Ramón's potential for decentering normative representations of the homosexual.

This querying of the trope is informed by a scopic understanding of the image and the body in relation to desire, as suggested by the scene where Ramón steps in front of the projection screen. The exercise of seeing — and I say "exercise" and not "action," as it is a repeated gesture that brings with it a certain training of the eye and a cognitive reassembly of the perceived as an adjustment to the seen — is reaffirmed in the final sequence of the film, immediately following the baptism of Rodolfo and Olga's firstborn. With Rodolfo reciting verses from Manuel Acuña's "Nocturno a Rosario," the camera pans from a seated Olga and a kneeling Ramón holding the baby to a standing Rodolfo and then, finally, to a seated Doña Herlinda.[6] Rodolfo benevolently gestures toward her as the camera moves in to a portrait shot of the matriarch, who stares at the lens, momentarily jarring the viewer from the perceived axiomatic anonymity of the scopic regime. The frame centers her just as Rodolfo is quieted by loud mariachi music: the aural disjunction of the montage temporarily blinds us to the out-of-frame characters and systems in the scene, as it is a moment of cultural and heteronormative reaffirmation as the baptism of the baby and the invited guests maintain the illusion of patriarchy in the household. We are beckoned to focus exclusively on Doña Herlinda, reigniting the scopic relationship of seer and seen provoked by the earlier projection onto Ramón, as the camera zooms out to incorporate the lovers and the child in a posed, implausible final image that is more appropriately seen in the static visual arts.

Doña Herlinda's looking directly at the camera is a narratological and technical acknowledgment of the scopic regime, something Ripstein alludes to in the scene in *El lugar sin límites* where La Manuela spies Pancho's brutal flirtations with La Japonesita, although, as in *El lugar sin límites,* the image of Doña Herlinda cannot probe beyond this simple acknowledgment.

As a portrait of the players and ties that bind them, the final shot of *Doña Herlinda* confirms the scopic relationship between viewer and gendered subject in Maricón cinema, where the ethical possibilities bestowed on being through viewership are avowed, though no further urge or action is explicitly requested. Maricón cinema is, then, political if we are to highlight the bringing into visibility of complex characters who, among other things, deviate from heterosexist norms, but it is also implicitly apolitical, in a de Certeauian and micropolitical understanding, as the image does not engender a tacit tactical relation between entities in the dialectic of seeing. The filmic photo, or an approximation, as is the case here, pushes a critical inquiry into the film as, through the temporal pausing implied by the particular medium, we are asked to consider exactly how these static bodies interplay and provoke a thorough examination of the erotics of the moving images and bodies beyond a simple narratological analysis, albeit only through that initial not-moving image.[7]

2.3. *A family portrait that fosters distance at the end of* Doña Herlinda. *Copyright Clasa Films.*

A similar dynamic is congealed at the conclusion of Francisco Lombardi's *No se lo digas a nadie* (1998), an adaptation of a novel by the same name by the Peruvian Jaime Bayly (published in 1994).[8] Presented as a sort of coming-of-age tale of the upper class in Lima, the film recounts Joaquín Camino's (Santiago Magill) sexual development from his early curiosity while attending a summer camp hosted by Opus Dei to his fleeing to Miami and finally his return to "decency" as a newly graduated lawyer with a girlfriend in the same social circle from which he had previously escaped.

The caveat to this tale of virtuous redemption, irony being here implicit in my description, is that Joaquín's old lover, Gonzalo (played by Christian Meier, who reprises the role of the closeted homosexual in another Bayly adaptation, *La mujer de mi hermano* seven years later), joins the graduation party. The film ends with a snapshot, a change-of-medium image that, as in *Doña Herlinda*, encourages a pause at and subsequent studied inquiry into the erotics of the still image, as stand-in for the visual and narratological trajectory preceding it.

While the novel established Bayly's reputation as the enfant terrible of the Peruvian mass media (I include his novels, as they too, of late, have been geared toward a pop sensibility), Lombardi's film catapulted the homosexual theme into the mainstream's collective conversation. While Ripstein and Hermosillo made homosexual-inflected films that fall into Martínez Expósito's second phase, they were marketed first to an international audience and then through limited local release. Lombardi's film, however, galvanized the Peruvian capital with its frank take on homosexuality in the country. While the film met resistance from the usual morality police, it did ignite a wider discussion of being gay in a society where sexual difference is taboo—as the protagonist's father affirms in the film: "one can be anything, except a maricón" [se puede ser cualquier cosa, menos maricón].

I am not interested in rehashing the narratological issues or sociocultural discernments of the film, as Foster, Joel del Río, and Gustavo Subero, among others, have already provided invaluable insights into these topics.[9] What I want to draw our attention to, though, pursuing a trajectory established in my earlier discussion of films by Ripstein and Hermosillo, is the relationship propagated by the film between the homosexual subject and the viewer and lens. Like Ramón in *Doña Herlinda*, Joaquín never fully asserts an intimate association beyond the flat celluloid of the montage but is, instead, visually, aurally, and affectively relegated to a dialectic site as viewed object, as Vieira argues, that holds an ethical potential.

Our first taste of this visual and, by implication, political geometry occurs early in the film, after an initial scene where a pubescent Joaquín is shown groping his tent mate. The image cuts to a much older protagonist confessing his weekly sins at church. The camera tilts rightward to include in the frame a close

2.4. *Framing the homosexual,* No se lo digas a nadie. *Copyright Lola Films.*

shot of the priest listening to the confession, overlaid by choral singing. Separated by the barrier of the confession booth, the image is split in two, akin to the image of Doña Herlinda approaching the two men in the garden: on one side sits the priest facing the lens, a symbol of the patriarchal order that regiments images and productions of the maricón; on the other, a well-coifed upper-class male with his hands clutched in penance, faces the priest. The angling of their bodies promotes a specific relationality with the viewer that calls attention to the dialectic of seen and seer, where only the priest can, through his posture, be allowed a position of contestation or reattributed subjectivity regarding the seer. Joaquín, however, is not allowed any such reciprocity as he faces and answers to the left side of the image, thereby rendering him as a viewed object in the field of vision of the voyeur audience. The lighting of this shot calls attention to the objectification of the sexual other, as Joaquín is backgrounded by bright light amidst a tiled background whereas the priest is shrouded in somber colors. The image therefore draws attention to the protagonist as object through a simple technique of hues and positions him and the viewer in an ethicovisual exercise.

This viewership strategy is furthered in a later scene, when Joaquín escapes the brothel he was brought to by his father to help him enter manhood. Going to a prostitute as a rite of passage is a trope in Latin American cultural production that merits its own study, and what happens in Lombardi's film is unsurprising, given the protagonist's hesitance to enter the masculine field of play despite repeated paternal coercion in several scenes throughout the film.[10] When things go awry with the prostitute, Joaquín runs from the brothel in a classic fleeing montage that is de rigueur in any Hollywood film from the 1980s, complete with a loud nondiegetic soundtrack of electric riffs, cutting images, tracking shots of the running subject from different angles, and a dissolve cut at the

2.5. *The protagonist in opposition to the lens,* No se lo digas a nadie. *Copyright Lola Films.*

very end that disperses into an image of an older Joaquín sitting in a university classroom.

At the moment of dissolution of a trope we see a frontal shot of a running Joaquín. He looks in the direction of the moving camera though not directly at the lens, evoking the cowering La Manuela in *El lugar sin límites*. Like the sexual dynamics of viewership posited by Ripstein's film, the frontal image of Joaquín evokes a reconsideration of the figure as not another stereotyped maricón but as a nuanced and precocious representation *and* exploration of the psyche behind difference. The visage and gaze of the homosexual character are not met in an explicit interchange of the seer and the seen but are brought closer to the viewer as a point of critical reflection that poses a cross-examination that goes beyond the flippant aesthetics and erotics of the *fichera* genre. By centering Joaquín and emphasizing his off-center gaze toward the lens, he is in effect reoriented from his original positioning as object in relation to the priest/patriarchy/normativity in the earlier scene and now occupies an openly tensile position that reaffirms the film's inclusion in Martínez Expósito's second phase of LGBT cinema in Latin America.

This modification or evolution in the regime of the scopic and its accompanying potential for an emancipatory action in the viewer conditions the final image of the film. I am unsure of Lombardi's influences in choosing to end the film in such a way but cannot discount the legacy left by Hermosillo's final print (although not completely static) of the bodies entwined in the erotics of *Doña Herlinda*. If the final image in the Mexican feature provokes a self-reflexive questioning of narrative components and trajectories, a similar effect is suggested in Lombardi's conclusion, where a "reformed" Joaquín returns from Miami and graduates with a law degree. As his family and close friends gather for a posed photograph, the camera is placed behind and to the right of a photographer who is peering into his lens. The action itself is banal, but its symbolism as instructions to the viewer, that is, instructions to *see,* is fundamental to the subsequent interactions between the posing bodies. They are lined up in hierarchical order, with Joaquín behind his seated mother and Alexandra (Lucía Jiménez), his betrothed, behind Joaquin's father. The camera snaps just as Gonzalo, standing to the left of Alexandra, caresses Joaquín's cheek and the latter gazes complicitly back while the impervious female smiles and looks forward, the butt of the joke. The caress suggests that the protagonist's acquiescence to reincorporating into the social order is only a tactic of passing as hetero. The image pauses as though focused now on a photograph, going a step further than Hermosillo's allusion to the still medium, and zooms in on the trio, fading to black and white. Centered (again) in the zoomed image of the photo is the female gazing back at the camera, in a knowing though defiant posture that reemphasizes Foster's affirmation that at times the best challenge to any hegemonic order is a structured, micropolitical set of tactics that undermines any systematic strategies of normativization. The final image suggests that Alexandra will turn a blind eye to her philandering partner and in doing so, posits a challenge to the order held up by the very social matrix that surrounds them in the photo.

The closing montage and sequence are central to any analysis of *No se lo digas a nadie,* but I want to draw our attention backward, immediately before the snapping of the photo that portrays the conflictive erotics of the film. Prior to the photo, the shot cuts to an image of the photographer instructing the group to smile. The camera, aimed at the viewer, positions us from within the vantage point of the insular group where the tensions of heteronormativity have been flexed throughout the narrative. The explicit location of the viewer-subject, although slight and not always noted in commentaries on passing and the closet in Lombardi's film, illustrates the potential for an ethical relationship between the visual and captured erotics and the viewer in a final push toward self-reflexivity as we are no longer allowed to occupy the vantage point of the extraneous voyeur. The viewer is included within the organization of patriarchy, signaling us as complicit actors who sustain or map out the matrices of power that maintain the reign of heterosexism over gender difference. The audience is no longer extrinsic to the plight and being of Joaquín and Gonzalo but integral as an intimate member of the multiple valences of power that keep the caress and its corresponding desire limited to the realm of the unseen (though the photographic capture brings it, albeit momentarily, into the visible). It is not implied that the viewer, though involved, will take any particular position vis-à-vis this desire, existing thus as a multivalenced entity housing the *potential* for pro-LGBT action and feeling.

Therein lies perhaps the greatest innovation in *No se lo digas a nadie* and another point of interest in this brief genealogy of a Maricón cinema moving toward a New Maricón cinema: the viewer is explicitly included (is not simply a voyeur, as in the Maricón and *fichera* genres) in the erotics of the image and is thus allowed the potentiality of positioning and choosing alliances that implicate an ethics of viewership that surpasses facile exercises of identification.

CHAPTER THREE

Final Notes on a Maricón Genre

Foster and Martínez Expósito highlight a preliminary final phase in homosexual-themed cinema known for its inclusion of homosexual characters and plot lines as secondary notes amid a broader plot concern. There are several films that can be included here, including Barbet Schroeder's *La virgen de los sicarios*, an adaptation of a novel by Fernando Vallejo, where the pederast relationship between the protagonist and the street youths of Medellín really serves as a spice note to a more complex titration of issues such as the drug trade, gang violence, and urban decay and poverty. While the film must be congratulated for its nonchalant portrayal of two social taboos (homosexual relations and intergenerational love), it does not engage in any sustained intervention about the role or existence of sexual difference, instead focusing heavily on how gang violence has decimated the protagonist's once cherished home.

If anything, his desires for same-sex relations is a catalyst for a deeper socio-thematic engagement, a process repeated in films such as Tomás Gutiérrez Alea and Juan Carlos Tabío's *Fresa y chocolate* (1993).[1] As José Quiroga so aptly observes, it is a film whose "characters are stock characters, and its plot is lifted straight out of an after-school special . . . an allegorical narrative" ("Homosexualities," 133–134). Though the film was seized by North American critics as a gay feature, Senel Paz, the writer of the original novel and film scriptwriter, was quick to dispel this facet of the film, arguing instead that the relationship between Diego and David shows the "need for sexual, religious, and political tolerance in Cuban society" [necesidad de la tolerancia—sexual, religiosa, política—en la sociedad cubana] (Ruffinelli, "Dime tu sexo," 62).

Dealing with a young Communist Party member (David) and a culturally conservative homosexual man (Diego) in late-1970s Cuba, the film develops their intellectual exchanges amid a political climate of censorship and cultural

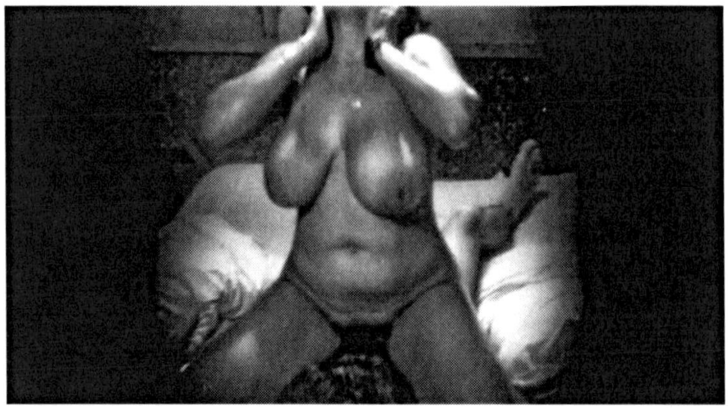

3.1. Matrices of seeing, or how Fresa y chocolate *engenders the scopic regime. Copyright* ICAIC.

repression. Sexual difference becomes, in *Fresa y chocolate*, a tired tropic set of clichés and stylistics, a rehashing of the *joto* in *fichera* films, albeit with an empowered sense of agency and taste. In fact, the representation of homoerotic desire is not much removed from that of the libidinous, almost perverse *locas* (queens, fairies, fags—a term, like maricón, that evades accurate translation) who populate the Mexican *sexi-comedia* genre, as the camera often fixates on Diego's gaze and his lips being licked in shot–reverse shot combinations. I would even go as far as to say that I am a few raunchy jokes and a pair of gratuitously exposed breasts away from including the film in less serious genealogies of Latin American cinema.

Such visual dynamics tied to the libido, with the potential for nonnormative expressions of desire, are dependent on and characteristic of the scopic regime of Maricón films, a detail emphasized early on, even prior to the appearance of the "homosexual element" in David's life. The film goes to great lengths to place sex (and the ethical positioning of the seer) at the center of its various narrative lines, emphasized in the first scene by David's bringing Vivian to a seedy hotel. While she prepares herself to be seduced, though she facetiously plays the naïveté card when David appears to uphold the moral values of heteronormativity and marriage, he walks over to a door dividing their room from another. He hears a woman moaning, and after checking on his partner like a cheeky teenage boy, looks into a makeshift peephole covered by tissue paper, undoubtedly made by men who understood the voyeuristic possibilities of these locales.

The image cuts to a point-of-view shot framed by the uneven boring into the wooden panel, and we see the busty torso of a woman gallivanting on top of a man. The dynamics of sight in this particular shot are not unlike the binocular-mediated images of normative sex in *El día del compadre*: the image signals a tacit dialectic of viewing that places the seer in a voyeuristic and disaffected location. This early image, as in the *fichera* genre and *El lugar sin límites*, to some extent establishes a praxis of perception regarding the erotics of the narrative that leaves no real room for any prolonged or incisive inquiry into sexual difference. It comes as no surprise, then, that Diego is never quite flushed out as anything more than a *loca* with high taste in literature and an interest in its free distribution under the new government.

The revolution and its legacy lie at the center of the film's project, as evidenced by a sequence toward the end where we are greeted with a panoramic long shot—a perception image—of Havana while Diego asks David (and the audience) to "let me take a good look" [déjame mirarla bien] prior to his impending departure from the nation. This request, coming at the end of the film, underscores two critical gestures that are calibrated and readjusted throughout *Fresa y chocolate*: an emphasis on seeing as the primal mode of perception, relaying thus a specific visual cognition of the erotic; and a heuristic focus on Havana as metonym of the revolution, *cubanidad* (Cubanness), and a higher social order and compromise that are the true object of study. The film, therefore, is less about the maricón, though he is central to the development of the plot, and more about external factors, placing it, then, in the latter phases of Foster and Martínez Expósito's pedigrees.[2]

All this talk of *jotos*, *locas*, and maricones leads us back to my initial argument for the chosen terminology, as what is ubiquitous in these films is male-on-male desire, perhaps reflecting social realities of visibility and taboo vis-à-vis lesbianism, or perhaps the need to reaffirm countertypes in creating the stereo-

3.2. The bodies of difference vis-à-vis the city at the end of Fresa y chocolate. *Copyright ICAIC.*

type of the macho, as is the case with any film and legacy of the *fichera* genre. In a queer sense, there is nothing exponentially decentering about the gender practices and portrayals in these films; they are more an exposure of the tactics and strategies that keep patriarchy in place. The reader will note, furthermore, that there is a distinct lack of women-centered narratives in these films, a detail highlighted by Foster in the introduction to *Queer Issues*. In fact, it is not until we transcend the poetics of the Maricón genre that we see films that place female sexuality and characters at the core of their gender interrogations, as is the case in films by Puenzo and Solomonoff, for example. In Maricón films, though, when women are present, they are less true visual and narrative conduits of homoeroticism and more what Foster calls "an allegory of the queer" (*Queer Issues*, xvii).

Perhaps it is easier to create an inclusive definition of nonnormative women within this genrification by including films that, although not explicitly homoerotic, do portray specific tactics and positions that decenter, and not simply uncover, heterosexist structures. In other words, we can include in a subset or, problematically, in a tangent a separate line of films that exhibit how women can and do undertake gender subversion.

The films of María Luisa Bemberg, as critics have already noted, are at the core of this subsection, though I find a less studied film by Hermosillo, *Amor libre* (1979), to be equally useful for this.[3] Hermosillo had already explored the topic of empowered *mujeres modernas* (modern women) in *La verdadera vocación de Magdalena* (Magdalena's real vocation, 1972), but he takes the potential for sexual decentering further in *Amor libre*, as the film not only advances the emancipation of women but also delves, albeit superficially, into the possibilities of female homoeroticism. It follows Julie and Julia, two young women who live together in an idyllic penthouse loft in the heart of Mexico City (quite incongruous, given their economic status, though one can easily forgive Hermosillo for portraying idealized urban lifestyles in the interest of focusing on broader themes such as sex and gender). The two are polar opposites—Julia, a sexually charged extrovert, Julie, a bookish loner—and are economically independent as a result of co-owning a store selling Mexican knickknacks and touristy kitsch. The film develops their friendship and cohabitation (the two female leads slowly begin adopting the idiosyncrasies and characteristics of the other in a subtle osmosis), culminating with Julie's fleeing with Julia's onetime boyfriend, Ernesto.

Roberto Cobo makes an appearance in the film, exhibiting some of the flair that lured Pancho in *El lugar sin límites*, as a street musician who rides the city's bus system and plays for tips. The song he repeats in several scenes, "En el mar" (In the ocean), becomes a metaphor for the freedom that Julie develops in her yearning to escape the structured lifestyle that is expected of her.[4] Cobo's char-

3.3. *Roberto Cobo gesturing toward the aqueous at the beginning of* Amor libre. *Copyright Conacine.*

acter and Octavio, the quiet foil to Ernesto's rampant machismo, can be interpreted as semblances of the homosexual countertype, though Hermosillo never fully explores the potential for male homoeroticism in the film. *Amor libre,* instead, and from the outset, develops an emboldened female agency on the part of Julia as a point of entry into the systems of gender (mimetic, so to speak, of a sociocultural reality) that the film puts on the table.

There are several points of contact that enable the inclusion of *Amor libre* in any genealogy of lesbigay Latin American films. First—and I argue that this is perhaps a side effect of Hermosillo's making films outside the mainstream—*Amor libre* demonstrates an acute awareness of the gaze's potential in framing and aligning the gendered bodies of the image with the viewer. This is perhaps most evident in the sequences in the loft, a modern structure with open and latticed windows that allows the viewer a voyeuristic, almost eerie, access to the actions within. In the first scene in which this space makes an appearance, the camera spies Julia after returning from a day in the streets of the city. We see her inside the apartment, reminding us of the dynamics of diegetic viewership in *El día del compadre,* and hear incessant ambient noise from the city streets below. This one sequence—appearing early in the film and therefore, I argue, a conscientious move by the director to indicate relationality between the seer and the seen in the moving image—captures the thesis of Maricón films as a voyeuristic, detached experience taking place almost exclusively within the urban as both a spatial and a semantic referent.

Lacking in the film is any exploration of male homoerotics—almost a sig-

3.4. *Framing, the urban, and sex and gender deviance,* Amor libre. *Copyright Conacine.*

nature of the director's oeuvre—though there are insinuations of female-on-female desire that, like so many other cultural manifestations of lesbianism, exists almost through its very palpable absence.[5] In the case of *Amor libre,* it makes an appearance through subtle insinuation and careful placement and movement of the camera. In the film's most explicit scene, we see Julia riding Ernesto through a sort of semitransparent screening device, in a position not unlike that spied by David in the opening sequence of *Fresa y chocolate*. The camera centers her voluptuousness and slowly zooms in on her face, neglecting Ernesto's corporality and, symbolically, subtracting him and masculinity (as a sign and organizing component of heterosexism) from the erotics of the image. Julia's gaze reaffirms the camera's movement, as she looks upward and away from her lover and expresses in a moment of sheer ecstasy: "You don't know what you're missing" [No sabes ni lo que te pierdes]. The recipient of her dialogue is the visually absent yet erotically present Julie, who becomes, thus, the principal designatum of Julia's desire. The camera reiterates this reading by continuing to zoom in on her head (the site of verbal and visual enunciation) until the image blurs behind the in-focus beams of the screening device in a long take that is punctuated by her sounds of pleasure.

This expression of desire, occurring almost a third of the way through the film, lays the groundwork for subsequent domestic sequences where the two women share their living space. Their interactions, at face value simple vignettes of cohabitational living, develop a distinctively amorous though not explicitly erotic tone. In one scene, they share a meal that assumes a visual language not unlike that of the classic heterosexual romantic dinner: by candlelight, seated at opposite ends of the table, facing each other and sharing glances typical of the exercises of courtship so prevalent in and perpetuated by the cinema. In another scene Julia and Julie share a double bed, the former wearing Ernesto's pilot's uniform and the latter in a demure nightgown. Julia adopts an almost masculine pose before falling asleep, and Julie covers her in a blanket before turning the lights off—on the scene, and on the overt possibility of the developing physical erotics between them. It is almost enough that Hermosillo characterizes the two protagonists through diametrically opposed sartorial and gesticular cues for us to presume an impending erotic connection (made possible only through the earlier filmic techniques employed in the heterosexual sex scene between Julia and Ernesto).

Amor libre exemplifies some of the tropes and techniques that are intrinsic in the Maricón genre, though the film, ironically, does not delve into any fictitious or real instances of "mariconness." Instead, it moves the genre further into a liminal space left largely untouched that pushes the barriers of sex and gender on the screen, suggesting that the possibilities (in terms of representation) of gender difference are more than the flat feminized and fetishized sissies that populate *fichera* films. This failure to go beyond the frontier of acceptability, to actively engage the viewer in an ethical exercise (beyond viewership) is the pitfall of these films and relegates the Maricón to a forgettable side of the cultural archive, one that New Maricón cinema will take as a starting point to renovate representations of sex-gender difference in Latin America.

Part II

NEW MARICÓN CINEMA

GIVEN THE NATURE OF THE REPRESENTATIONS OF sexual difference in Latin American cinema (and here I am not referring to any possibility of a distinctly queer cinema but of simple instances in which characters and themes of same-sex relations or bodily difference are treated), a reflection on recent trends is warranted. In the preceding pages, and in dialogue with previous criticism, I have attempted a brief overview of what I call Maricón cinema. I have drawn attention both to the systems of representation and to how these, in turn, have encouraged a particular affective relationship with the image. In the case of Maricón cinema there is, more specifically, a lack of relationship, as the notion of difference is treated more as deviance that is meant to be seen and heard but not necessarily connected to.

This, however, is not to say that these films embarked on a purely negative venture or furthered a politics that only served to ostracize bodies and identities that fell outside the binomial parameters of Latin American gender normativity. Instead, Maricón films brought to a wider audience the issues and real experiences of sexual minorities. While homophobic violence has been and continues to be a reality, how many viewers saw for the first time in *El lugar sin límites* the results, albeit fictive, of homophobic beatings? How many (again, for the first time) saw themselves invited to view the real experiences of a homosexual male in a revolutionary society in *Fresa y chocolate*? In addition to making the heterosexist viewer privy to the intimacy of difference, these films furthered a social consciousness of self for non-normative or gay-labeled viewers, who were able, finally, to identify with the protagonist of the matinee. Maricón cinema, like its literary antecedents, broke ground by creating a communal sense of sexuality that cemented what would later become identitarian transnational movements toward gay identity in the region.[1]

Though these films made strides in visibility and acceptance, they did not engage a truly transnational or global audience in the struggles for sexual and identitarian emancipation. If anything, as I outlined earlier, these films unknowingly weakened the politics of the image by connecting sexual difference to broader themes that were already being hashed out in the critical and cultural collective. Topics such as social violence, the role of democracy after revolution, the changing social demographics of urbanization, and the practices of economic subservience all feature heavily in Maricón films as broader superstructures onto which the question of sexuality is neatly and, at times, casually tagged.

Homosexual-themed cinema produced and filmed in Latin America has, however, undergone a seismic contextual shift from its antecedents. Starting in the first decade of the twenty-first century, a slew of films began to address the issue of difference through style, aesthetics, and ethics that broke with scopic visions of sexual difference. In keeping with the nomenclature I favor in part I, I propose that what we see today in Latin American and international film festivals and movie theaters can be called New Maricón cinema, an evolution of the Maricón parent with some vestigial characteristics still in place, namely, the failure to completely break toward a true queer cinema. New Maricón cinema can be described by the following, though not exhaustive, list of characteristics: a qualitative focus on sex and gender difference that is not treated as a subset or subtheme of a broader debate; the minting of varying aural and visual affective intensities—often engendered by an engineered hapticity to the viewing experience—that stimulate an empathic viewership experience; and the use of nonurban spaces, metaphors, and movements that shift the reference of the subject away from the gendered tautology of the city. The urban, under Maricón films, served as a spatialization and point of reference for heteronormativity; though the Maricón materialized and was allowed to walk through its streets, he/she never reached acceptance or generated empathy from a heterosexist audience while there. The structures of the urban, namely closed, framed spaces and scopic roads and alleys promoted a perception of this figure as an abstracted and abjected object.

These same characters, however, are allowed to break from the confines of urban gendered normativity in New Maricón cinema, as the narratives and images employ a stark juxtaposition to the urban or, at times, a complete disassociation from it. In my analyses of *Contracorriente, El último verano de la Boyita*, XXY, and *El niño pez,* I show how the moving image dialogues and contrasts with the urban as a semantic and visual narrative device. In these films, the nonurban, or rural, space allows for a nuanced and studied exercise of approximation to sexual difference that, through various affective registers, encourages viewership and the circulation of empathy.

These films, then, permit and perform an "outing" of Latin American cinema from the Maricón closet and from the spatial contract of heteronormativity that the urban propagates. They out difference from clichéd and politically flawed exercises to a productive and fecund terrain where Latin American gendered bodies enter into a broader dialogue with global movements and an ethically engaged audience, where difference is not merely symptomatically viewed but also allowed to enter into personal and political action. They, in fact, demonstrate a mindful and almost deliberate topical preoccupation with the nouns and verbs of outing, whether with the subject who tries to escape the normativity of the domestic or the body that constantly resists the camera's attempts at framing and thereby encloses itself within a carefully curated and constrained medium and praxis of viewing. These films often project a critical understanding of the relationship between the camera and queerness and forward, through various technical and narrative devices, an alternative that in effect creates a categorization of the New.

A useful reference in distinguishing the ethical projects behind both genres is Murray Smith's distinction between *recognition* and *alignment* in reference to the spectator's relationship with certain characters. While Maricón cinema is exemplary of recognition, or "the spectator's construction of character: the perception of a set of textual elements, in film typically cohering around the image of a body, as an individuated and continuous human agent" (Smith, *Engaging Characters*, 82), including, I may add, their gender identification and sexuality, New Maricón films provoke an alignment of the spectator with certain characters, "placed . . . in terms of access to their action, to what they know and feel" (*Engaging Characters*, 83). Alignment, furthermore, possesses a relationship with the generation and movement of affect, including how it shapes and leaves imprints on surfaces and bodies. In Ahmed's understanding of affective circulations, alignment can be viewed as one manifestation of "orientation," a positive facet of the term wherein the subject seeks proximity and ties with the object at hand. She underlines that "the orientations we have toward others shape the contours of space by affecting relations of proximity and distance between bodies . . . orientations shape not only how we inhabit space, but how we apprehend this world of shared inhabitance" (*Queer Phenomenology*, 3).

Alignment, then, is an empathic orientation brought about by the transmission of positive affective intensities between the subject and the object, thus rendering both and their spaces as reshaped surfaces. This fundamental difference between recognition and alignment is, I argue, encouraged through the various technical and narrative traits I identify below, proposing thus the collective realignment with the *joto* and the maricón so prevalent in the history of Latin American film. I do not mean for these concepts and definitions to be exhaustive in their current iteration but hope that the following discussion provides individual and holistic reflections that will lead to a work-in-progress notion of a New Maricón cinema in and from Latin America.

CHAPTER FOUR

Outing Contracorriente

ON SPATIAL CONTRACTS AND FEELING NEW MARICÓNNESS

JAVIER FUENTES-LEÓN'S DIRECTORIAL DEBUT, *CONTRAcorriente* (2009), has garnered both critical interest and success, winning rave reviews from respected international print and Web outlets and coveted Audience Awards at Sundance, Chicago, Miami, and Cartagena. The film recounts the archetypal love triangle of a gay man (Santiago), a closeted man (Miguel), and an unsuspecting wife (Mariela) in a quiet fishing village somewhere in Latin America. It explores issues such as religion, death, and homophobia, all within a magical ghost story. It comes as no surprise, then, that some reviewers have called *Contracorriente* "*Brokeback Mountain* meets *Ghost*," tacking Fuentes-León's film onto a growing corpus of mass-market homosexual-themed cinema that shares the populist project of raising "awareness" of homosexuality.

What interests me, however, in reading and, to some extent, feeling *Contracorriente*, is its placement within a critical Latin American canon of gay cinema, which has been ignored as a negotiating agent in global discussions of a Queer cinema. The title of this chapter is necessarily in dialogue with the theorization of Maricón film, as my suggestion of a "new" cinema is grounded in a tangible shift from a defined "old," which I identify to be the traditional scopophilic nature of LGBT-themed cinema in Latin America. In the following pages, I will negotiate points of contact between these two genres in an attempt to underline how cinema produced in the region is undergoing a shift that is more in line with Anglophone notions of queerness or the broader lesbigay agenda that Foster highlights. My study is by nature preliminary and not meant to be exhaustive, yet I am also categorical in my intent to identify aesthetic and poetic traits that serve as a blueprint for contemporary cinema.

I want to argue that Fuentes-León's love triangle in an idyllic fishing village breaks from the tradition of Maricón cinema and can instead be read as New

Maricón cinema, in dialogue with, yet not a direct subset of, Ruby Rich's New Queer cinema, as the film presents, instead, a paradox of competing positions and postulates on gender that problematizes its inclusion within Rich's and Foster's respective genealogies. It can be considered a "New" iteration of films by Hermosillo and Lombardi because it undertakes a "queerying," on several levels, of the representation of homosexualities in Latin America.[1] The most obvious facet of this shift involves an authorial focus on the haptic and its affective potential in reorienting the viewer's positionality vis-à-vis the queer subject.[2]

Unlike in the films that I identify in part I, the camera in New Maricón cinema does not sustain a particular heteronormative gaze but instead encourages the viewer to be placed in motion with the nonheteronormative subject; that is, we as viewers are explicitly moved to identify with the queer body and desire through several auditive, visual, and generic (in terms of a Maricón legacy on the silver screen) cues. What I am proposing is the notion of the cinema moving beyond a visual space to that of a representational and empathetic art form in line with Marshall McLuhan's notions of the "audile-tactile" (McLuhan and McLuhan, *Laws of Media*, 45).[3]

In the most obvious sense, *Contracorriente* relocates the homosexual problematic to the nonurban and nonterritorialized seaside space, breaking with previous films that typically maintain the urban as a topological referent. There is a spatial queering in the geographic sense of the homosexual subject away from the masculine and feminine space of the public and private in urban settings. The subject is, instead, relocated and renegotiated in a nontraditional geography that lays a foundation for more substantial cognitive and haptic approximations to the subject. With this spatial queering, gender and sexuality are treated outside the contextualized sociopolitical systems of oppression that are characteristic of Latin American gay cinema; in effect, we can argue that *Contracorriente* succeeds in outing Latin American cinema from the domestic and urban space.

An earlier example of this shift is signaled in Eduardo Nabal Aragón's study of *Y tu mamá también*, where he argues that Alfonso Cuarón's film manages to delve into the homoerotics of a very homosocial relationship only through spatial displacement away from the city and toward the rural oceanside (*El marica*, 176). The move away from the urban, arguably, allows the two male protagonists to share a drunken kiss—an event that goes unmentioned and forgotten on their return to the city.

A similar structure can be observed in Julian Schnabel's *Antes que anochezca*, as the film queers the macho sex symbol (Javier Bardem) in the homoerotic and liminal geography of the coast. There is a relocation of the subject away from the city as a voyeuristic space in which the viewer is mainly asked to see the object of difference, to a scenic un-urbanity that reframes our viewing practices. I am not suggesting that the city is by nature a site of heteronormativity, as it is the urban that has often been the space of "coming out" that Karen Tongson and Judith Halberstam identify; rather, its usage as a cinematic setting is often accompanied by a heteronormative gaze that fixates difference as non-affective. *Contracorriente,* however, moves us away from this cinematic legacy in several steps that the director employs to accentuate the fact that the film breaks with several generic conventions.

There is, furthermore, a narratological queering of the Maricón genre, as Fuentes-León employs and, to an extent, problematizes the magical-realist aesthetic that is, in itself, polemical in contemporary cultural production from the region. Unlike previous films that have tended to spoon a healthy dose of reality onto the urban chronicles of sexual exploration, *Contracorriente* engages a magical break, explaining, in part, the critics' comparison to *Ghost.*

The final, and perhaps most interesting, queering can be deemed affective, as the film decenters stereotypes such as the closeted male, the cheated-on spouse, and the scandalized village through a carefully framed tactile and aural experience of heterosexual norms.[4] There is a recalibration of the stereotype, which, as understood by Rey Chow, is an "objective, normative practice that is regularly adopted for collective purposes of control and management" (*The Protestant Ethnic,* 54). This latter process, however, is intrinsically spatial, as Fuentes-León frames and unframes homosocial and homosexual relations relative to what Waugh terms the private and public function of space (*The Fruit Machine,* 183–184), as *Contracorriente* plays with the scopophilic and the haptic in creating a more nuanced and emotionally intense relation between the viewer and the onscreen image.

The director is acutely aware of the role of space as genderized and genderizing and pays particular attention to its role in the poetic characterization of the homosexual. This is observed from the opening image of a tight close shot of Mariela's very pregnant stomach. Its rhythmic rise and fall, which induces a maternal or paternal emotion in the viewer, is interrupted by the image of a cross dangling from Miguel's neck, underlining the triangle of sexuality, organized religion, and procreation. We can, here, return to Foster's definition of queerness and its visibility in Latin American cultures, as the film's triangulation stresses the structurally complicit facets that maintain and proliferate heteronormative notions of subjectivity and the family. By centering this triangle in the establishing shot of the narrative, Fuentes-León sets up a deconstructive practice — an unpacking — that will call into question each of the apices of the structure that oppresses difference. The two characters play up this representation as Miguel spiritedly questions the gender of the baby, leading Mariela to chastise him for possibly "confusing" the child.

From the outset, heteronormativity is placed in a dialogue with noncon-

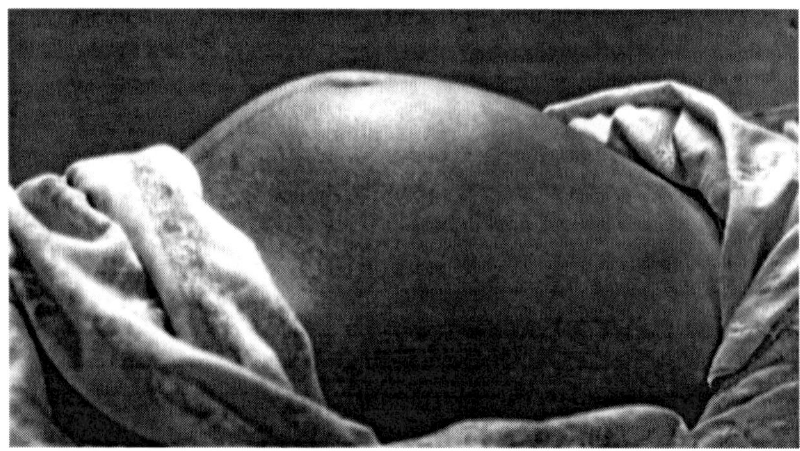

4.1. Setting the tenor of normativity, Contracorriente. *Copyright Elcalvo.*

forming subject positions and possibilities, as Mariela's words reprise traditional discourses of homosexuality's being a choice/a disease/a confusion. By voicing the notion of confusion, she evokes the heteronormative stance of there being a "right" or a "correct" sense of identification, based again on the binary of gender and sex that is founded on the possibility of procreation (so intrinsic to any monotheistic tradition). This stance is signaled by her rising and falling pregnant belly. The fact that the first scene takes place within the confines of the heterosexual bedroom only serves to amplify the film's underlining of heteronormativity as a thematic point of departure and suggests that what is to come is an exploration of the very "confusing" nature of the queer.

Succinct and repeated spaces in the film are further codings of heteronormativity. The bar where Miguel, Héctor, and the rest of the village's male population go to drink and play cards is an important example. A scantily clad blonde pinup reminds the viewer that this is a distinctly masculine space, unwelcoming of Santiago as he invites the men for a beer to commemorate the passing of Héctor's brother and Miguel's cousin, Carlos. Santiago is presented as an outsider, a *forastero,* not to be trusted because he comes from the city (the name of which is never mentioned). The film mints the urban male artist stereotype (he is a painter and photographer), as there is a suggestion that he is somehow different because of his disinclination to follow the behavioral patterns and gender performance of the other men in the village.

Difference, here, brings us back to the notion of the urban as a site of coming out or of going beyond gender norms. Evident in Santiago's characterization is the seeming paradox that is built around the urban vis-à-vis viewership, as the characterization codes for the potentiality of the queer. Yet it is visually evocative of simply seeing queerness in the Maricón genre. The men initially reject Santiago's offer but acquiesce to the gesture upon Miguel's taking a swig from a bottle, foreshadowing his clandestine relationship with Santiago. Miguel's actions succeed in bringing Santiago momentarily into the spatiality of homosocial acceptability that the cantina advocates and also succeeds in gently guiding the viewer to what is to come, as the eroticism of his lips touching the phallic bottle are not lost when we discover later that he is having a clandestine relationship with the artist.

Miguel and Mariela's house, through the carefully placed marriage portrait next to the door and several Catholic-themed prints, further illustrates the domesticity of heteronormativity that the cantina evokes on a communal level. The diegetic entering of characters into the house and visual aids that emphasize the importance of the localized space and the scopic in characterizing the subject constantly remind the viewer of the sanctity of heterosexual marriage. Fuentes-León continues to build the triangulation of heteronormativity into the spatiality of some of the film's settings, as though to emphasize that the film will actively engage in unpacking these norms.

As a result, the bar, the house (that is, the living space of the protagonal nuclear family), and the church in the small fishing village are reference points for establishing a topology of gender practice and acceptability in *Contracorriente*. The first shot of the diegetic village accents this notion of a topology of gender. It is a long shot split between the ocean and the desert, which are set up as two oppositional spaces constructed by their differences and their relationship with and to acceptability. If one is colorful, dynamic, and full of life, the

4.2. Specifying the spatial contract of heteronormativity, Contracorriente. *Copyright Elcalvo.*

other is somber, dreary, and dead. The gendered spaces of the village exist in between the binary geographies, as a symbolic point of normalcy that evades the (semantic, geographic, symbolic) extremes attributed to the sea and the desert.

It is, therefore, unsurprising that Miguel and Santiago can express their homoerotic desire only when spatially shifted away from the ground zero of topographic normalcy; that is, they are allowed to manifest their love and desire only when located at the extremes of the spatial spectrum that the film establishes. Their first embrace is captured in an empty and unfinished house in the desert, separated from the village by a steep hill that Miguel quietly climbs. It is worth noting that the images only show him negotiating this spatial shift away from the point of normalcy, as he, unlike Santiago, must function within the norms of heterosexuality demanded by the house/bar/church triangle, whereas his lover is already gender marked by his profession and origin (the city). By climbing the hill and coming out on the other side, Miguel in effect leaves behind his heteronormative shell and can fully express his homoerotic desire for Santiago. He goes from room to room in the empty, unfinished house, perhaps a metaphor for a Latin American political project of gender emancipation that is structurally in place but that requires consistent and substantial construction. Graffiti on one of the walls fuels this reading: "defecating in this house is prohibited" [se prohibe hacer caca en esta casa], underlying the biopolitical sanctity of the queered domestic space as vital to any sustainable progress in bringing all gendered bodies into acceptability (though one can equally argue that perhaps a better strategy would be a deconstruction of the actual assemblages of acceptability). Though not adhering to the heteronormative principles of the village house, the desert/homosexual space demands its own sense of domesticity, as it is an impromptu living space for the homosexual couple.

Of note in the spatiality of their encounter is the very need to frame it within the domestic space, as though the film is looking for an inclusionary notion of queerness along preestablished norms and systems of heterosexuality. This is akin, in a sense, to the debates surrounding gay marriage, as such political and juridical gestures do nothing to actually contest the notion of marriage as an organizational point.

The film, additionally, queries other heteronormative spaces, such as the fishing boat, the site of homosocial work, which is also definitive in establishing a belonging to masculine hegemony in the cantina. The boat's genderizing potential is established early in the film as Miguel and the other men salute the priest on the beach as they haul in a catch. The gesture of acknowledgment establishes a symbolic union between the masculine cultural space of work and the organizational semiotics of the Catholic Church, elaborated later when the fishermen participate in church activities. Their simple wave can be read as a connective line between the apices of heteronormativity that are erected in the

4.3. Homoerotic expression in the spatial calque of the household, Contracorriente. *Copyright Elcalvo.*

film's first composed shot, in which the father, the cross, and the pregnant belly are featured.

The second homoerotic encounter, unsurprisingly, occurs in a similarly queered boat, as Miguel and Santiago meet in the empty, landlocked carcass of a ship. Akin to the location of the first homoerotic encounter in the desert house, this boat is located away from the heteronormative space of the village and the metonymic entity of the fishing boat. Like the desert house, the boat is code for a simulation of heteronormativity, suggesting that the two men can partake of homoeroticism within the spatial confines of homosociality.

What is of note in the juxtaposition of the first two homoerotic scenes in the movie, however, is that in the second, the focus on locating homosexual desire in the space of homosociality directly confronts Miguel (and, to a lesser extent, Santiago) with the expected and allowed behavior of the space. In the desert house, Miguel's actions are analogous to his behavior with his wife in their village house, though a male substitutes as the object of his desire. In the abandoned boat, however, his actions break with the normalized behavior attributed to the homosocial; that is, as Eve Sedgwick has noted, his expression of male desire toward Santiago eradicates the invisibility allowed this same desire in compulsively heterosexual male groups.

In this scene, Miguel reveals to Santiago that Mariela will be having a boy. The film encourages a scopic viewing through the frames of the ship's scaffolding within the frames of the multiangled medium and close shots that capture the interchange. The images invite us to look in on this private moment of homoerotic relations, as though the men have been painted as a couple within a wooden frame, not quite unlike the framed marriage portrait at the entrance of the village house; this once again emphasizes the substitutive nature of Santiago vis-à-vis Miguel, and of Mariela vis-à-vis her husband.

There is, furthermore, the paradox of being in relation to the spatiality of the scene. The film plays with the concepts of being in/invisible and being out/visible, as though homosexuality exists within closed spaces in the film. It is visual and scopophilic, as the viewer is permitted and encouraged to witness Santiago and Miguel through the open walls of the unfinished house and the empty skeleton of the fishing boat. This scene builds, perhaps, on the legacy of the Maricón in Latin American cinema, as we are explicitly urged to see the two men exchange words and gestures as opposed to identifying or aligning with either of their positions.[5]

The juxtaposition of heteronormative and queer spaces, in addition to the paradox of being that the boat and the house posit, provides the underlying substrate for the theorization of gendered spaces and spaces of acceptability within the diegesis. The film highlights the notion of a spatial contract of heteronormativity in Latin American film. Miguel's and Santiago's inability to express their emotions within heteronormative geographies points to the existence of a spatial contract of acceptability, where gendered bodies must act out certain gender roles. Any notion of a "contract" concerning gender (norms, behavior, performance, speech, etc.) is built on an axiomatic relationship between the creation of individual and collective subjectivities and their placement within particular topologies and geographies, as we take as imperative the relationship between the self and its space. In a sense, such a contract is built around the lack that Michel Foucault identifies when theorizing space: "Space [is] treated as the dead, the fixed, the undialectical, the immobile. Time, on the contrary [is] richness, fecundity, life, dialectic" ("Questions," 70).

By theorizing a spatial contract, however, we are imbuing space (both real and diegetic) with life and richness, allowing it to enter into a dialectic with the construction of the subject. As a result, gendered subjects must act out certain roles within culturally specific loci of heterosexism. These loci may be defined as semantic, physical assemblages of the lines and structures of power that keep patriarchy in constant motion. Such spaces may include a church, a school, a single-family home, or even the neighborhood bar. Miguel, for example, must be manly, powerful, and domineering within the household, which partially explains Mariela's making him watch soccer instead of the afternoon soap opera when she first hears of his relationship with Santiago. The creation of a spatial contract here is not a legislative gesture but a loosely held together notion of gendered subjectivity that, through its interactions with space, places the subject either inside or outside, yet always in dialogue with the boundaries of specific sociocultural acceptability. Subjects enter into and agree to a "contract" with their respective topological referents (referents as code for heteronormativity) to enjoy and partake of the benefits of heterosexism.

The idea of a spatial contract, which in the case of the films studied here allows for homoerotic desire to be expressed only away from the topological sites of patriarchal power (usually located in the urban, or the semblance of it), in a way breaks from the traditional gay migration narrative, that is, that non-heteronormative bodies and desires somehow always end up moving to the big city with its possibilities of market erotics and anonymity from the hetero gaze that seemingly stagnates in the rural. Judith Halberstam theorizes metronormativity as evolving from David Bell's ideas of metrosexuality. She argues that "while the story of coming out tends to function as a temporal trajectory within which a period of disclosure follows a long period of repression, the metronormative story of migration from 'country' to 'town' is a spatial narrative within which the subject moves to a place of tolerance after enduring life in a place of suspicion, persecution and secrecy" (*In a Queer Time*, 36–37).

What is brought to our attention in the spatiality of *Contracorriente*, however, is how the characters seemingly move away from the topologically urban (the village) and instead favor the desert, or the rural. I am, of course, speaking in relative terms, as the village in no explicit descriptions can be equated with the urban, but if we remember Edward Soja's (*Postmetropolis*) notion that the urban is everywhere in the global age, then the rural, too, can microrepresentationally stand in for its macro referents. In other words, the spaces and sites of power within the rural village in the film are relatively and symbolically urban in relation to the spaces of queer expression that the two men favor.[6]

The notion of metronormativity can be used to explain the composition of Santiago, as he represents, on an altogether different scale, the relationship between the rural and the urban. He is emblematic of the urban as being a site of homosexual existence (and not necessarily of coming out, as we are not privy to his youth) and openness and plays into the stereotype of the young, urban, artistic gay man. His coming to the village highlights the paradoxical position of the urban vis-à-vis erotics in Latin America, as the village is not always an essentialist site of queer being but, in terms of representation, a topological reminder of the institutions and laws of patriarchal gender (and social, economic, racial, etc.) oppression.

The contract, in a way, explains that the first scene of lovemaking between Miguel and Santiago can only take place outside the village, in a place where neither is subject to the gendered demands of the church, the house, the cantina, and so on. Panning long shots from right to left capture them making their way to a secluded beach cave that cannot be accessed during high tide. The dry desert that backgrounds Santiago's journey is contrasted with the vivacious vibrancy of Miguel's boat ride. We can revert to the spectrum of spatial acceptability that I underlined earlier, as the film seems to suggest that their meeting is a subversive spatial act. Their coming together can be interpreted as a symbolic meeting of the desert and the sea, which in this case does not occur within the village, where they meet in a real sense, as the village stands between the desert and the ocean.

By backgrounding the shots of movement toward each other with their respective binary settings, Fuentes-León suggests that the village as a gendered spatial construct is in fact a fallacy, thereby deconstructing its affirmation of heteronormativity. A further contrast can be found in the framing of these shots, as while the desert is open and uninhibited by diegetic framing devices, the ocean is at times framed and closed in by rocky outcroppings. The diegetic framing of Miguel's moving shots in contrast with the fluid ocean can be interpreted as a simple metaphor for his being closed or closeted in his sexuality, whereas the free and unrestricted angles of Santiago reflect his acceptance of desire. They meet in a cave (another substitute for the house that Miguel shares with Mariela?) and engage in a sensual and erotic episode that is emotively jarring in its subtle compliance with the coital aesthetics of heteronormativity.

The film frames their lovemaking through a stylized sequence of close and unsteady shots that capture semantic parts of the homosexual subject and his homoerotic actions without ever portraying the body or desire as a complete whole. A series of shots focus on the hands, the back, the buttocks, and the hair, to the point that viewers at times forget that they are watching two men engage in foreplay and then sex. The film's montage of frantically moving yet disconnected pieces of the body brings into focus an important point regarding the

4.4. *Perception images that put into motion affective circulations,* Contracorriente. *Copyright Elcalvo.*

4.5. Homoerotic bodies at the cusp of the aqueous, Contracorriente. *Copyright Elcalvo.*

aesthetic of homosexual sex in New Maricón cinema, as we are not presented per se with a "body in pieces" (Féral, "Performance," 171), but with what Elena del Río rightly calls "bits and pieces of the body" (*Deleuze*, 95).

Working through a Deleuzian platform to examine affectivity and performativity, del Río argues that the excised and curated "bits and pieces" of the performative body are "a body without organs that neither results from an original unity, nor strives towards its definitive restoration" (*Deleuze*, 95). She positions the body (as assemblage) at the core of performativity—in our case, that of homoeroticism—and argues that any sustained thesis must go beyond discursive approaches ("performing femininity/masculinity," etc. [*Deleuze*, 7]) that "remain philosophically insufficient" (7).[7]

The alternative, then, is a structured examination of the corporeal facets of performance, something brought to the fore in the cinema through strategic framings that present the body as bits and pieces, never affectively guaranteeing a nonframed whole. Del Río works with Deleuze and Guattari's ruminations in *A Thousand Plateaus*, noting specifically that the resulting "body" is only an aggregate "whose elements vary according to its connections, its relations of movement and rest, the different individuated assemblages it enters" (*A Thousand Plateaus*, 256). In cinematic terms, then, the bits and pieces of the body implicate performativity and its affects, going beyond the frame and the celluloid and gesturing toward multivalenced intensities and flows that rest outside yet are connected to specific loci of the corporeal body, strategically framed, curated, shown in motion. The bits and pieces of the body—a characteristic of all New Maricón film—engender thus a cinema of affect (as opposed to the scopic) wherein the body is not purely a narrative device "performing" genders, so to speak, but one wherein discordant and multidirectional affective ties are allowed to intersect and enter into contact with the viewer.

This theorization, when juxtaposed to the montage of male body parts in the film, provides an understanding of how the images—which are in no way representative of a real material aggregate—evoke particular affective intensities through their condition of being carefully framed and segmented pieces and not a whole; in *Contracorriente*, this translates into a parsed-together performativity of sex that escapes labeling. There is, however, a very real authorial consciousness of framing (by intentionally deconstructing the body as a whole in favor of curated loci of corporeal and visual desire) that permits an affective opening.

Paradoxical yet intrinsic to this montage of bits and pieces is a praxis of framing that allows us into the affective opening, just where we notice the void that the body as bits and pieces logically leaves bare. We must remember that though the scene's framing chooses the parts and pieces that become part of a set (where one may argue that the body as pieces only manages to affirm a heteronormative gaze), the set is itself only "relatively" closed (Deleuze, *Cinema 1*, 18). Therein lies the route that the film asks the audience to take, as the bits and pieces evoke affective intensities in a viewer who sees beyond the frame, that is, beyond the relatively closed set that explicitly (though only half-heartedly) resemanticizes the gay body within heterosexual aesthetics—and senses and is reshaped by the impending *and* flowing affective currents emanating from the corporeal pieces.

The scene begins with Santiago on top of Miguel, a configuration that is quickly flipped as Miguel adopts the missionary position on top of Santiago, in effect queerying any notions of Latin American homosexuality's being a binary of a decidedly macho top (*activo*) and an effeminate, taken bottom (*pasivo*). In fact, *Contracorriente* completely resists identifying either man as the penetrator, as Miguel and Santiago interchange subservient and "feminine" roles throughout the film. This is perhaps most importantly observed in a postcoital shot, where Miguel rests his head on Santiago's naked and hairy chest, adopting a traditionally female position. The two leading men add to this observation, as neither is aesthetically feminine or "sissified"; this evokes a further break from Maricón cinema, which is quick to visually and epistemologically characterize the penetrated male (de la Mora, *Cinemachismo*, 113). Santiago and Miguel are hairy, virile, assertive (and all the other characteristics that are systematically and arbitrarily attributed to the heterosexual male), and masculine for all intents and purposes, except for the fact that each is in love with a member of the same sex. The character portrayal breaks, for example, with *Doña Herlinda* (perhaps the least fetishistic of Maricón films) as even Hermosillo is guilty of contrasting the hairy, "masculine" Rodolfo with the corporeally feminized Ramón.

The aesthetics of the sex scene in *Contracorriente* and the affective intensities it generates by calculatedly not producing discomfort in the viewer may be attributed to the camera's focusing on Miguel's buttocks while he is in the missionary position. Their rhythmic rise and fall, reminding us of Mariela's pregnant belly in the first shot, can be read within the aesthetics of heteronormative sex, not unlike a later scene in which Miguel makes love to his wife. In fact, we can, for a second, completely forget that Miguel is having sex with a man. The men's penises, furthermore, are never captured in the same detail and setting as their buttocks and are instead relegated to long, grainy shots that reveal the men's nudity without exactly portraying the (unwatchable) penis. The languid framing of the distinctly male sexualized buttocks in no way regiments our understanding of their kinesthetics in relation to homoerotic sex. By suturing the viewer's gaze to the male buttocks and other undifferentiated parts of the two lovers' bodies, the film embarks on what can be called a Trojan horse strategy of deceptively bringing the viewer into the erotics of queerness, without necessarily creating a distance (encouraged by the heterosexist gaze in Maricón cinema) that sabotages any change of an affective connection. The director addresses this disconnect by emphasizing the affective potential of the moving image in relation to its reception by Latin American audiences: "I made this film for as many people as can get to see it, but I had the Latin American audience in mind, and I wanted to highlight the romance and the love between the two men, and be a little bit careful about how much to push that envelope. I didn't want to lose [the audience], especially because [scenes with Miguel and Santiago] come early in the movie" (Fuentes-León, "Interview"). The coital aesthetic of heterosexuality that the film seizes to frame homosexual sex is fundamental to the notion of not making the film "unwatchable" to unconditioned Latin American viewers.[8]

What I am getting to is the critical shift toward affect that *Contracorriente* necessitates in contrast to earlier Maricón films, as "the material presence of the image competes with, and often supersedes, its representational power" (Beugnet, *Cinema*, 68). The geography of the film, in combination with alternating long and close scenic shots, emphasizes the haptic in inviting the reader to touch and feel the spaces of the nonurban, namely, the desert's grainy sand in contrast to the warm, wet, and bustling ocean. Herein we evidence the spatial tactics deployed in *Contracorriente*, as the kinesthetic and symbolic shift away from the urban permits a strong textural focus on the haptic in the nonrural. In a sense, the film works through the belief that the city is a bombardment of sensorial impulses that mute and numb the viewer into not feeling (or empathizing with the queer subject) and, as such, proves to be a locale that is better for viewing. In fact, our experiences of the urban are less about touch or the sensation it provokes (as is the case with the relatively unmarked seaside or the rural setting) and more about seeing (people and landmarks) and other sensorial processes that place an emphasis on consumption (commerce, entertainment, etc.) instead of affect. *Contracorriente* places the queer subject and the viewer in a space that is not compromised by mass cultural production, where what we are encouraged to feel is the contact and emotion that is generated by the diegetic environment, suturing our bodies (in their capacity for the tactile) to the filmic image, which is thereby a haptic site of empathy, and not simply viewership. In a sense, the nonurban audile-tactile long shots (which are, it is important to note, time-images in the unraveling of the plot) present in *Contracorriente* and other New Maricón films can be identified in Deleuzian speak as vectors, which, as Felicity Colman explains, "cues us to the *organization of sensory stimulation* on screen through systemic shifts in the direction and quality of things in the cinematographically constructed world" (*Deleuze and Cinema*, 121, emphasis in the original). The natural and the aqueous, materials and materialized intensities present in these transition images, are a key stylistic characteristic of the New that engages viewers in a nonnarrative image that allows them to enter into physical and tactile contact with the erotics of the film.

The focus on the haptic as a sensorial and a spatial site or point of contact, furthermore, brings to the fore the film's relationship with what is "watchable" or, more important, how the image can reorient our cultural and archival practice of simply viewing queerness as an other. Working with the axiom that the filmic image is not only visual but also tactile, Asbjørn Grønstad theorizes the existence of the "unwatchable" as "not just . . . graphic violence" but also "virtually anything in the image that may insult our sensibilities, that makes us want to avert our eyes, or that forces us to reconsider our investments, be they visual/aesthetic or political/moral" (*Screening the Unwatchable*, 15). The unwatchable, significantly, is "a means to an epistemological-ethical end" (Grønstad, *Screening the Unwatchable*, 15), leading us, in turn, to consider what the ethical drive is behind resemanticizing the homosexual along an aesthetics of heterosexual sex and around a generation of affect instead of a suturing of the heterosexual gaze to the nonnormative body.

To return to the former point, the buttocks, that corporeal and epistemological site of male homosexual desire (one cannot forget the camera's focus on La Manuela's tightly clothed backside in Ripstein's film), are recalibrated along heteronormative visuals to not be a site of penetration or effeminate prancing but, rather, the corporeal motor behind the penetrating (heterosexual) phallus. This allows a sensitive audience to not feel "unpleasure" in watching the buttocks rise and fall in the scene between Miguel and Santiago, as we later see the same thing in the sex scene between Miguel and Mariela when the husband must prove his virility to the suspicious wife.

Of note in this juxtaposition is the sequencing of the sex scenes, as we first

4.6. Bits and pieces of the body, Contracorriente. *Copyright Elcalvo.*

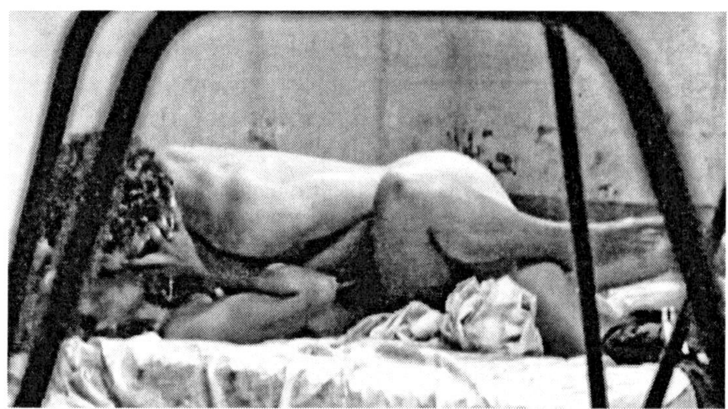

4.7. Corporeal calques of desire, Contracorriente. *Copyright Elcalvo.*

see Miguel's buttocks in a scene with Santiago and then in a scene with his wife. The film breaks with a certain logic of viewership here, that is, that an easy association could be created if the scene with Mariela were to background the viewer's experience during the homosexual scene on the beach, thereby creating a simplistic and almost banal exercise of comparison between homo and hetero sex. By placing the beach scene first, however, the film subtly foregrounds the homoerotic instead of simply framing it as an alternative or second place to hetero/procreative sex.

While *Contracorriente* is not unwatchable, it can, however, be approached through the notion of Grønstad's "inwatchable" cinema, as "it contains elements that actively try to withstand the endemic reduction of all experience and epistemology to the totalizing work of the visual" (*Screening the Unwatchable,*

85). There is, as I cite above, a narratological queering, as the filmic narrative forces the viewer to peel away the façade of the visual and to consider the textual, cultural, and literary layers behind the image: inwatchable films invite the viewer to peel "away . . . the visual layer of the image to reveal the tactile substance underneath it, thus exposing itself to the haptic" (Grønstad, *Screening the Unwatchable*, 97). An inwatchable film, furthermore, "defuses the sway of the image by displacing aesthetic pleasure from the domain of the visual to that of the tactile. Granted, the film is not an object to be touched, but that does not mean that it cannot itself enact tactility in the form of visual (and sometimes aural) gestures" (Grønstad, *Screening the Unwatchable*, 97).

We can in effect "touch" the image in *Contracorriente* by means of the spatial and its referents, the sea and the desert. Homoerotic sex is, as a result, haptic in the film, as the scenes of coitus are displaced from the scopophilic settings of the apartment bedroom, the cinema, or the back alley (all urban spaces that invite the gaze and that are prevalent in Maricón cinema) and are, instead, reinscribed onto the tactile spaces of the beach, the sand, and the ocean. Close and tightly composed portrait shots of Santiago and Miguel after making love invite the reader to feel the textures and sounds under the visual layer. In a close shot in which Santiago lies naked as a wave washes over and caresses his post-orgasmic face, the viewer is treated to the cold and smooth texture of water running over grainy sand, evocative of the macrogeography of queerness that exists right outside the heteronormative village, that is, in the desert space or in the sea. The water running over their bodies combines with the shot's emphasis on feeling and touch, displacing the viewer from a position of viewership to one of association, as we too imagine or feel the rich textures of water on sand. The scene cultivates a haptic visuality, which, as Laura Marks notes,

> frees the viewer from the illusion that cinema is capable of representing the profilmic event . . . The image indicates figures and then backs away from representing them fully—or, often, moves so close to them that they are no longer visible. Rather than making the object fully available to view, haptic cinema puts the object into question, calling upon the viewer to engage in its imaginative construction and to be aware of her or his self-involvement in that process. ("Video Haptics," 342)

This shift in positionality, read in relation to the bits and pieces of their bodies, generates an affective connection between the queer subject and a now possibly empathetic viewer who identifies with and is oriented toward (and not simply watching) the othered body.[9]

Contracorriente can also be considered haptic in the sense that it appropriates the magical-realist aesthetic, almost as if we were reading Fuentes-León's

4.8. Engineering hapticity and the audile-tactile image, Contracorriente. *Copyright Elcalvo.*

images on a page written to chronicle Macondo Latin America. Note here the generic shift from traditional LGBT films, which are in the urban, the space par excellence of McOndo, to these rural queer spaces (belonging more to Macondo), which are anachronistic in a sense, as the film plays with the temporality of Latin American cultural production.[10] The use of magical realism queers the film's cultural and literary archive in that it moves us aesthetically backward (while seemingly forwarding an emancipatory message of sexual rights), returning us to an erotic paradigm that foregrounds heterosexual relations. Magical realism is introduced as the two men disagree and fight about Miguel's inability to come to terms with his desire for Santiago. Santiago, as a result, flees in anger, accidentally drowns, and comes back as a ghost.

The magical-realist aesthetic, which successfully makes the film inwatchable, is nothing new in cinema coming from or about Latin America. What is original, however, is its use to discuss and problematize queer identities, as Fuentes-León's film in effect queers the narrative mode. We can view magical realism as an "aesthetic mode" (Pérez Melgosa, *Cinema*, 106), though *Contracorriente* might better be termed a postmagical film as it both acknowledges a cultural and historical connection to magical realism and puts forth a path to transcend it. This transcendence is made possible by decentering the aesthetic mode from traditional narratives to an uncomfortable zone that forces the viewer to reconsider preconceived judgments and perceptions. Unlike our reaction to the character played by Patrick Swayze in *Ghost*, here we are asked not only to reorient our epistemologies of viewing to accommodate the spectral but also to consider the homosexual experience within a patriarchal system of homophobia. The aesthetic mode, as Adrián Pérez Melgosa argues, "frequently attempt[s] to bring comfort from the cultural anxieties insistently brought about by [the] constant realization of the gap existing between languages that evolved in a different history and continent" (*Cinema*, 109). The film queers this notion of magical realism through a semantic substitution of "language," in Pérez Melgosa's theorization, as it reframes a narrative mode often used to negotiate parallel yet exclusive cultural paradigms to analogically parallel gender expressions of difference.

The director can be congratulated for this narratological innovation, as the magical in *Contracorriente* seemingly alleviates the anxiety of the other, the maricón who threatens heteronormativity. By reverting to an existing schema of spectrality and the magical in Latin America, the film calms any sense of violence or terror at being faced with the unknown or the queer, as heterosexual audiences, both inside and outside Latin America, are somehow already used to living with these othered subjectivities.

Language and its enunciation, however, are intrinsic to the construct of the homosexual male, as the film captures the typical silence around him as something that cannot be named yet that always exists, veiled in a hypocritical secrecy. The rumors that mill around the homosexual/artist/foreigner/other articulate Chris Straayer's notion of homosexuality's often being an open secret, where "the act of coming out often exposes an elaborate structure of *unknowing*, a deliberate ignorance induced by a fear of continuity" (*Deviant Eyes*, 163). Miguel's unknowing, for example, is so ingrained that he cannot see the penis in an ultrasound of his baby, as to do so would somehow engage him as a homosexual subject. This inability foreshadows his fear of being discovered as he insists on his heterosexuality until the end of the film.

Borrowing from Eve Sedgwick's theorizations of the closet, Straayer furthers the notion that homosexual relations are kept secret, as "by maintaining the secret, one hopes to contain homosexuality in the bodies of others" (*Deviant Eyes*, 164), in this case, in the character of the urban maricón painter. When the secret is enunciated, as when Héctor confronts Miguel about the nude paintings of his body found in the now-deceased painter's home and calls him a maricón, violence is the only answer, as language cannot acknowledge the other, as doing so implies contagion.

A further postmagical characteristic may be evidenced in the queering of space, or the breach of the spatial contract of heteronormativity. Like other cinematic narratives that advocate a post- or antimagical stance, *Contracorriente* "depict[s] geography as an imaginary category in order to reject any ontological link between culture and territory" (Pérez Melgosa, *Cinema*, 109). It is clear, even within the narratological queering of the genre, that spatiality is fundamental in understanding how *Contracorriente* brings something "New" to the aesthetics and politics of Maricón cinema.[11] The film posits a symbolic spatial lattice that emphasizes the geographic and imaginary contract of heteronormativity, away from traditional signifiers of gender in the urban. This shift is evidenced by the death of Santiago after the two men fight about Miguel's inability to break the spatial contract and to openly affirm his relationship with the painter. Santiago dies off screen, his death explained posthumously by the magical-realist spectral figure that recounts how the waves crashed his body onto the rocks before the undertow dragged it below the surface.

The title of the film, it is important to note, originates from the elimination of the queer male body (as, unlike Miguel, Santiago aims to decenter the structure held in place by the triad of spatial institutions and their corresponding discourses). The title stresses the processes leading to Santiago's demise and also the fact that this death is the engine behind Fuentes-León's appropriation of the magical-realist aesthetic. This, in turn, sets up the inwatchability of homoerotics. Santiago is killed by and in the symbolic spaces of queerness in the film, as the fluid and haptic ocean sacrifices his body to the arid and grainy coast, articulating thus the intrinsic connection between body and space. The shots immediately following the men's fight are underwater and devoid of sound, focusing on subtle yet distinctive rays of light that break through the waves and invite the viewer to look downward. A similar directionality is evoked in the next sequence as the camera focuses on sand being blown across the beach, again in a motion downward to the static camera. The quietness of the marine element is contrasted with the aurally uncomfortable wind, which evokes the haptic in that the viewer can visualize the wind and the coast and also feel the grains of sand rush against the body, akin to the tight close shot of a postcoital Santiago gazing lovingly at Miguel/the audience. The downward movement and the unforgiving nature of the windstorm foreshadow the metaphysical being/not being that Santiago experiences as a magical-realist ghost that comes back to haunt Miguel, and the audience can infer through literary imagination that he has now descended to a spiritual purgatory.

The focus on the natural movement of sand and light implies that Santiago is also in the process of moving between states of being and temporalities. This latter facet is thought provoking if we take into consideration the normative temporality of the (Western) subject as moving from "birth, marriage, reproduction, and death" (Halberstam, *In a Queer Time*, 2). Santiago's passage or lack thereof occurs between the temporalities of reproduction—albeit in a nonprocreative sense, no matter how heterogenizing the aesthetics of the buttocks are—and death, as he does not follow the "natural" progression to not being. The magical-realist aesthetic allows for what Halberstam identifies as "Queer time," in which "Queer subcultures produce alternative temporalities by allowing their participants to believe that their futures can be imagined according to logics that lie outside of those paradigmatic markers of life experience" (*In a Queer Time*, 2).

Santiago's nonliving yet nondead transition state sets up two distinct queer markers: on the one hand, he queers the temporality of Western Judeo-Christian systems by refusing to move on, evidencing the queer subject's break with heteronormative notions of "time"; on the other, his living-dead condition decenters traditional epistemologies of cinematic reality at a time when the real (versus the fantastical) is valued in Latin American cinematic and literary production. Santiago's deadness is in fact an anachronism or exception that belies a broader thematic of demonstrating the sociopolitical realities of the region through a dedicated compromise with cinematic realism. Magical realism is in this case a queering element that deflects the viewer's expectations and forces a stark epistemological shift wherein we must recalibrate our notions of the real to understand how powerfully Santiago can decenter the erotics of the village.

The abrupt yet to some extent foreshadowed switch to the magical-realist aesthetic mode highlights the larger part of *Contracorriente*'s relatively short 100-minute running time. The switch in narrative mode can be read as what Mary Louise Pratt calls a "contact zone," or geographically delimited "social spaces where cultures meet, clash, and grapple with each other, often in contexts of highly asymmetrical relations of power" ("Arts," 34). The magical-realist aesthetic is one such zone in the context of there being a contact between a heteronormative and a queer temporality, as the focus of the men's meeting is to bring Santiago toward "death"; it is a contact zone between the ethics and the physics of the real and its complementary queer space. Therein we can find at least another gesture that deviates the film from any true queer politics or compromise, as the pressure seems to be on bringing Santiago back to Judeo-Christian temporality.

The spectral mode in the film represents another zone, where the queer male can come into visual contact with the spaces and systems of homophobia previously deemed off limits by the spatial contract of heteronormativity. The film emphasizes the linkage between the aesthetic mode and the contact zone through Miguel's panic at seeing Santiago inside the village house. The first contact with magical realism is decentered by quick-moving shots of the three characters in the living room, of Miguel alone, and of Santiago and Mariela, as if the director refuses to allow the viewer to completely identify the visual telos with the magical-realist tradition. We are instead invited to situate the magical within the epistemology of the real through carefully constructed shots that emphasize that not all points of view share an experience of or can be located within the contact zone. The aesthetic mode is decentered by Miguel's initial incredulity at the spectral presence, quite unlike what happens in traditional magical realism, which normalizes the supernatural. In *Contracorriente*, instead, the two male protagonists struggle with the magical, refusing at first to acknowledge its existence. This pushes the film further into inwatchability, as the viewer and the diegetic characters must negotiate a position in relation to the contact zone between the magical and the real. We (and they) are asked to tear away at the filmic image as a site of the homogeneity of the real and the heteronormative, to unearth a substrate where alternative systems, bodies, desires, and gazes can proliferate and come into contact.

The gay characters' perspective, however, evolves when they realize that the spectral permits a violation of the spatial contract, as Santiago openly interacts with Miguel inside the latter's house. It is within this mode of contact that we can unearth an epistemological and ethical theorization of the queer in the film, permitting a "New" reading that actively juxtaposes systems and beliefs of difference with heteronormativity.

The film proceeds to move the breach of the contract to other gendered spatial referents such as the church and the bar. Miguel is at first uncomfortable with the spectral presence of Santiago during Sunday service, but the film effectively uses aural strategies such as the meshing of the reading of non-homophobic scripture with full-body shots of Santiago standing among seated parishioners to renegotiate the presence of the queer within the church space. The spatial framing of this scene emphasizes the queer body's nonbelonging to patriarchal religious systems yet at the same time invites the viewer to deconstruct the visual structure through the aural cue of nonprejudice, followed by Santiago's sitting next to Miguel in a pew.

The film thus presents the possibility of a heteronormative space accommodating difference (albeit through the nonrealist trope) by means of a consciousness of the magical. By placing Santiago next to Miguel in the company of his religious community, Fuentes-León encourages us to view alternate temporalities and spatialities as possible and positive future realities to replace current environments of gender oppression.

This possibility is later clarified in one of many nightly encounters in Miguel's living room, when Santiago expresses that he cannot stand being alone and that it is horrible to not exist. The paradox here, of course, is that Santiago has never *not* been alone in the village, as the villagers have always viewed him with suspicion and as an outsider. What Fuentes-León succeeds in posing is that it may be better to be an ostracized homosexual seeking acceptance within a spatially coded society than simply not to exist. There is, then, an implicit call to make difference visible and spoken rather than living in a culture of aural and visual silence—to overlay these alternative temporalities/spatialities/realities onto their heteronormative counterparts and to engage thus in epistemic disobedience.

Miguel's anxiety at seeing Santiago in the public/out space is gradually alleviated as the two men reacclimatize themselves in an unfinished house at the periphery of the village. Note in this movement a shift toward the outside of the urban, where it meets the rural in another sort of symbolic contact zone.[12] They accept the magical-realist aesthetic, creating a contact zone that permits an exploration of the spatiality of nonheteronormative gender configurations. After what can be seen as a warming-up period, Santiago proceeds to leave the confines of the open/closed space and invites Miguel to follow suit. He beckons him to come out, and when Miguel asks where, replies almost casually: "just outside" [fuera pues]. The shot that captures this exchange is backgrounded by the fluid, haptic space of the ocean (as vector of the potentiality for the queer), with Miguel located between the viewer and Santiago. The scopophilic angling is directed toward the haptic water, asking both Miguel and the viewer to step out and to break the spatial contract of heteronormativity, with the ocean as a gendered signifier functioning as an ethico-erotic compass. There are frames within frames in this shot, akin to the earlier boat scenes, as the filmic image emphasizes a metanarrative of coming out from multiple spatial closets and resists simplified Anglocentric narratives of leaving the figurative closet (or the figurative space of the rural, for that matter). Miguel joining Santiago *fuera* is a complex move, both politically and epistemologically, and cannot be attributed to a reductionist "coming out." Even in a later scene when Mariela confronts Miguel about the paintings found in Santiago's house, he asks her: "What picture?" [¿Qué cuadro?], evoking the multiple frames that Fuentes-León's composition elicits from the viewer trying to understand the matrix of Miguel's gendered struggle with subjectivity and identity. The framing (¿Qué cuadro?) of the coming-out experience in *Contracorriente*, instead, posits that the Latin American closet is a very different space; as such, any epistemology of it, or phenomenology of leaving it, must be socioculturally sensitive and not necessarily directed by Anglo notions of gender identity or emancipatory politics.[13]

The subsequent shot is of Miguel peering out from behind an unfinished wall, alternating with a medium shot of Santiago inviting him out, even going as far as to talk to people who cannot see him. Santiago exists on the outside of the metonymic house, though not really in a corporeal sense. This is perhaps symbolic of a broader cognitive dissonance between gay rights and homosexual movements in Latin America in relation to both traditional structures of patriarchy and Anglo movements inspired by a greater visibility and "watchability." Santiago, in fact, can only be *seen*, in a spatial sense, when he affirms that "nobody sees me, dumbass" [nadie me ve, huevón], highlighting, ironically, I argue, the homosexual's absence from the heteronormative aesthetics of coitus evidenced in the homoerotic lovemaking scene; homosexuality can only be seen, spoken, and worked through by the film and the audience within the magical mode of narrative and through other such contact zones.

Santiago seems to affirm this disconnect when he affirms: "It's better this way . . . outside" [Mejor así . . . afuera], as soon as Miguel steps outdoors. The camera invites us to see the homosexual in a public space, but also asks us to feel the breach of the spatial contract through the haptic reading of magical realism as an unpacking agent of the visual image. The audience must, therefore, not take the men walking hand-in-hand through the village as a simple representation of how much easier and normalized an acceptance of homosexuality can be, but, instead, as a polysemantic exploration of systems and spaces of narration that permit such representation, exemplified by Santiago repeatedly stating: "Nobody sees me" [Nadie me ve]. This statement slowly loses its value through repetition and leads to the contrasting assertion that "someone sees you" [alguien le ve], that someone, of course, being the audience, which is asked to build an empathetic bridge with the newly "outed" couple.

With that being said, however, it is equally fundamental to acknowledge that *Contracorriente* does not affirm a queering or decentering of all norms of patriarchy, as what is representative of acceptance is the ability to hold hands in public just like heterosexual couples. We can read a subtle critique of the drive to share straight rights, which produces no real epistemological challenge to extant systems in which the social structures that limit us to systems of heteronormative familiar life would be brought into consideration. There is no real queering of the norms of heterosexual structures, as the two men experience an intense emotive reaction at the birth of Miguel and Mariela's son, reaffirming the value placed on procreation vis-à-vis sexuality, as depicted in the opening shot of Mariela's rising and falling belly. Their paternal instincts are unveiled to the audience as though, in their estimation, bringing babies into the world is the real purpose of life, akin to the feelings shared about paternity by Ramón and Rodolfo in Hermosillo's *Doña Herlinda*. We can, in this regard, view the resistance to completely doing away with the aesthetics and structures of heternormativity in *Contracorriente* as a return to the director's need to make a watchable film for the Latin American audience, though it remains highly inwatchable to the informed viewer, who must peel away the layers posed by the magical-realist aesthetic mode behind the visual image.

The spatial and epistemological coming out of Miguel (from the closeted unfinished house) and Santiago (as a seen and unseen specter within the spaces of heterosexuality) allows the film to enter, albeit ephemerally, into a lighter tone, as the two men engage in the type of hijinks permitted when one character is invisible. Even during these lighthearted scenes, Fuentes-León does not allow the viewer to completely disassociate the magical-realist aesthetic from an ethical exploration of the contact zone between queerness and heterosexuality. He uses, for example, the typical caper of the invisible accomplice reading the hands of the other players during a card game. This lighthearted moment is subtly placed within a power system of contention, as Miguel, holding only a pair of queens, coyly symbolic of the two protagonists, wins a hand of poker against a bluffing member of the homophobic male homosocial that controls the village. The simplicity and humor of this detail are balanced by the potential of the two queens being capable of overpowering the homophobe within a previously outlined space of heteronormativity, albeit through the paradoxical visible/invisible narrative mode. The poker hand also foreshadows Miguel's coming out to the community, thus visibly being seen, too, as a "queen," as he agrees to offer Santiago's cadaver to the ocean, thereby allowing him to return to normative time.

Miguel symbolically comes out to the village by offering Santiago, that is, by bringing him back from a Queer temporality to the accepted progression in Western epistemology. He thereby highlights the importance of the aesthetic mode, on the one hand, and the disconnect between local and foreign epistemologies of the closet, on the other. Coming out in *Contracorriente* occurs through an engagement with the magical-realist narrative (as contact zone and epistemological axis). Miguel tells Mariela of his plans, and she leaves him and their home, which loses its affective sense of place within the spatial contract of heterosexuality. The coming-out scene is not only visual, in the sense that the narrative is located in the scopophilic frame of the kitchen, but also haptic, as the audio repeats the rhythmic and tactile sound of waves, reminiscent of the close shot of a postorgasmic Santiago on the beach. We must remember here Marks's assertion that haptic visuality is erotic, as "eroticism is based more upon interaction than voyeurism" ("Video Haptics," 342). The collection of images of Santiago coming out, then, is not pivotal solely as a narratological element but also as a key denominator in the structures of feeling that the film engenders.

By collocating this aural cue with a framed visual of coming out, Fuentes-León invites the viewer also to feel the conflicting politics of Miguel's identity. Miguel subsequently leaves the domestic space, and the camera lingers over the doorframe, emphasizing his outing and also reminding the viewer, with the wedding portrait that hangs next to the door, of the power of spatiality over gender. The portrait is framed in an earlier scene as a fundamental referent in determining Miguel's sexual politics, as it hangs in the background, behind a standing Miguel, who is framed by a door. The shot invites the viewer to see him in a frame within frames, as he affirms to his suspicious wife that "I am not like that, I swear to you" [Yo no soy así, te lo juro]. This double framing suggests that there are several layers or processes of coming out that are in play within Miguel's progression throughout the film, as though we cannot read onto his body the traditional Anglo narrative of outing oneself by simply opening the closet door.

By leaving behind their marriage, Miguel is also severing himself as a subject in the village's topology of heteronormativity. The uncloseted man's decision to publicly acknowledge a relationship with Santiago is, moreover, problematized as he can come out to his community only in the symbolic liminality of death (and its adherence to a nonqueer temporality), and within the spatial liminality of the ocean, as he takes Santiago's body into deep water. It bears noting that they are never caught in flagrante, as the villagers label Miguel as a homosexual only after seeing the nude painting of him, which, in a parallel fashion, emphasizes the haptic process behind peeling away Santiago's thick and expressive brushstrokes to unearth sexual practices that are never seen by the audience and the diegetic characters.

Reading Miguel's homosexuality in *Contracorriente* is really about touching the semantic and tactile bonds of desire that the painting evokes. The film ends with Santiago's body being offered to the sea, a final kiss between the two men, and Santiago's specter disappearing from the film, bringing full circle the narratological and spatial queering that *Contracorriente* has embarked on. The viewer is left with a dose of uncertainty and is asked to ponder whether it is the magic of the offering that liberates Santiago's ghost, or if it is the act of coming out by Miguel that liberates his own conscience, as, prior to offering up Santiago, Miguel has to first come out to his lover. He tells Santiago that he had found his body but had decided to leave it tied to a rock, as he enjoyed their magical-realist relationship, which allowed him to be out while really being in.

Either option, however, requires a full buying into of the magical-realist aesthetic by an empathetic audience, which is already, as the film concludes, deeply laced into the affective ties that the images and sounds create. The film, therefore, does not suggest a clear path out of the Latin American closet but succeeds in problematizing its space and posing an alternate epistemology that underlines the sociocultural matrix that differentiates global gender expressions from a seemingly uniform norm.

The film's promotional materials also deserve some consideration, as Fuentes-León evokes the archetypical love triangle of Maricón cinema that is perhaps best captured by Lombardi's *No se lo digas a nadie*. The interpretation of Bayly's novel ends with the homosexual members of the triangle seemingly agreeing to live a silenced relationship without public acknowledgment. *Contracorriente*, however, reframes this triangle, as Miguel actively comes out to Mariela, severing the visible and invisible lines that hold together the geometric shape in favor of a spatially undifferentiated paradigm. This suggests that the film, at least, questions and decenters the archetype of female complicity. The movie poster and DVD cover show Miguel, Mariela, and Santiago seated on the living room sofa, which has cleverly been relocated to the beach. The image is jarring in its juxtaposition of the domestic with the public, the inside with the outside, and the symbolic space of heteronormativity with the haptic symbolic space of queerness. The composition of the characters in relation to the film's spaces underlines the reading of a spatiality of queerness or, equally, a spatial contract of heteronormativity that not only places the erotics of the film but that also is central in the development of alternative sexualities and identities not limited to the narratives and scopics of metronormativity. By placing the three characters on a couch by the sea, Fuentes-León obviates previous strategies of LGBT film in Latin America and examines, instead, both the spatiality of the genre and the potential for empathy that affective strategies generate in a willing audience.

The film, as what may be termed a "New" genre within Latin American cinema, is acutely *expressive*. I am referring to Steven Shaviro's discussion of what he terms "post-cinematic affect," or how cinema can be "*expressive*: that is to say, in the ways that [it] give[s] voice (or better, give[s] sounds and images) to a kind of ambient, free-floating sensibility that permeates our society today" (*Post Cinematic Affect*, 2, emphasis in original). Shaviro goes on to define how expressive cinema is both symptomatic ("they provide indices of complex social processes, which they transduce, condense, and rearticulate in the form of what can be called, after Deleuze and Guattari, 'blocs of affect'" [2]) and productive. The latter acceptation is of particular interest in the location of *Contracorriente* within a genre separate from and subsequent to Maricón film, in the sense that the film does "not *represent* social processes, so much as [it] participate[s] actively in these processes, and help[s] to constitute them" (Shaviro, *Post Cinematic Affect*, 2). What I am posing, then, as we move into a discussion of several other films within this conception of a New, is that *Contracorriente* is not solely representative of a widening of queer identity (or, at the very least, gay identity) and representational politics in Latin America; instead, it is an active dialoguing and ontoformative agent (in the capacity that the film is inwatchable) in specifying what Quiroga calls "lateral identifications" (*Tropics*, 197), or shifts and destabilizations that tease out sites and conceptions of difference left unmarked (or theoretically homogenized) by Anglo studies.[14]

MATERIAL BODIES IN NEW MARICÓN CINEMA

Contracorriente ends with Miguel offering Santiago's body to the sea as the magical-realist mode comes full circle and the viewer is left with a feel-good vibe that now Santiago's soul and body can finally rest. The film, however, does not cue us in to what happens to Miguel after coming out. Does he go "back in" and mend his relationship with Mariela? Will he now occupy Santiago's space and role as the queer other in the quaint fishing village? Or will he simply embark on the metronormative route to the big city—perhaps Lima or even Miami? The film concludes with a sequence that shows Miguel alone on his boat as he guides it toward shore. The mobile camera languidly undulates as though it too is located in the water, tracking the boat's progress as the sun sets (on the film, on their relationship, on Miguel's passing as a married heterosexual man).

In the final shot, as the boat moves from right to left, the camera suddenly pauses (though it continues to waver as though in the water), and Miguel exits from the frame. The subtle shift away from the tracking shot leaves the viewer lingering over the water and the sun in the background, just as a bolero cues the ending credits. The subsequent shot during the credits retakes the motion of a moving camera as we see a vast scenery of static and unoccupied boats, not very different from that in which Miguel makes his departure, suggesting that his story is just one of many others. Thus we see how the film moves toward a conception of the New, as the film is both symptomatic and productive; that is, we must understand that Miguel's story is not a solitary one and that, conversely, a political process of emancipation out of the spatial contract must be encouraged, wherein "coming out" does not necessarily mean embracing a gay *internacional* identity (based on identity politics that do not conform to the traditional *activo* and *pasivo* dyad), but coming to terms with the structures and powers of heteronormativity and heterosexist privilege that permit a hiding or abjection of the gendered other.

Of note in the screening, or materiality, of the symbolic possibility of outing in the ending credits is the audio overlay of Celso Piña and Café Tacuba's version of Santiago "Chago" Díaz' bolero "Aunque no sea conmigo" [Even though it isn't with me]. The song is gender neutral, though music videos and live performances by Piña and Enrique Bunbury, in addition to Paulina Rubio's upbeat pop rendering, script its erotics along heterosexual lines.[15] The song, a bolero, after all, is always "measured within the space of desire—desire, of course, not as an index of the real but as a mental construction *imposed* on the real" (Quiroga, *Tropics*, 152, emphasis in the original). Its inclusion in the film, especially in relation to the "giving" of Santiago's body, in effect queers its gender registers, moving us away from the imposed gender dynamics of its performances, as the viewer does not necessarily associate the sung lyrics with the hetero version. That is, we no longer overlay Díaz' sense and schema of longing onto the distinctly masculine and feminine voices that call to the gendered other (within a heterosexist dichotomy) but open up, instead, the possibility of a queering of desire, akin to the director's sharp use of montage and bodily "bits and pieces" to link homosexual and heterosexual coital aesthetics in the film.

If boleros are indeed about desire (and the possibility of its queering), they are also about erasure. As José Quiroga rhetorically postulates: "What other

4.9. Spaces of normativity coming into contact with the vector of difference, Contracorriente. *Copyright Elcalvo.*

musical genre can be so invested in its own sense of disappearance that it seeks to proclaim absence by belting out songs claiming that the only thing that remains is disappearance itself?" (*Tropics*, 152). The conclusion of *Contracorriente* stresses this paradox in that we are left without bodies (or their bits and pieces) or certainty in the queer story arc of Miguel, but we have lyrics that emphasize the centrality of desire and love and their corresponding affective intensity in the human experience. Necessary in this final note is the disappearance of the nonheteronormative body from the materiality of the screen, as we are left with only its symbolic prosthesis (the fishing boat).

While *Contracorriente* is an effective foray into the spatiality of desire and its possibilities of being, the concluding bolero poses the question of where can or does the body reside?[16] Its absence within the lyrical queering of the musical/filmic genre, and of the "Latin American audience," is arguably necessary, as we move away from seeing the queer to feeling it. That, however, is not to say that the body (and/or a distinctively queer body) cannot be a screened locus of erotics or an assemblage of gendered power dynamics that puts into contention the saliency of cultural heteronormativity (which really was and is the case in Maricón film). There *are* films within the New inflection of the corpus that emphasize the body as an entity on the screen and not necessarily as a "bits and pieces" way into a broader discussion about the possibility of a queer Latin American cinema. These films can be affiliated, in a more intimate sense, with transnational (or, really, Anglophone) queer cinema in that they move beyond a simple telling of "coming out" or of refusing to "pass," tropic elements that have been otherwise exhausted in a context of cultural production that went through Stonewall and the subsequent move toward identitary politics, and focus instead on decentering notions of desire, orientation, and gender that are housed within the dichotomies of sex that are otherwise taken as axiomatic in heterosexist discourse.[17]

The next three films in this part of the book share aesthetic, poetic, and affective traits with *Contracorriente* but place a stronger onus on the role of the body vis-à-vis gender, which Fuentes-León seemingly obviated in the interest of making his film more watchable. These films encourage, instead, a broader engagement with transnational notions and studies of the queer, allowing therein a line of flight away from a conservative cocooning of Latin American film in queer anthologies.

CHAPTER FIVE

Outing El último verano de la Boyita

ON MASCULINITIES AND THE MOMENT OF ENGAGEMENT

OFTEN GROUPED WITH LUCÍA PUENZO'S *XXY* (FOR issues regarding intersexuality) and Albertina Carri's *La rabia* (Anger, 2008, as another Argentine film presented from the perspective of a child or adolescent), Julia Solomonoff's *El último verano de la Boyita* merits special attention within the aesthetic and poetic shift that is New Maricón cinema. Told from the perspective of Jorgelina, a young girl who, up until the point of the narrative that the film takes up, shares everything with her older sister, Luciana. The film moves us through her process of coming to terms with her sister's puberty and how this, in turn, affects her own development and individuation.

Their parents divorce, and Luciana and her mother decide to spend the summer at the beach. The disenchanted Jorgelina (disenchanted because she is now excluded from "big girl" activities such as trying on bras and from her sister's living space, as Luciana now has her own room) decides to spend the summer with her father in their country farmhouse away from Rosario. There she reconnects with Mario, the shy young son of the farm's caretakers. He, like Luciana, is experiencing physical changes. Therein lies the first decentering of heteronormativity in the film, as the viewer soon learns that Mario, too, is beginning to menstruate.

Coproduced by Agustín and Pedro Almodóvar's El Deseo, the film deals with intersexuality as a topic left unexplored in Latin American film, as what often passes for gender movement or change is the figure of the transvestite or transgendered man-to-woman.[1] The film locates the viewer, then, within an organic heteronormative temporality, where the sexuation of the subject from child to adolescent and the possibility of its queering takes place. Unlike Maricón cinema, which thematically and aesthetically isolates the nonheteronormative and, in some cases, carnivalizes the queer, Solomonoff's film can be located

5.1. Setting the directionality of difference, El último verano de la Boyita. *Copyright Travesía.*

on a queer continuum of global cinema if we take into account its fixation on moving past lesbigay topics of coming out or passing, which *Contracorriente* effectively deals with, albeit in a new aesthetic mode that encourages empathy and an acknowledgment of politicality.

Working with David Halperin's definition of the queer, which falls in line with Foster's theorization (that is, considering the queer as LGBT and Q), Santiago Peidro argues that *El último verano* is a "queer film" in that it displaces the gaze and individual subjectivity from being complete positions to disassociated and complex constructions ("Dos casos," 68). Deborah Martin's reading and association of the film with Puenzo's XXY, furthermore, notes that both movies "constitute a quite unprecedented intervention on the part of Argentine cinema into international debates on intersexuality, as well as into global queer filmmaking" ("Growing Sideways," 35).[2]

From a genealogical standpoint, then, the film is placed at points on multiple axes that lay the groundwork for the potential for politics in the moving image, away from an intimate and nonallegorical treatment of gendered bodies in an outward gesture that pushes geographic and thematic boundaries. One such gesture places *El último verano* in a direct relationship with the spatial demarcations within *Contracorriente,* as the film uses aural and visual cues to establish a sense of space away from the gendered and genderizing urban reference. Unlike the latter film, which creates a microurban visual topology in relation to the sea and the desert (and, partly, in relation to Santiago's coming from the big city), Solomonoff's film explicitly addresses the spatial, temporal, and political move from Rosario toward the Pampas and then back.

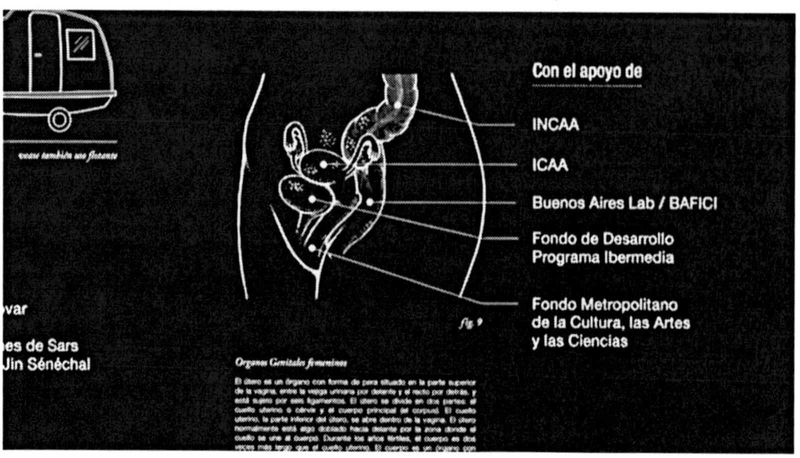

5.2. The use of scientific diagrams, El último verano de la Boyita *and New Maricón films. Copyright Travesía.*

The first scene, which showcases young Mario taming a horse among the homosocial, is juxtaposed with the suburban streets of Rosario through an abrupt visual cut, though the aural characteristics of country and city are both characterized by ambient noise, including the sounds of animals (flies and horses in the former, dogs barking in the latter). A quick montage of a static shot of a street is followed by a medium shot of clothing hanging to dry on the roof of a house. The first image of the quiet street suggests a directionality from left to right, contrasting with the introductory credits, which flow from right to left. Several critics have focused on the credits as being didactic signifiers of the film's themes (including the nature of the Boyita, or mobile home, anatomy and gender, etc.), but their significance is quite elementary as they imply nothing more hermeneutic than a simple correlation between the scrolling image and the development of the plot.

What is of importance, however, is the direction of movement in the credits, as they contrast with the initial suggested angles in the urban. Solomonoff establishes a praxis of directionality vis-à-vis the city and vis-à-vis the nonurban, as the characters and the camera follow a structured move from left to right and right to left when moving between both specific tropes. In a later long shot, for example, Jorgelina and her father move from Rosario to the farmhouse and traverse a dirt road from right to left. Of note in this perception-image are the trigonometric characteristics of the roadway that the car follows, as it replicates almost exactly the angles of the suburban road in the establishing shot of Jorgelina's house, implying a movement between spatial referents akin to the shots immediately prior to the lovers' rendezvous in *Contracorriente*.

The second shot in this early montage of the clothes drying over the household furthers the spatial contract evidenced in Fuentes-León's film, as it stresses the position of the roof over its inhabitants; that is, it explicates that those living within the roof's confines are constricted to the spatial contract of heteronormativity. The following shot in this carefully staged montage is of a standing fan inside the domestic structure. The viewer is encouraged to go beyond the visual and to engage the image as a haptic space. This process, akin to that of *Contracorriente*, is forwarded in the previous montage through the overlay and augmentation of aural cues (the animals, stressful ambient sounds) that, when combined with the image of the fan, engender the notion of the scene being a montage of audile-tactile images. The sense of heat and perspiration that the fan evokes, a trait captured perfectly in Lucrecia Martel's *La ciénaga* (The swamp), seemingly connects the urban house to the farmhouse, as establishing shots in the film's later geography will also use the fan to evoke heat. By situating the visual in line with the aural and the tactile from the onset, Solomonoff quickly and effectively severs the film from any possible scopic praxis. In other words, we are made aware early on that the film cannot be linked to a genealogy of the Maricón and must instead be considered outside the parameters of Maricón viewership and politics.

In fact, prior to any move to the nonrural in this gender exercise, which is allegorically performed in *Contracorriente* (and XXY and *El niño pez*), a nondescript yet timely scene before the move to the Pampas establishes the film's interpellation of the urban into the hapticity of water and the marine as a potential space of becoming and feeling. Though Luciana cannot swim because of

5.3. *Perception images that out desire away from the urban,* El último verano de la Boyita. *Copyright Travesía.*

her period, the two girls join a score of male and female friends in the river to play, splash, and swim in reaction, presumably, to the heat evoked by the establishing shot of the standing fan. The water's sounds are amplified over the screaming voices as the film almost forcibly pushes onto the viewer the fact, or an acknowledgment, that the river makes possible a different state and sense of being, akin to the purpose of the maritime in *Contracorriente* as a spatial designation of nonheteronormativity. The water, its sounds, textures, nonsolidity, is a Deleuzian vector in New Maricón films, "useful for the recognition of constituent genre elements, [and] the diversity of historical screen information" (Colman, *Deleuze and Cinema*, 129). In a shot that foregrounds the children playing in the water, we see in the distance the skyline of Rosario. The composition of the image (as a set) is uncompromising in that it juxtaposes the fluidity of the river as an audile-tactile space (or an image within an image) with the static and scopic urban setting in the background. We are explicitly invited to *feel* the water, its sounds, and the young bodies playing in it, and to *see* the city behind us. One experience is interactive and heuristic; the other is strictly voyeuristic, yet it reminds the viewer of the *usual* space of othered and/or queer narratives. The city in the background evokes Jean-Clet Martin's conception of the city-image. Writing in Greg Flaxman's early yet timely *The Brain Is the Screen*, he reminds us that

> neither the profile of a city, variable to infinity, nor the construction of a panoramic territory refers to a state of things. Rather, they refer to an errant line that runs through space as a scaffolding of relations, a maze of depths, relative to the more or less typical place that one occupies—which implies that every landscape is a virtual construction in relation to a memory able to stock piles of images in all their encroachments upon one another. The human universe is open to a variety of changing perspectives, adjusted according to the axis of the gaze that cuts through the city, accumulating facades, stockpiling walls along the axis of a depth that is already memory. So there contracts a découpage of images, cut out upon the blue background of the sky, which is nothing like an objectively realized solid. ("Of Images," 66)

The skyline is purposely blurry as the lens focuses on the playing children, suggesting thus the notion of the city as a spectral or virtual space that is relational yet not ontoformative for the development of the diegesis. We must view the skyline not as a real space or referent but as a historically constituted and remembered virtuality that materializes as not a real space but as a compendium of all those other urban shots that placed the queer subject in space in Maricón film. Therein one notices the initial, and perhaps starkest, point of

5.4. *The city as a virtual space in the background of narrative and affective developments,* El último verano de la Boyita. *Copyright Travesía.*

difference in the genealogy of a queer cinema in Latin America, as Solomonoff's (and Fuente-León's and Puenzo's) films are situated in the foreground of this shot, in contraposition to its urban, Maricón antecedents.

Returning to the geospatiality of gender, the tension implied in the film's use of directionality is not limited to these tracking shots of movement from the urban to the rural; they are in fact also present in several shots in the central part of the film, that is, when the narrative is located in the Pampas. On arrival at the farmhouse, Jorgelina and her father rest after the long trip. The standing fan is central to this scene, as we not only see it and feel the heat that its presence logically implies (as present in the urban household) but also now hear its rattling, as, unlike its urban counterpart, the fan in the farmhouse is more unstable. I hesitate to overanalyze such a detail, but the fan's positioning in the composition of spatiality in the film cannot be ignored, as the second, loud, fan is the subject of Jorgelina's critical gaze, as it seemingly bothers her while she reads. The child's gaze directs us explicitly to the fan and draws attention to its relationship to its urban counterpart. What seems to be suggested is that the nonurban household (housing a spatial contract of gender) is akin to the urban in that both are regimented by a certain ordered structure; the rural, though, somehow breaks with this representation as the fan's clanging blades create an audile-tactile space that keys the viewer in to a different image altogether. The fan blowing in the urban house is both an affection-image and a perception-image, though its silence heavily accentuates the latter; the nonurban fan, however, is highlighted like the former, especially if we take into account Jorgelina's curious and disapproving gaze. The loud fan establishes a feeling that, like the foregrounding of the splashing children in the river with the skyline in the background, pushes us away from a scopophilic cinema.

I highlight this short montage of sounds and shots in the first real images of the farmhouse because they precede a tableau of four medium and long shots that are spliced together and interrupt the narrative. A medium long shot of cows running from left to right is connected to a similar shot (in terms of directionality) but with Mario now present on his horse and herding the cows. The use of a jump cut is thought provoking in that we can read Mario's presence in terms of a gendered directionality; that is, by splicing his body onto a movement-image that implies a geopolitical shift from left/rural to right/urban, the image suggests that his actions in the shot approximate him to a practice and identity of gender that is housed by symbolic urbanity. In other words, his riding of the horse and learning the ways of the gaucho are intrinsic to the insertion of his body into the structure of masculine hegemony.

The montage, however, while initially implicating Mario in the geospatiality of gender in the film, also suggests a problematization of his masculine becoming, as subsequent shots reveal a tension in directionality, as though the film refuses to allow us to assume the character's clean move into heteronormative maturity. The image cuts to an extreme long shot that places the viewer within the vastness of the Pampas, but also shows movement of the gauchos and the cows from right to left. Another tracking shot shows ducks flying from left to right. This back and forth between the topos of normativity that the initial water/skyline shots establish complicates the initial shots of Mario on his horse moving from the direction of the rural to that of the urban and suggests that his gendered becoming or maturation is problematic and possesses a potential queering of both body and heteronormative time.[3]

Through this brief sequence, then, we can see that the directionality implied by the car tracking away from Rosario is less about Jorgelina's perspective of the shift to the Pampas and more about Mario's coping with his changing body and position in relation to the men who work the land.[4] Solomonoff centers the narrative not only on Mario (and Jorgelina) negotiating his corporeal markers in relation to the established norms as represented in diagrams in Eduardo's anatomy books, but also on how this negotiation in turn impacts his blossoming into a member of the male homosocial.

We must remember, after all, that the film's shift to the nonurban is immediately preceded by Luciana's own negotiation between changing body and adult femininity, compounded by Jorgelina's childlike gaze and relation to this change. It is thus not a surprise that the tracking shot of the car moving to the Pampas precipitates a similar crisis state in which what is now negotiated is the masculine corollary. Touching on this plot point, Deborah Martin notes that the film opens with a highly tactile image, where "extreme close-ups permit the

5.5. *The use of movements and perception images to create tension in the moment of masculine becoming,* El último verano de la Boyita. *Copyright Travesía.*

viewer little control of the image" ("Growing Sideways," 40); the image here, of course, is of young Mario participating in the subjugation of a horse, this "being a traditional marker of *gaucho* masculinity" ("Growing Sideways," 40). Important in the first sequence, which Martin focuses on to establish a queering child gaze in the film, is the explicit depiction of both a coming-of-age and an identitarian act that establishes the parameters of and membership in the rural homosocial.

Shows of strength and of taming the natural are, furthermore, characteristics cultivated in the regional and sociohistorically specific hegemonic variant of masculinity. Readers familiar with masculinity studies will note that my usage of the qualifier "hegemonic" invariably evokes Raewyn Connell's orientation of masculinities into a "gender structuring of practice" (*Masculinities,* 73). Connell creates a matrix of power relations that describes relations within (and, to some extent, outside) the specific grouping. The matrix of masculinities—composed of hegemonic, subordinate, complicit, and marginal positions—is in actuality a virtual structuralization composed of matrices within matrices, wherein local masculinities enter into dialogue with other local, global, and regional masculinities, and, it is important to note, with their respective historical masculinities. In other words, and as Connell reiterates, hegemonic masculinity, for example, is "not a fixed character type, always and everywhere the same. It is, rather, the masculinity that occupies the hegemonic position in a given pattern of gender relations, a position always contestable" (*Masculinities,* 76).[5] What is of note in any theorization or praxis of hegemonic masculinity is its creation of other gendered masculine positions that are held in a virtual orbit around the point of power. Subordinate masculinities, most often represented by the homosexual male, are a sine qua non for the condition of hegemony.[6]

El último verano de la Boyita specifies the characteristics of the hegemonic position in several ways: in the initial sequence, which shows a group of men, including Mario, taming a horse; in the gaze of his father and male peers when Mario is shown to be a good equestrian; and when Eduardo mentions that Mario's racing and participation in a local festival allow him to "prove himself as a man" [probarse como hombre].[7] The second of these examples is stylistically linked to the earlier montage of movement from left to right and right to left, which inserts the maturing boy's body in a poetics of directionality. This time, however, Solomonoff uses an abrupt and jarring jump cut to reiterate the parental position and gaze vis-à-vis Mario's abilities as a racer. Jorgelina's gaze mediates this sequence, as she first fixates on Eduardo and Mario's father watching the young rider. A cut to a medium shot of her face is overlaid with the father yelling words of encouragement to his son. The father moves toward the trajectory (of left to right) left by the speeding horse, and a jump cut inserts a separate shot of the father yelling "faster" [más rápido]. The effect of this technique is to sever the parameters of linear temporality in the scene, as the images suggest that the practice sequence seen in the film is only one of many and crucial to Mario's integration into the homosocial (in that he is able to master a characteristic of the hegemonic position).

The second shot in this jump-cut sequence, however (like the tension created through directionality in the previous jump-cut montage), also evokes a certain anxiety regarding Mario's integration into the masculine. As in the first shot of this sequence, the camera focuses on his father as he walks forward—away from the camera—and in the direction of a speeding-away Mario, who traverses the image from left to right. The second shot, however, introduces an important shift, as the camera suddenly attempts to track Mario on his horse, leaving behind the father as he edges closer to the left margin of the frame. The camera moves with the horse but reaches a tensile point that does not permit a complete tracking shot, as it maintains the father within the frame. The image slightly jerks from right to left as though having *touched* an invisible frame that evokes the matrices of gender relations extant in the film. The resistance in the jerking motion suggests on a technical level tensions and anxieties as the narrative progresses. We see in this subtle movement another clue to Mario's impending point of contact with the masculine order, as his actions of integration are juxtaposed with stylistic and thematic topos that seemingly *interrupt* his coming of age.

These sequences of the intersexed subject on the horse underline the film's preoccupation with what Connell terms the "moment of engagement," or "an

5.6. Mario negotiates his masculinity, El último verano de la Boyita. *Copyright Travesía.*

active appropriation of what was offered, a purposeful construction of a way of being in the world . . . the moment in which the boy takes up the project of hegemonic masculinity as his own" (*Masculinities*, 122). In the film, the moment of engagement is more accurately a process that leads to the moment, which is the actual competition that Mario enters with his horse.[8] The shots of him practicing, interspersed throughout the film, accentuate the moment as a process, wherein the gendered subject approximates the tenets of hegemonic masculinity in an attempt to prove belonging.

Important in Connell's theorization, however, is the role and conception of the body: "A key part of the moment of engagement, then, is developing a particular experience of the body and a particular physical sensibility" (*Masculinities*, 123). It comes as no surprise that the subsequent scene shows Mario disrobing in his bedroom, in a barn away from the main farmhouse that he moved into immediately after having his first period, six months prior to the events of the film. It is the first image that indicates that something is *different* about him, that his body goes against the aesthetics of masculinity expected in the hegemonic position.

In a dimly lit medium shot, we see him facing away from the camera, slowly unbuttoning his shirt and then removing his undershirt. To his right we see a dirty mirror that reflects his face and shoulders, creating a doubling effect that complicates the perception of his/the body. As he removes his shirt, we see him glancing downward, beyond what the mirror captures and out of sight of what we can see from our vantage point behind him. His gaze indicates or hints at the possibility of difference when read in tandem with the previous scene, which underlined his position in regard to the moment of engagement. Upon removing his garments, we see that his upper torso near the pectoral region is bound in bandages, keeping in check and out of (public) sight his budding breasts.

This shot immediately cuts to a close-up of a silent Jorgelina resting at the side of an aboveground swimming pool, her eyebrows furrowed in thought. Her gaze, when overlaid with the previous scene of a disrobing Mario, corresponds directly to the position of the mirror in his bedroom, as though establishing a geometry of sight that explicitly places her in a position of full disclosure, unlike that of the viewer, who is situated behind the disrobing body. Jorgelina's gaze correlates with a position of privilege wherein she is given full rights to seeing and identifying Mario. Her silence and pensive facial expression, an affection-image, translates perhaps into what the audience also feels at seeing Mario's bound chest, as we (like her) are asked to negotiate just what that means in relation to the previous sequence of his racing the horse. How can he *probarse como hombre* when we know that his bodily experience defies the norms of the masculine gender, which is (among other things) "a certain feel to the skin, certain muscular shapes and tensions, certain postures and ways of moving, certain possibilities of sex" (Connell, *Masculinities*, 52–53)?

Of further importance in this montage of temporally and spatially disconnected, yet thematically and affectively connected, shots is Jorgelina's placement near a swimming pool. The lens foregrounds and focuses on the textures of her body, leaving the water behind her out of focus. Its blurriness is a bipartite image in that it establishes the liquid as an ambient prop but also, by virtue of its actual representation over an extreme close-up or a low camera angle that backgrounds the sky, underlines its poetic importance in signaling a "queerying" of the body. Jorgelina's brooding gaze, then, contextualized within

5.7. The disrobing of the body of difference, El último verano de la Boyita. *Copyright Travesía.*

5.8. Dialectics of seeing and feeling difference; Jorgelina in the water, directing the viewer's orientation toward Mario, El último verano de la Boyita. *Copyright Travesía.*

the liquid as a visual and affective referent, situates the film's discussion of the intersexed subject (vis-à-vis the moment of masculine engagement) within the parameters of a New Maricón cinema.

The image of the foregrounded female protagonist is followed by a reverse-angle shot showing an equally pensive Mario sitting at the edge of the pool. This is followed by a medium shot from outside the pool area that shows the boy's full body. He is seated on an improvised ladder and is holding between his legs a piece of wood that he is carving into animal forms. The phallic symbolism of this shot is unmistakable, as the shape of the branch evokes the boy's anatomical lack. He grasps a long section of the branch that sticks out from his groin and whittles away at its base. The action as symbol is a simple (and quite logical) follow-up to the previous sequence's disrobing, as we wonder in what other ways little Mario is *different*. He holds onto the longer, phallic, part of the branch and cuts away at its base, suggesting that his current gender expression is incongruent with his sexual anatomy, and that the cutting is symbolic of a need to rid himself of the masculine. Conversely, the cutting may be the fashioning of a prosthetic penis that would then allow him full membership in the male order.

Mario's engagement with masculinity is further complicated in the next scene, as he accompanies Jorgelina and Eduardo to the local watering hole, El no tengo [The I Don't Have]. The locale's name stresses a lack or void, as one naturally asks, "What is it that you don't have?" which in Mario's case is a pertinent question. Once inside, he is met with the disapproving gaze of the local teenagers, his would-be competitors in the horse race, and therefore aspiring members of the local gender hegemony. They tease him for drinking cola instead of wine, yet their disapproving gaze reveals something more than simple male goading to consume alcohol. It is as though they, too, know something is different about Mario, but unlike the viewer, they are not able to articulate what that difference is.

The spatiality of this scene returns us to a similar interchange in *Contracorriente,* where Fuentes-León stresses the spatial contract of heteronormativity in relation to the cantina as an assemblage of masculine being and relating. Solomonoff, however, takes this association one step further and presents the bar as a space of masculine becoming, where the male-gendered subject partly enters into the process of engagement.

Masculinity in this particular diegetic sociocultural context is defined by the traditional coda of virility—corporeal, behavioral, and aesthetic—but also by the male's ability to control nature. Our suspicions of Mario's condition are confirmed immediately after he displays this control, when Jorgelina sees his menstrual blood in the woolen saddle pad. Riding the horse is both a key action in the move toward engagement and what exposes Mario, or symbolically outs him from the heteronormative contract. It is the action of engagement that reveals his genital composition, which was previously only hinted at through the symbolic woodcarving. Unlike the protagonist of Puenzo's XXY, who has both sets of genitals, Mario is sexually female but his sex is misconstrued at birth due to a larger than "normal" clitoris. This misidentification regiments his upbringing, sartorial aesthetics, and communal role as just another farmhand who helps with the animals and the daily upkeep of the land.

In fact, it is when his father, Óscar, realizes that something is different in his son that Mario is severed from the process of engagement. Jorgelina precipitates this by telling her father that Mario menstruates. Eduardo talks to Mario's mother, Elba, about the boy's condition. We then see Mario lying bloodied and facedown on his bed as Jorgelina comforts him.

The next scene of daily life on the farm is initially nondescript, as we see Elba picking oranges. As the camera follows her, however, we are jarred by the image of a visibly beaten Mario holding a container to collect the fruit. He is in effect resemanticized along a different gendered line of flight potentially leading toward feminine becoming, as his daily tasks now correspond to his mother's activities, as though they "naturally" correspond to his anatomical condition.

A prior perception-image hints at this assumption, as we see Eduardo entering the farmhouse to talk with Elba. In the foreground, Jorgelina's gaze directs us toward her father as he crosses the threshold, signaling that something is about to change. He enters and confronts Mario's sense of self within the confines of the heteronormative domestic structure. The spatial demarcations of this shot remind the viewer that though much of the film is presented through

5.9. The body inescapable and the performance of femininity, El último verano de la Boyita. *Copyright Travesía.*

5.10. The hapticity of the natural as Mario is outed from the masculine order, El último verano de la Boyita. *Copyright Travesía.*

the child's unassuming and innocent gaze, there are real structures of power that regiment gender codes and behavior in the Argentine countryside.

Next to Jorgelina in this shot are a mass of ripe and fallen oranges. The shot immediately prior (if we can conceive of Eduardo entering the house as a vector) is a close-up of ants crawling into and desiccating one of the felled oranges. This affection-image not only situates the viewer in relation to Mario's outing within his community and family but also emits a negative affective intensity that signals the oppression faced by such outing, negative, of course, in terms of orientation. The image of the ants, which take away chunks of the fruit's flesh, when juxtaposed with the scene of Mario helping Elba with the fruit picking, suggests the dematerialization into bits of the subject as agent in a frustrated process of gender-becoming.

Mario is also shown helping the men collect wood for a fence, which he had earlier helped build as part of his insertion into the process of engagement. But he is told by his father to remain at the farm when the men go to the bar after the day's work. Aware of his difference, and therefore the impossibility of his engaging with hegemony, Mario is banned from the spatial topos of masculinity in the town. What follows is unsurprising: Óscar sells the boy's horse, Yayo, to one of the other adolescents who in earlier scenes in El no tengo sent a disapproving gaze in the direction of the boy. In this scene, Mario is told to go to the barn but stops at a distance from the other boys looking over the horse. The camera is placed directly behind him and orients us to consider his relationship between his own "bodily experience" and the possibility of engaging the masculine. In a symbolic and subtle gesture, he takes out his knife and whittles away at a large fence post, noticeably larger than the prosthetic phallus he earlier carved into an animal shape in the swimming pool scene, as though emphasizing his phallic privation and corresponding bodily need to belong to what he has so long worked toward, that is, integration as a *normal* member of the male homosocial.

The camera cuts to a reverse angle, where we see Mario staring angrily at the men buying his steed. The steady, cold anger in his eyes is intercalated with a puncturing gesture as he mindlessly strikes the post with his blade (his actions are visceral and unconscious) as though his self yearns for the very thing that punctuates his rejection from the group.

This action is repeated in the subsequent shot, where he is shown sitting on a fence. A low-angled camera behind him almost confuses the piece of wood for a fashioned penis as it stands erect out of his groin. His repetitive carving of the piece of wood (presumably the same piece from the earlier swimming pool scene) could be confused for prepubescent masturbation, another event in the process of male-becoming, as the long strokes of the knife against the wooden grain evoke a stroking of the absent male appendage.

Of importance in this not-so-subtle shot is the sound of thunder and an impending storm. We observe and feel meteorological disturbances as vectors of a possible queering in *Contracorriente*. A long shot of blowing sand precipitates Santiago's queering of both the village's spatial contract and the magical-realist aesthetic mode. A similar assemblage of distinct events and images is conjured in *El último verano de la Boyita*, as the camera cuts to a long shot of Mario glancing longingly from a window in the barn, just as the wind intensifies. The barn is backgrounded by billowing trees and foregrounded by waving grass—both images that signal an affective intensity of change. Almost on cue, the subsequent long shot shows sand flowing over a dirt road. This perception-image of an affection-image is, as in *Contracorriente*, an image vector of queer possibilities; in *El último verano*, it precipitates Mario's leaving the village and a queering of the masculine moment of engagement. Following this shot is a montage of shots overlaid with guitar instrumentals that collocate portrait shots of different masculine sites and actions belonging to the farmhouse, including the workers' cart, the boy's quarters and his collection of wooden carvings, and a violent image of Óscar severing the jugular of a young cow. This real cutting of the jugular vein is also a metaphorical cutting of the son by the father, as we learn that Mario has fled the farm.

Mario's flight is also a challenge of roles because by leaving the farmspace, he leaves behind the feminine gender roles that it (the space as assemblage of gender discourses) assigned to him upon the discovery of his difference. Returning to the vector image of the long shot of moving sand and the audile-tactile vector of the storm, we see how the film uses the natural as a semantic precursor of the queer, as Mario queers notions of bodily experience and prescribed anatomic congruency vis-à-vis becoming/belonging, and his leaving further decenters the gendered order imposed by the local hegemony. Mario's disappearance is followed by a montage of medium and long shots that locate the apparatus either behind the subject (Jorgelina, Elba) that is always looking toward the right of the frame, or in a tracking gesture that follows it, again, from left to right. The directionality of the shots in this montage of searching images takes on new meanings when dialogued with the earlier shots of movement from the urban to the rural, as they imply that he has physically and symbolically left behind the spatial contract of the countryside and its gender regime.

Mario's return, unsurprisingly, occurs during the village festival where he was supposed to take part in his own moment of engagement with the masculine order, that is, by his winning a horse race. The image of his return, also expectedly, shows him moving from left to right, in a trajectory similar to that of the long shots of Eduardo's car traversing the Pampas to the farmhouse.

The geometrical vectors of this shot place the intersexed subject in a trajectory of liminality and becoming, as he moves from the outside to the inside, where he can regain the possibility of engagement. He promptly mounts his steed, to the protest of its new owners (though Eduardo is quick to buy the animal back) and lines up to race. Ridden by Mario, Yayo easily beats his competitor, and the camera cuts to several shots of the crowd's jubilant reaction. One of these quick shots shows Óscar smiling approvingly at his different son/daughter, highlighting the assertion that the race and prowess on the animal are definitive of the moment of engagement and belonging. The quick smile,

5.11. Winning the race and moving away from the confines of space, El último verano de la Boyita. *Copyright Travesía.*

furthermore, suggests the possibility of masculinity's being more than a bodily experience of anatomical construction, as Mario's winning of the race proves his manhood, even if he is sexed as a female.

The image immediately following the vignettes of communal approval (including Óscar, Elba, and Eduardo) depicts Mario riding off into the distance, symbolically breaking the masculinist regime and, in turn, the heterosexist gaze and its approval. This gesture also breaks with the spatial geometry of the film, as the horse moves from bottom right to top left, thereby inverting the dynamics of semiotic and topological movement in the film's earlier scenes. Mario's final ride away from the festival outs him in the sense that he consciously removes himself from the masculine moment of engagement after having successfully negotiated its rules. His action is one of challenge, a line of flight that epistemologically breaks with any regimen of becoming and signals a queering potential that is understated yet powerful in its rejection of normativity. The image cuts to a shot of birds in flight moving from the bottom of the frame to the top, an act that also breaks with the film's geometry, underlining Mario's previous directionality as a decentering trajectory. We are then presented with a long shot of an outcropping in the river and of Yayo resting by a tree. Mario sits by the water and casually tosses a small twig away. Unlike earlier scenes where he is almost violently cutting into a larger piece of wood, the small twig, almost like a nervous gesture, nearly goes unperceived by the viewer. The inference I am making is that Mario no longer *needs* to fashion a physical vector of the masculine onto his body; the prosthetic possibilities of the whittled wood no longer apply as he has already met and surpassed the moment of engagement with the hegemonic order. His gesture of tossing aside the branch attests to this act, negating and at the same time demythifying the social practices of belonging to and constructing the masculine position. His actions successfully queer the process of masculine becoming and question the primacy of its origins and correlative praxes and aesthetics.

Immediately following this gesture comes the arrival of Jorgelina, who, unlike the other members of the community, knows exactly where Mario has headed after breaking its social contracts. The river is, after all, the original site where Jorgelina and Mario engaged in a sort of protoromantic courtship, where their childish playfulness and innocent wrestling evoked the first encounters with love (not necessarily desire). It is easy to identify something more between them prior to Mario's outing as a different body, which will later be compounded by a floating Jorgelina repeating his name in the swimming pool, in a scene that hints at her increasing romantic fondness for the blond boy (girl).

In this earlier scene by the river, she asks him to join her in the water, which he repeatedly refuses to do, as to do so would mean removing his clothing and accepting (and bringing into the social matrix) his budding breasts and changing body. In a scene immediately after their playful flirtation, the two children are seen lying on the ground under a tree. Jorgelina asks him why he doesn't want to swim in the river, to which Mario answers: "The water is treacherous" [Es traicionera el agua]. The child's worldview confronts the broader notion of queerness in this scene, as Jorgelina innocently replies that she would prefer to be bitten by a snake in the water than to roast in the sun, unaware that Mario is really referencing his body and the water's potential to betray his "passing." Almost instinctively, his reaction is to pull his shirt down to cover his body, in-

5.12. *The river and queer desire,* El último verano de la Boyita. *Copyright Travesía.*

dicating to the viewer that something is different, as we, at this moment in the film, are unaware of his physiology.

Fast-forwarding, we see the two protagonists on the shore of the river at the end of the film, at their original site of intimacy and where Mario first demonstrated signs of difference. The image cuts, after a complicit gaze between the characters, to the flowing water and them wading into it. The audile nature of this image bears underlining, as the soundtrack foregrounds the bubbling noises of water and, more important, bodies breaking its rhythm and cadence. The image is not solely visual, but an audile-tactile experience that is spatially demarcated by the sounds of touch and movement (and their impending possibilities), as Jorgelina and Mario allow the water (as haptic, and, following the tenets put forth in *Contracorriente,* queering) to play out its *naturaleza traicionera.* With Mario's back to us, Jorgelina unbuttons his shirt, exposing his bindings, which she also discards into the flowing water. This action, and its interpellation in the broader scene of Mario entering the water after having surpassed the moment of masculine engagement, brings to mind Alain Badiou's words about the cinematic capture of sex and gender. Writing in reaction to Antonioni's *Identification of a Woman,* Badiou moves us through the following:

> Let's begin with the title. *Identification of a Woman* is a true translation of the true Italian title. Let's say that it's a true title, or rather the title of a truth. Which truth? This one: what cinema is capable of with respect to sex or sexuation, or even what it alone is capable of, is giving sensible, corporeal form, not as is too often thought, to the distribution of sexed roles or to the images of that distribution but rather—and this is infinitely trickier, and more original—to the process of identification of what being sexed means for a subject . . . In this sense, cinema, or at least one kind of cinema, albeit an essential one, is an art of love, a witness in thought of love as the identification of difference. (*Cinema,* 151–153)

Jorgelina removing Mario's clothing not only is a realization on the part of either character of being sexed but also is a recognition of difference; in this case, however, difference is not necessarily the dyadic distinction between male and female, but a realization of sameness that queers the prototypical child-romance narrative. The subsequent shot conflates this statement, as we see the two characters holding hands and moving closer together. The impending kiss, however, is cut by a temporal fast-forward of Eduardo and Jorgelina driving back to Rosario, with Jorgelina's father gazing concernedly at the sleeping child, suggesting that whatever happened during that cut sequence changed the notion of self in Jorgelina, that is, that her stripping and movement toward Mario and his difference (and the possibility of a kiss) might also have moved her away from the center of heterosexist becoming, which was initially the point of tension between the two sisters in the film.

The sequence then cuts to the two children wading into the water, embracing the substance of gender fluidity and haptic empathy that resignifies them, and us, along a different axis, wherein *their* difference is not simply viewed or signified, but viscerally connected to and felt. The audile tactility of the aqueous as both a scenic and a thematic vector yet also a means of perception and affection moves the viewer to connect with "the process of identification of what being sexed means" and to assimilate the "identification of difference," akin to the first postcoital scene between Santiago and Miguel in *Contracorriente*.

The direction of the shots as Eduardo and Jorgelina leave the nonurban accentuate the decentering of the praxis and aesthetics of heteronormativity and masculinity in the film, as the car now counterintuitively moves from left to right, that is, the trajectory followed when coming from the city to the countryside. The film, however, introduces a different image in this movement montage, a low-angle shot of the cables and central tower of a suspension bridge, which breaks the thematic continuity of movement that was stressed in earlier montages of the car and of Mario on his horse herding cattle. The interruption of the montage by this image severs the physics and metonyms of movement previously stressed in creating a spatiality of/to sexuation, as though indicating that the characters' lives will no longer be the same, or regimented by the spatial contract of heteronormativity that maintains difference and subordinate masculinities at a safe and ostracized periphery. Any reading of the "move back to the city" is thereby decentered, as the cutting bridge paradoxically disconnects our modes of viewing the rural and the urban and specific gendered spaces, thereby outing the film from static spatial narratives of subjectivity.

Commentary on the film is incomplete without a consideration of the Boyita in the title. The mobile home, which originally appeared only in prerural scenes, is central to the film's conclusion as its images alternate with the ending credits, which are white-on-black stills. In setting the stage to analyze the practices of reading in *El último verano*, Irma Vélez comments that mobile homes are "a metaphor of change, both of the values that they transmit but also of the geographies they may or may not allow to cover . . . That closed and amphibious space is symbolically the itinerant space of (de)construction" [una metáfora de los cambios tanto en los valores que trasladan como en la geografía que permite o no recorrer . . . Ese *huis-clos* confinado y anfibio es simbólicamente el espacio itinerante de la (de)construcción] ("Género," 13). The images of its inside in the ending credits are mediated by Jorgelina's not-so-childish gaze, as we see artifacts of childhood, that is, a life stage prior to adult sexuation (Tragabolas, a chessboard, and Playmobil figurines), and torn pages from the Hollisters books, which appear in the Boyita prior to the move to the countryside.

Now torn and scattered, these books represent a letting-go of the symbols and structures of the heteronormative (heterosexual, white, middle-class) nuclear family that Andrew E. Svenson used as a backdrop for his thirty-three books. The image of these scattered pages reverberates throughout the scenes in the countryside, as one of the first things Jorgelina asks Mario when seeing his room is if he liked the Hollisters books she sent him. Their presence in the destroyed Boyita signals it as a spatial metaphor of normativity, where children are children and learn the structures of gendered power through didactic texts. The shot of the tattered books, an image of images, fosters a meta-ethical questioning by the viewer of the social and moral tenets alluded to in the Boyita, even as it lies broken in half by an upended tree. Its destruction or, more accurately, the sequence of events that leads to a reflection of what it holds, return us to the scene of Mario's disengagement from the masculine, where he decides to run away from the farmhouse. The rain and wind, and the nature-vector of the blowing sand precipitate his outing and the queering of the norms of sexuation in the Pampas, which then seemingly resonate in the upended tree; that is, the Boyita as a symbolic space is parted in half by the very audile-tactile vector images and sounds that originally deconstructed gender, returning us to these cinematic strategies as not simple filler or ambient shots of the natural, but as key stylistic and ethical interventions that produce a definitive *New* in regard to Maricón cinema.

CHAPTER SIX

XX-

Lucía Puenzo's XXY (2007) should perhaps be located at the start of this discussion, given that it was produced and screened earlier than *Contracorriente* and *El último verano de la Boyita*. I am purposely situating it after having discussed the other two films, however, as it ties together several links of the chain that I have attempted to create on New Maricón film. I am, furthermore, entering XXY in dialogue with Puenzo's *El niño pez* to find aesthetic points of contact within her oeuvre, even if there are several with *Contracorriente* and *El último verano*. Several critics have already addressed Puenzo's XXY in relation to Solomonoff's *El último verano de la Boyita*, as a means of opening a debate in relation to the queer. Deborah Martin, for example, argues that the two films "constitute a quite unprecedented intervention on the part of Argentine cinema into international debates on intersexuality, as well as into global queer filmmaking, which had hitherto passed over this theme" ("Growing Sideways," 35). Both films, like *Contracorriente*, enter into this global filmmaking through what I argue to be a haptic visuality or circulation of connective scenes and images that encourage an empathic reaction. Note here that empathy is an emotion generated or conduced from specific positive affective intensities that engender a psychic alignment between the subject and object, the observer and the observed. My understanding of empathy or an empathic connection in relation to viewership in these films follows Ahmed's theorization of emotions as "relational: they involve (re)actions or relations of 'towardness' or 'awayness' in relations to such objects" (*The Cultural Politics*, 8).

In the case of New Maricón films, the former circulatory mechanisms are stressed through specific techniques of placement and audiovisual characteristics. It comes as no surprise, then, that Puenzo uses several of the audile, tactile, and visual cues analyzed in the two later movies, albeit without directly explicating their importance to initiating a different viewing experience, which Fuentes-León mastered in *Contracorriente*.

XXY, or perhaps more accurately, *XX and a broken X*, is a vignette of the coming-of-gender/-age of Alex, the fifteen-year-old intersexed child of Néstor and Suli Kraken, an Argentine couple who now reside in a quiet fishing town on the Uruguayan coast. The family moved from Buenos Aires to escape the perceived problems of rearing an intersexed child. The film thus undertakes a spatio-imaginary outing from the urban/center that is Buenos Aires to peripheral spaces, though in this case, the film (unlike *El último verano*) does not take place in the Pampas. Instead, Puenzo designates the Uruguayan coast as another peripheral and therefore subordinate area to the Argentine capital, just as she suggests in her later film, *El niño pez*, where the periphery is another neighboring country, Paraguay. There is, then, a mapping rudimentarily based on a center and periphery and what these code for.

XXY begins and ends with the visit of a surgeon (Ramiro), his wife (Erika), and their son (Álvaro) to the Krakens' house at the invitation of Suli, who, unbeknownst to her husband and child, has invited Ramiro to explore the possibilities of sex-reassignment surgery or, perhaps more accurately, sex-affirmation or -realignment surgery. The film develops the dynamics of Alex and Álvaro and the relationship between the family and the villagers, who, immediately prior to the events of the film, have begun to hear whispers about Alex's otherness. The events of the film coincide with this outing and with Alex's decision to stop taking the hormones that have retarded her masculine traits.

Alex has been reared as a female, and her body is going through a second puberty during which maleness directly confronts her nurtured and natured femaleness. The film chronicles this development and includes a discussion of whether she should be operated on, sexual relations between her and Álvaro, and a rape scene, where young men from the village violate her in an attempt to *see* her sexes.[1] The film ends with the fallout from this rape, as Ramiro and family leave the coast, and Puenzo leaves us with an open ending as to Alex's "choice."

Puenzo deploys the haptic potential of the aquatic from the onset of the film, as the credits show undifferentiated subaquatic life forms foregrounded by the muffled sounds of movement in the water, akin to the underwater shots in *Contracorriente* when the film begins a queering of the magical-realist mode. Puenzo, however, intercuts the computer-generated images (CGI) of the marine beings with action images of Alex running through a forest with a large knife in hand.[2] The sharp contrast in sounds in this montage is significant, as the audile-tactile subaquatic image enters into dialogue with the audile-tactile image of the protagonist running between trees. Of note is Alex's constant entering and escaping from the multiple frames provided by the trees, akin to Miguel and Santiago's constant need to move out of the many frames (windows, boat structures, doorways) in *Contracorriente*. Unlike in Maricón movies, which are willing and effective in framing or representing the homosexual subject, Puenzo's characters constantly and from the outset shift away from any diegetic framing, perhaps, I would speculate, as a sort of intertextual referent to the historical aesthetics of representing LGBT characters in Latin America.

The alternating images of a heavily breathing Alex moving in and out of frames in the woods is met with a sharp cutting action and sound immediately prior to a shift back to the CGI marine imagery, as the film's mutilated title appears ominously in the darkened recesses of the water. The protagonist's cutting motion can be interpreted in multiple ways: perhaps it signals a cut of the third X in the title, referencing the foreshadowed possibility of bodily cutting that Ramiro is bent on performing; perhaps it evokes the violent decentering force that is at the core of the film's phenomenology; or perhaps it furthers the notion that Puenzo is cutting the film away from a previous genealogy that so poorly attempted a "queer filmmaking." Of note in the ambiguity of the opening credits is the focus on the visibility of movement and the foregrounding of the audiosensory mechanisms that establish a semiotics of viewing that will later be developed by Fuentes-León, Solomonoff, and Ricardo de Montreuil in *La mujer de mi hermano*. The credits montage obviates subtlety in favor of a brash affirmation of what the film is *not*, that is, a puerile and sterilized depiction of lesbigay lifestyles and subjects, or, alternatively, of a politicized intersexual agenda. As Jeffrey Zamostny notes (and I quite agree with his evaluation): "XXY would probably be a less engaging film if its sole aims were to buttress activist discourse and to indulge in a politically correct celebration of the ideals set forth by the intersex movement" ("Constructing Ethical Attention," 193).

This theme reverberates throughout the film and is especially evoked when Álvaro first enters the Krakens' household. A roving point-of-view shot that follows his gaze moves through several framed portraits of the young Alex that show a posed child, followed by a markedly younger image of her playing in the water, more or less at the life stage of Jorgelina in *El último verano*, followed by two framed photos that break with the seeming innocence of prepubescence. These images—shown in a darker, somber light—evoke a particular storyline, of a child who is coming, and then has come, to terms with her condition of difference. The first image of this dyad is almost a replica of the posed portrait, except that Alex is looking despondently downward with an evaluative gaze that focuses on the body outside the frame and invites the viewer to engage in a dialectic of naming that will struggle to identify her as male or female for the rest of the film. The gesture toward that which lies just beyond the frame is also

6.1. The aqueous in the credits of XXY. *Copyright Historias Cinematográficas Cinemania.*

6.2. Alex escaping the frame, XXY. *Copyright Historias Cinematográficas Cinemania.*

explicit in Mario's disrobing, as the mirror in *El último verano* provides a needed gendered framing—that is, is he a boy or a girl—for the viewer.[3]

The second portrait in the dyad, however, reiterates the trope of escape that is present in the credits montage. Alex's palm is held up to the camera, blocking her face but, more important, blurring it as the camera's autofocus fixates on the hand. This gesture, read in tandem with the former, underlines the role of escapism (both subjective and spatial) in depicting the queer, because to do so requires a decentering or unframing of norms. It also stresses the barriers placed in and around Alex as a reference point, as much of the film deals not solely with her coming to terms with gender but also with how those around her, namely, her parents and her male peers, manage their relationship with her as she/he undergoes the changes that come with stopping the hormones.

Herein lies the crux of a critical intervention in the film, because beyond simply showing the changes that come with being an intersexed person, XXY more deeply explores the tangential interactions between intersexed and sexed bodies (which Solomonoff also develops, albeit in a less intense and more playful manner, between Jorgelina and Mario). Perhaps more fittingly, XXY probes just what happens to supposedly fixed categories of gender and orientation when they come into contact with the intersexed state. Álvaro, a teenage boy, is surprised by Alex while he sketches at the beach. Álvaro's proclivity for the arts, reminiscent of the schoolteacher who erupts into the young Reinaldo's household in *Antes que anochezca* and tells the family that the boy has an affinity for poetry, clues the viewer to the fact that he is not the stereotypical young male who belongs to the heterosexist homosocial that we see later in the film. His quiet demeanor, slender frame, and inclination for the arts props him up on a semantic field of otherness that is common in Latin American cultural production where the man of arts is relegated to the passive, symbolically penetrated position.

The first meeting between Alex and Álvaro occurs immediately upon the latter's arrival at the beach house. Unlike in *El último verano,* where there is some mystery around Mario's condition, we know from the outset (through the hormones in the bathroom, the dolls with prosthetic penises attached, and

6.3. The resistance to framing, XXY. *Copyright Historias Cinematográficas Cinemania.*

the movie's title) that Alex is gender-different. This heuristic detail decenters the film's initial approximation to the intersexed subject, as, unlike in other films that deal with gender-body-sexed disjunctions, the surprise of seeing and then knowing is not what arranges the progression of sequences in the film. What substitutes for the surprise of unveiling intersexuality (or transvestitism/transgenderism) is, as stated previously, the intimate surprises that the state produces in seemingly differentiated and fixed bodies—in this narrative, Álvaro.

Their first encounter by the sea is punctuated by an offhand conversation about masturbation and Alex propositioning sex. As a counterpoint to her invitation, close shots of Álvaro's face show his reaction to her nonchalance. These images, which at first glance provide comic relief, subtly accentuate Álvaro's own becoming vis-à-vis the intersexed body; that is, Alex's body duality provides a catalyst for Álvaro's own maturation. More important in this first interchange, Álvaro never responds to Alex's invitation of sex. When she asks: "Would you have sex?" [¿Vos te acostarías?] he replies: "With whom?" [¿Con quién?]. When she answers "With me" [Conmigo], his reply is still an interrogative "With you?" [¿Con vos?], as though the thought of sleeping with a (seeming) female had never really entered his mind. Álvaro's relative lack of sexual interest in a willing female is particularly surprising in a teenage boy and leaves the viewer with a nagging suspicion. After all, aren't all virile teenage males a bundle of charged hormones?

The subsequent scene amplifies the notion that the plot is concerned less with the ontopolitics of intersexuality and more with how it makes possible a queering of heteronormative positions. As the two families gather around a table for a meal and some wine, the camera fixates on Ramiro's gaze as he watches Alex for the first time. His gaze, coupled with a sly twinge of the mouth, suggests an almost perverse act of looking because he (like the viewer) already knows that *she* is also a *he*. His looking is met contrapuntally with an almost reverse shot of Néstor, whose cynical furrowed gaze has already identified the fetishistic look and is thus wary of Ramiro's intentions. Ramiro, after all, aligns with the homosocial and heterosexist gaze that Néstor and Suli fled in Buenos Aires.

This characterization will be repeated during the movie, perhaps most potently when Néstor confronts his daughter's rapist. Ramiro intervenes in this tussle to restrain him, and Néstor promptly attacks him and affirms: "You're the same as them . . . worse than them" [Vos es igual que ellos . . . peor que ellos]. Ramiro, in fact repeatedly throughout the film, reaffirms his belonging to the (urban) gender hegemony. He displays looks of distrust and discomfort when he spies the two teenagers together and debases his son for being a vegetarian. Again the implications of his actions speak to an audience that quickly learns to juxtapose Álvaro's salient, forming identity with the overpowering masculinity of his father. If we return to Connell's theorem of masculinity, Álvaro has already entered into the moment of engagement with the hegemonic group, choosing to practice and occupy a subordinate position.

The relationship between Álvaro and Alex, if we are to take it as the line of flight in the film, develops further through conversations and the use of thinly veiled symbolism that describes Alex's condition and the possibility of surgery, that is, the very reason that brings Álvaro to the coast. While helping Alex's father rescue a maimed sea turtle, Álvaro asks if it will survive. Alex responds, again with an explicit reference to her own possible mutilation, that it will but that it can never return to the sea. The sea and the maritime function again as heuristic vectors that gesture toward the queer and the plural possibilities of leaving heteronormativity behind; Alex's "maiming," real or symbolic, is a surgical intervention that writes onto her body a conformity to the binary of permissible sex and gender (in the capital and beyond, no matter how isolated Néstor and Suli feel the coast is).[4]

The association of the animal and Alex is furthered when in the next scene she asks Álvaro how many breast augmentations his father has performed. The implication is that she is considering a change, although we cannot know whether she is choosing the female over the male, as higher testosterone levels will likely stop or at least counteract the growing breasts that the viewer sees in several scenes.

These superficial phenotypical referents to sex are the only clues given about Alex's body difference, as even when other characters (forcibly or consensually) see her genitals, the camera carefully leaves them unframed. Not allowing the viewer to see, leaving her difference to the imagination (in terms of the gaze and the symbolic) and therefore in the realm of unrepresentability, the film implicates the viewer in the collective homosocial fetishism of wanting to see her penis and her vagina. Her budding breasts, furthermore, are not erotically charged, and do not have the often vacuous heterosexist appeal of the nude female torso. They are less a true point of entry into any real discussion of the eroticism of the image and more a perverse aspect of homosocial entertainment. We see them first in an informative scene prior to the turtle rescue, where Alex is lying half-clothed on her bed with the turbulent sea in the background. She is wearing only a pair of shorts and, in a close shot of her breasts, places a hormone pill on her chest. The image centers the pill between her nipples, and our gaze is drawn to her fingers flicking it across the room. Of note in this image is a decentralization (or, arguably, a demythification) of the nipples and breasts as erogenous zones, as here they are vacant, almost inert, extras that are excised from the eroticism of the visual. What is charged with eroticism, however, is what we cannot see, what is suggested yet never fully represented in the voyeuristic state that the moving image permits, though, of course, suggested by the hormone pill. The pill thus becomes the true erotic locus of the shot. In

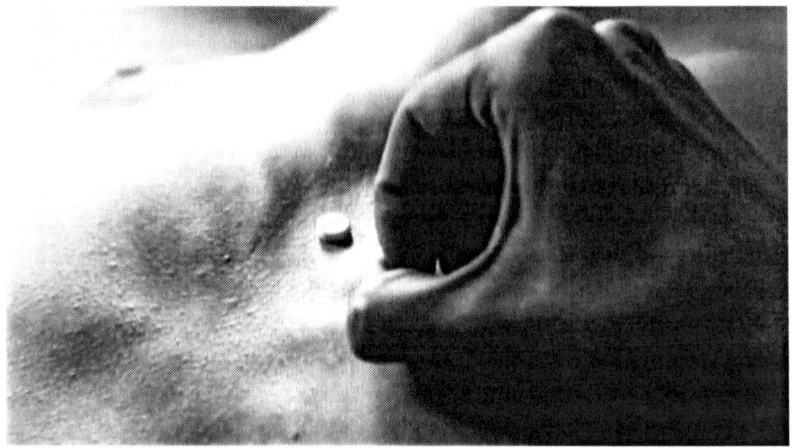

6.4. The de-eroticized body, XXY. *Copyright Historias Cinematográficas Cinemania.*

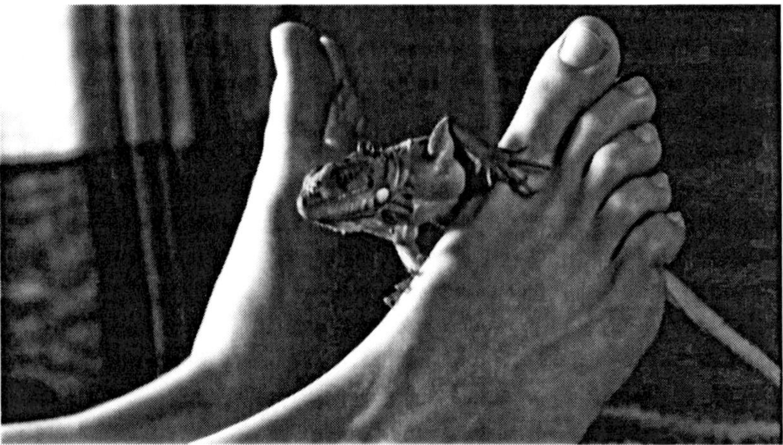

6.5. Visual cues to tactility, XXY. *Copyright Historias Cinematográficas Cinemania.*

subsequent images we are presented with Alex calmly resting her hands over her genitals then removing them, followed by the image of her pet iguana running up her legs.

The montage of both sets of images and their emphasis on eroticizing the unseen (versus the seen naked body) and the movements of the camera lens underline the erotics of intersexuality that *XXY* poses. The film locates the viewer as a malleable and participatory entity in the framing and becoming of the sexual body, not as a detached observer who is directed toward *what* to see, but as a subject that is tasked with peeling away the layers to reach the unseen.

Returning to her conversation with Álvaro after observing how Néstor cures the maimed turtle, Alex's question about implants emphasizes the superficiality and ubiquity of (naked) breasts on the screen. What is central to the eroticism of the image is the unseen and the unmarked, not the perfunctory presence of nipples and mammary glands. Álvaro's reply, though brief, calls our attention to the film's originality in terms of aesthetics and content in Latin America: "You're *weird*" [Sos *rara*] (my emphasis). The term "*rara*" in Spanish is perhaps the closest approximation we have to the English "queer," as it signals both difference (and hence a decentering epistemology) and, in colloquial (including Mexican and Argentine) speech, homosexuality. Of note in the second meaning is the homogenizing semantics of LGBT as Q, which, arguably, thus collocates *XXY* in global filmmaking.

Perhaps more important in this brief interchange is Alex's reply: "So are you" [Vos también]. Her response brings us back to the thesis I proposed earlier, that the film is less about her coming to terms with her body and self and more about how Álvaro (and, by extension, the viewer) comes to terms with the attraction he feels for Alex's difference. This position is only made clearer in a shot after a sequence showing them flirting with each other. Both teenagers hop off a pickup truck, and Puenzo provides us with a carefully segmented image traversed centrally by the road that leads the two characters to the frame. To the north of the central line lies the beach and ocean, vectors of nonheteronormative and homosexual desire. Given Álvaro's difference from the norms established by the patriarchal order, it is unsurprising that his first inclination is to move toward the water as a subtle symbolic gesture toward difference that serves to emphasize his earlier characterization as also *raro*.

6.6. Álvaro exposes his queerness, XXY. *Copyright Historias Cinematográficas Cinemania.*

In fact, Álvaro repeats his previous affirmation of Alex's difference, of her as *rara,* in a later scene where both characters lie on the beach. In response to her previous invitation to have sex, Álvaro reiterates: "You are not normal. You are different . . . and you know it" [Vos no sos normal. Vos sos distanta . . . y lo sabés]. His rejection is founded on how others in the village *see* Alex and not on any tangible, corporeal sign or quality of nonnormalcy. The onus placed on seeing and the visual (versus the real or audile-tactile) is responsible for Álvaro's anxiety, which can be simplistically attributed to a form of heterosexist panic.

Alex, predictably, flees from him after the rejection, and a close image of his face and gaze tracking her as she leaves shows again an affective switch that evidences confusion and misrecognition, as though what is really unseen and, therefore, *raro* lies beneath the mask of his bewilderment.[5] The affection-image is complemented by the sounds of seabirds and the persistent and repetitive rumbling of the sea, coupling the affective potential of the face with the audility-tactility of the natural. As seen more explicitly in the postcoital images in *Contracorriente,* the image seeks a point of empathic contact with the viewer, a polysensorial movement and feeling of embodiment that momentarily invites the audience to escape its own framing in favor of a phenomenological break that then positions viewers within the emotive and perceptive plane of the subject of the affection-image. In other words, the image invites the viewer to occupy Álvaro's confused state of desire and rejection vis-à-vis the corporality of unsettling difference that Alex embodies. The viewer moves from simply being an implicit and largely unconscious fetishist-voyeur to an actively decentered subjectivity engaged in a conflicting dialectic of perverse scopophilia and, more important, coming to terms with what this entails. Jennifer Barker's thoughts on contact and viewership inform this theorization:

> We do not "lose ourselves" in the film, so much as we exist—emerge really—in the contact between our body and the film's body. It is not a matter simply of identifying with the characters on screen, or with the body of the director or camera operator, for example. Rather, we are in a relationship of intimate, tactile, reversible contact with the film's body—a complex relationship that is marked as often by tension as by alignment, by repulsion as often as by attraction.[6] (*The Tactile Eye,* 19)

Álvaro's rejection prompts Alex to flee to a barnlike structure that is separate from the main house (akin to Mario's living quarters in *El último verano*). The structure is a skeletal homologue of the sanctimonious domestic space so central to the spatial contract of heteronormativity and therefore allows for a representation and praxis of queer sexual contacts. In a darkly yet sensually lit montage of images, we see Álvaro make his way to the loft where Alex is lying despondently. What first provides a sense of disjointedness in this sequence is the presence of what seems to be nondiegetic music, as though the film is suddenly breaking out of character and entering a Hollywoodesque aesthetic of seduction where casual musical and lyrical sound overs provide an affective prompt for the prescribed kinesthetics of viable (and vanilla) heterosexual coitus. The presence of music as Álvaro enters the dimly lit space speaks of the allure of the intersexed body, which Steven Shaviro (working with the ideas of Graham Harman) notes as "the way in which an object does not just display certain particular qualities to me, but also insinuates the presence of a hidden, deeper level of existence. The alluring object explicitly *calls attention* to the fact that it is something more than, and other than, the bundle of qualities that it presents to me" (*Post Cinematic Affect*, 9).

Predictably, the two teenagers begin kissing and clumsily undressing each other on the floor, again within the visual aesthetics of acceptability forwarded by heterosexist cinematic antecedents. In an act of self-reflexivity, however, Alex severs the sound-image from this genrification of eroticism by switching off the radio, which has provided, up to that point, what has been perceived as nonambient music. This action (which comes immediately after the first sight of Alex's already de-eroticized breasts) confuses not only Álvaro (an image of his once-again furrowed face is spliced in as a counterpoint to the interruption) but also the viewer, who at this point has assumed a generic montage of sounds and images that foreshadows heterosexual sex. The switching off of the radio, then, is not only an act of real coitus interruptus, but also a semantic act that decenters and interrupts the progression of images from an aesthetics of prescribed eroticism.[7]

It may be useful here to think of Jennifer Barker's notions of viscera and the cinema. She argues (focusing largely on rhythm) that there are certain techniques and motions that slow the sequence of images to a point of self-reflexivity, akin to feeling one's heartbeats to realize that the human body is a set of mechanical organs in constant motion. What happens, however, if we expand this notion of viscera to also include other seemingly self-evident and nonmoving elements of the image? Alex turning off the radio is one such example, as by her doing so, the seduction scene immediately slows down, and the viewer is left to grasp the movements and generated affects of the scene without the overtones of sensualized lyricisms. Our reaction, then, to Álvaro's penetration is a visceral one, as we realize the magnitude of our previous empathic affiliation with him and feel our own sphincters give way to momentary pain, which later turns to pleasure.

What takes the place of the sanitized music as their foreplay resumes is the reverberant and pervasive echo of the sea, as though the film returns us to its possibilities as a vector of the New in Latin American depictions of nonheteronormative subjects and actions. An erratic mobile camera frames parts of their bodies and never captures them as a whole, evoking Elena del Río's theory of the framing of "bits and pieces," which precludes any real sense of the subject's wholeness. In a scopic sense, we are pushed again in the direction of wanting to see Alex's difference on the off-chance that the roving, insatiable camera will capture what others in the village have heard of (and in the rape scene, will want to see). This movement, however, is paradoxically offset by a separate audile-tactile process that returns us to the visual points of empathy already traced through previous affection-images of Álvaro's incredulity and confusion, most recently evoked when Alex turns off the radio. The viewer, thus, is segmented and incised, asked to occupy conflicting yet convergent points of being vis-à-vis the eroticism of the image.

The disjunction (or queering) of the viewer that is brought about by Alex's simple action comes to the fore in the immediacy of their passion, as she flips Álvaro over and exposes his (our?) backside to her still unseen pelvis. With their faces to the camera, we *hear* Alex's penetration of Álvaro in a coital dynamic not very different from traditional representations of homosexual sex on the silver screen.[8] Shaviro develops the theory of attraction in a concept he calls "vicarious allure," which perhaps is most indicated in the film by the presence of the intersexed body; what draws us to it is specifically what hinders any possibility of intimacy. In XXY, Alex is in essence vicariously alluring, affectively charged because she can only be grasped and seen through contacts of absence. In other words, we never see her difference but are allowed to intimately feel it by her vicariously penetrating Álvaro, in a gesture that displaces both us and the subjects in the image.[9]

In fact, we hear only Álvaro's grunts and then whimpers of pleasure throughout the scene, as Alex becomes an almost invisible penetrating body. We do, however, see a "piece" of her in the next shot, as the camera lingers over and frames her buttocks, which, as discussed earlier in *Contracorriente*, align the eroticism of the image with a possibly heteronormative aesthetic, as though what is being seen in XXY is a man penetrating a woman. This conjecture, though, is largely unfounded, as the audio track never deviates from Álvaro's low grunts, thereby never allowing for a complete dissolution of the queer into a disinfected heterosexual piecemeal of sex.

This is made clearer when he reaches around to her buttocks (again, heterosexual bits and pieces) and encourages Alex's thrusts. Herein we note the queering potential of the intersexed body, not solely as ontologically queer, but in its ability to resemanticize seemingly rigid sexed bodies by their (physical and/or visual) association. The only coital scene in XXY reaffirms what had already been suggested in various earlier scenes, that Álvaro is not only unwilling to follow in his father's power/aesthetic/relational footsteps but that he is

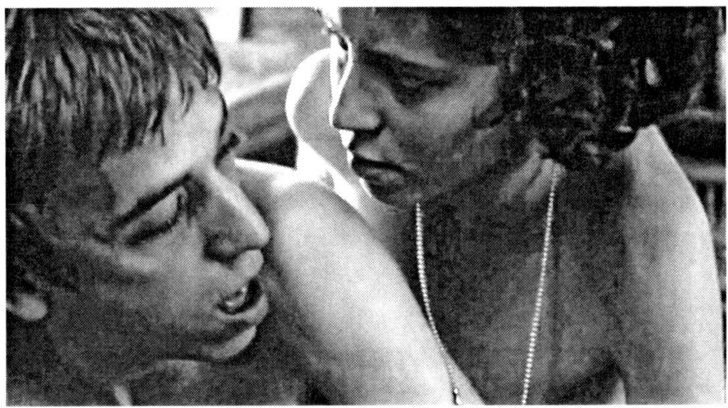

6.7. The moment of reckoning, XXY. *Copyright Historias Cinematográficas Cinemania.*

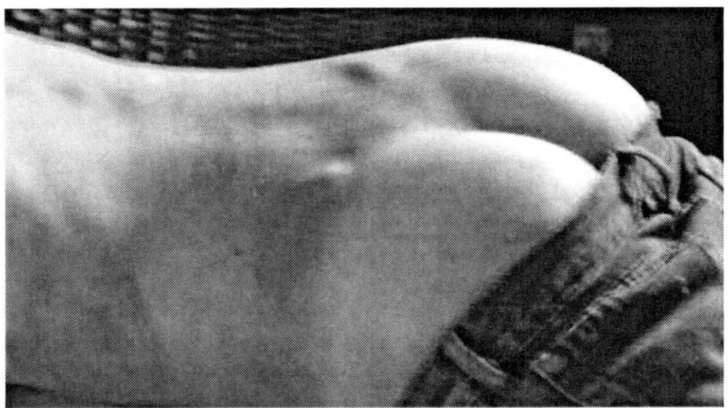

6.8. Disarticulating desires, bodies, and identities, XXY. *Copyright Historias Cinematográficas Cinemania.*

also completely rejected by the structured norms of hegemonic masculinity. By being penetrated (and enjoying it), Álvaro is also *raro,* albeit in the behavioral sense, to Alex's organic difference.

Álvaro's difference triggers a moment of panic that the camera captures in a slowdown reminiscent of the opening credits, as he walks between trees and frames away from the scene and the act of queerness. The camera cuts sharply to an image of him leaning against a tree, and we are placed at a vantage point behind him, returning us as viewers to the position of voyeur after having momentarily shared in the pain and pleasure of penetration. A moving medium image shows him frantically stroking his penis as a sort of reaffirmation of his masculinity and heterosexuality, evoking his interrogative "¿Con vos?" when he was first asked about having sex with Alex.

It seems from this sequence of images, sounds, and shifting referential points of view that Álvaro, though he already breaks with the model of masculinity embodied by Ramiro and the paternal order, never once considers himself to be nonheteronormative. I hesitate to use the word "homosexual" here as Álvaro instead problematizes desire and orientation, having fallen in love with a girl-boy who successfully penetrates him and produces pleasure. Again, Álvaro is also *raro*, and not only for enjoying penetration but for also being incapable of coming to terms with a preassigned gendered identity.

This disconnect is addressed in a zoomed-in voyeur image that profiles his distraught crying. Of note in this particular image is its deviance from the close affection image used in earlier scenes, where what was sought from the viewer was a point of empathic contact. In its place, the viewer is consciously displaced and now sees Álvaro as just another queer body, akin to the cut-in image that follows of a similarly sobbing Alex. The connection being made is that Álvaro is also *raro* and therefore to be seen and not felt.

While the framing of this image and the placing of the camera liken the representation of gender difference to earlier films about LGBT characters, we cannot lose sight of the previous affection-images that link the viewer empathically to the penetrated orifice. In essence, the voyeur-image in the forest provides an acute juxtaposition of how the cinema can reorient our appraisal of and contact with the queer, again assuming a largely heterosexist and heteronormative target audience (returning once more to Fuentes-León's quotation about watchability and the moving image in Latin America).[10] What is posed in this exercise, then, is a sort of genealogical self-reflexivity that in realigning the viewer with how we see difference, the image, conversely, emphasizes a New or less scopic way of feeling the previously taboo.

The importance given to Álvaro's moment of becoming is highlighted in a scene after he returns from the forest. At the dinner table with his parents and their hosts, he is quiet and is drawing; the emphasis is again placed on his relationship with the dominant masculine. Ramiro takes the sketch and shows it to the others at the table, affirming: "Look how well my son draws" [Mira qué bien dibuja mi hijo]. This oral appreciation, however, is a double-edged sword, as he immediately pours a protesting Álvaro wine, arguing that he is old enough. Ramiro, knowing the signs of archetypal Latin American effeminacy (read: an inclination for the arts), attempts to reintegrate his son into the homosocial through the consumption of alcohol (see Mario and the teenage boys in *El último verano de la Boyita*). Having been through the genealogy of such films, it wouldn't surprise us at all if his next action were to take Álvaro to a local brothel, akin to the ill-advised strategies of the domineering father in

Francisco Lombardi's *No se lo digas a nadie*. It also comes as no surprise that Néstor comes to the aid of the teetotaling teenager, especially when he reminds us that "I can't stand arrogance . . . we left Buenos Aires to be far away from a certain type of people" [No soporto la prepotencia . . . nos fuimos de Buenos Aires para estar lejos de cierta clase de gente]. The film's praxis of a spatial outing is emphasized in this moment of hegemonic challenge and reminds the viewer of the gendered topologies of subjectivity in Latin American cinema that were so present in the Maricón age.

From the moment of penetration, the narrative continues to explore Álvaro's queerness and how this is created and impacted by his contact with and desire for the intersexed body. In a dimly lit sequence, he is shown looking through Alex's belongings. One particular image in this scene is striking, as we see him in profile flipping through a book of her childhood drawings. Immediately behind him and clearly marked in white letters is the word "*raro*." The image could not be clearer in its dialogue with previous conversations, with the coitus between the two protagonists, and with Ramiro's attempts to masculinize his son: Álvaro has become the point of queerness, or the "*raro*," in the film, a detail signaled by the stark white letters in the dark room.

His coming to terms with the pleasure he felt during penetration directs the ensuing moments of contact between the two teenagers. In one scene, an overhead angle shows a seminaked Alex floating in a lagoon, not unlike Jorgelina in the above ground pool in *El último verano*. With Alex's uneroticized breasts exposed to the air, the camera cuts to a languid Álvaro on the shore, slowly disrobing, presumably to join his love interest. The aquatic vector is again present as a site of queering, but it does not signal contact between the two, nor does it situate the floating intersexed body. Instead, its queering potential is reflected by Álvaro's entering the water. By doing so he is complicit in and accepting of the earlier penetration, thereby placing himself as a *penetrado*, or within the traditional corporeal semiotics of the maricón or *joto*.

Alex's resulting panic and flight from the water address this supposition, as she, too (though intersexed), does not necessarily understand or acquiesce in the decentering of the subject produced by Álvaro's penetration. In other words, her rejection of him hinges on the knowledge of his being different, of his allowing and enjoying sodomy. These tensions are developed as Álvaro chases her into the forest looking for answers. In response to his confusion about her being able to penetrate him (remember that he, like us, never sees her penis), she almost nonchalantly states: "I am both things" [Soy las dos cosas]. What follows is at the core of any theory of queerness and eroticism in the film, as each character attempts to unravel the identification and orientation of the other. For example, when Álvaro asks, "Do you like men or women?" [¿Te gustan a los hombres o a las mujeres?], Alex replies, "I don't know" [No sé].

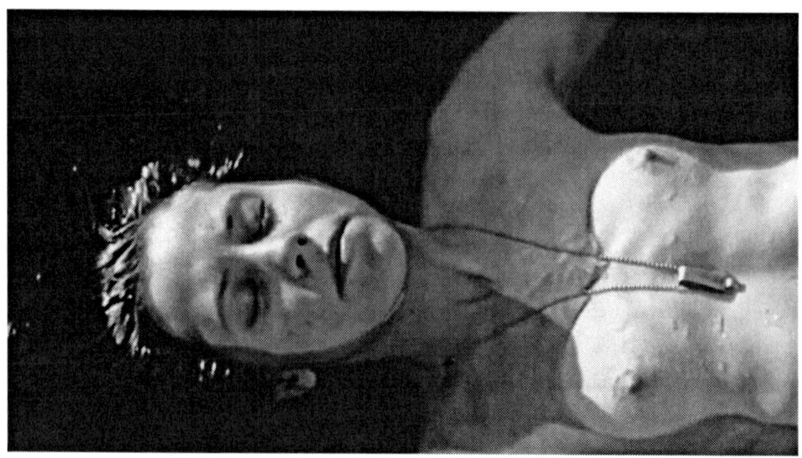

6.9. Floating in the vector of difference in XXY, *a repeated motif in New Maricón cinema. Copyright Historias Cinematográficas Cinemania.*

They both, however, agree that they enjoyed their one interrupted tryst, albeit for different reasons. When he wants them to have sex again, to finish what was interrupted, she rejects him and states: "I want something else" [Yo quiero otra cosa]; that is, she enjoyed the phenomenon of penetration, but not with a willing male partner and his anus. Alex, we can gather, is a heterosexual male who happens to also have a vagina and budding breasts, though these will slowly disappear as the undisturbed hormonal cycles slowly make her into a he.[11] Álvaro's only reply to this rejection is a reiteration of difference, although his decenters him from the praxis of heterosexism: "I also want something else" [Yo también quiero otra cosa]. The scene ends with a dejected Álvaro retracing his steps through the forest, the mobile, handheld camera catching him between tree trunks in an aesthetic similar to that employed in the opening credits. Like Alex's body-subjectivity in the credits, he too is now constantly entering and escaping frames, becoming a queer entity that decenters the normative expectations of the homosocial of the maturing teenager.

What Álvaro wants, that *otra cosa,* is evoked at the end of the film when Alex bids him farewell right before he and his family return on the boat to the city (and, therefore, away from the queer periphery). He reiterates his desire, and now love, for her, but she again rejects him, retorting that "Something else happened to you" [A vos te pasó otra cosa]. This *otra cosa* lies at the center of the film's development of a queer problematic, as the presence of conflicting and nonhomologous desire supersedes the presence of intersexuality. How can a man enjoy penetration? If he does, is he a homosexual? Does his enjoyment preclude notions of identity and orientation? Where is the viewer in all this? Are we, too, penetrated by Alex? Such are the questions that the film asks yet leaves unanswered, decentering notions of sex, gender, and identity that are otherwise cleanly designated by action and orientation paradigms of self. Álvaro's *otra cosa,* furthermore, is never explained, quite unlike Alex's difference, leaving, then, the implication that perhaps the unnameability of his desire is what is truly queer about the film.

The film, then, is really more conservative than one would initially suppose (from the thematic matter and the open portrayal of sex), suggesting that what is really different, unnameable, and shocking (as evidenced by Alex's rejection of Álvaro) is a queer desire that is never fully articulated or explained. Perhaps this conservative tinge can be attributed to what Fuentes-León calls watchability, as the intersexed body is never a visual site of contention or a shock to the viewer. What takes that body's place, however, is both the moment and the sound of penetration and the subsequent desire, which aligns the eroticism of the film with a broader trajectory of cinema that probes *joto*-ness or maricónness, though Puenzo is masterly in not completely revealing the underpinning axes of desire and emotion in the male subject. We are left, instead, with the possibility of male homosexuality, though by not naming or identifying it as such, the film points to a different possibility: the taboo of penetration and ambisexuality that bends identitarian notions of gender and self to open a true queery of desire that dissolves the maricón/gay debate.

The reader here should recognize that the film only "outs" Álvaro or displaces his subjectivity in the sense that the sequence of images and the eroticism of the narrative succeed in unveiling something unknown or a difference in him, and not in Alex, as there is no effort to hide the fact that she is intersexed. Quite unlike *El último verano de la Boyita,* Puenzo's film is an exercise in the politics of coming out (when Álvaro confesses his pleasure at being penetrated) and the rejection that this produces. There is a circularity to this process that is evidenced by the spatiality of the diegesis as he is shown twice opening the gate that allows him and his family access to the space of queer intersexuality that the Kraken household makes possible.

The second image in this series, of Álvaro closing the gate, is almost forgettable for its lack of dialogue and simple representation of an everyday action. It gains importance, however, when read in juxtaposition to the initial scene when he opens the gate, thereby allowing for contact with Alex and her house. We must remember that the domestic structure houses a series of facile representations of difference (the portraits, dolls, pictures, etc.) and that his entrance is a symbolic moment of engagement with queerness as a potential subject position and as a strategy out of the conflict in which he is engaged with the hegemonic masculinity of his father. There is, in a sense, an inversion of the politics of the spatial contract in XXY, as, unlike in *El último verano* or *Contracorriente,* the domestic structure portends all that is nonheteronormative. By having him close the gate immediately prior to his departure back to the city, the director suggests that Álvaro has entered the space and then come out a different person, more aware of his individual desire and self vis-à-vis the gendered order that awaits him in Buenos Aires.

We see signs of this impending deviance from masculine engagement in a scene immediately prior to their leaving, where a dejected Álvaro sits by a bonfire. Ramiro joins him, and the two have a heart-to-heart, and his father tells him that he "more or less" [más o menos] likes him. This moment of frankness is taken further when Álvaro expresses admiration for his father's work and "talent" [talento], and asks him if he has the same skill. Ramiro's reply is wrenching and brutal; the "no" reverberates not only through this brief dialogue but also through the previous and following images in the film, and we come to understand the disconnection felt between the hegemonic father and the nonheteronormative son. Ramiro then asks if Álvaro has fallen for Alex. When his son is unable to form a definite answer, Ramiro takes his silence as a yes and replies: "Perhaps you'll make me happy . . . I was afraid of you being a faggot [Igual me das una alegría . . . tenía miedo que fueras puto]. He slowly walks away, and the camera lingers on Álvaro's partly confused and partly guilty face, returning the viewer to the initial affection-images, which demonstrated his confusion and bewilderment at being propositioned by Alex. It is again silence that marks the libidinal and identitarian quandary posed by the character, leaving the viewer to ponder and envision the future that awaits him as he leaves the queer periphery for the heterosexist city. We can almost imagine a future film where Álvaro must come to terms with this initiation into personal and communal sexuality and negotiate his own interpersonal relations inside and outside the family unit back in the rigid, classist structure provided by his parents and "a certain type of people" [cierta clase de gente].

The film ends with Alex walking away from the port with her parents, Néstor's arm over her shoulder, suggesting that she and her parents have come to terms with her condition and choice. A subtle glance as the camera pivots indicates Puenzo's use of the aquatic as a metaphor for gender, as Alex looks knowingly at the calm sea. The camera tracks their movement from right to left, but then stops and lingers over the water, moving slightly back and forth, as though finding itself within the background sea, akin to the camera's struggle with framing Mario's training on the horse prior to the race in *El último verano*. This scene returns us to Barker's description of the audile-tactile image and the viscera as the image's self-consciousness provokes a deeper-than-skin relationship to the film. By resting on the now calm waters, the camera suggests a closed ending and an acceptable resolution to Alex's growing pains. One can equally argue, however, that the symbol of the tumultuous sea now follows

Álvaro as he makes his way back to the urban. We may, again, conjecture that any sequel that focuses exclusively on Álvaro's coming to terms would be rife with aquatic images and metaphors, where the pulsating waves and their accompanying audility-tactility would provide a haptic backdrop to a narrative of queer potentials.

Without meandering too far into hypothesized possibility, we can, however, see several points of contact between XXY and Puenzo's next film, *El niño pez*. The latter is narratologically more ambitious than XXY, recounting the romantic entanglements of Lala (Inés Efron), the daughter of a judge, and Ailín (Mariela Vitale), one of the family's maids.

The movie begins with the death of the judge interpellated with shots of Lala crossing the border into Paraguay and Ailín evading the press, suggesting that the girls' actions are in some way related to the judge's demise. From there the film crosses over temporalities and recounts, in several plot lines, the blossoming of attraction between the female leads, the sexual relationship between the judge and the maid, and the events of her childhood that cause her to leave Paraguay. This last storyline likely includes an incestuous relationship between the Guaraní girl and her father and the drowning of her baby in a lake.

The film delves into a magical-realist aesthetic mode in this trajectory, as Ailín suggests, though never clearly states, that her drowned child has become the mythical Mitay Pyra, or Fish Child, that takes the drowned to the bottom of the lake. As a result, her childhood home becomes a sort of shrine for believers who leave offerings and dolls at the gate in homage to the creature.

As in other films in the grouping of a New genre in Latin American film, the aquatic and its metaphors are present from the outset in the guise of a CGI marine space for the introductory credits. Aside from reflecting on the Fish Child myth that the film explores, the marine conditions a structure of feeling that, returning to Sara Ahmed's notions of circulation, establishes empathic and affective channels with a wider audience. A further point of contact may be found in the motif of outing (in its plural meanings), which I highlight in the discussion of *Contracorriente*, as the initial montage of images shows Lala on a journey away from the center/urban, Buenos Aires, to the peripheral/rural, Paraguay. As in XXY, Puenzo sets up this semantic and topological sense of movement between the metropolis and places outside of it, though she places Uruguay and Paraguay as the periphery to the Argentine state, as though moving away from "cierta clase de gente" requires a move away from the nation, farther still than the Pampas and the *gente* who terrorize Mario in *El último verano*. We see this deliberation come to life in a later scene where the two female leads plan their escape from the patriarchal stranglehold imposed by the judge. In a dimly lit image, they are shown kissing passionately on the floor, their heads and roving lips backgrounded by a road map that clearly indicates

6.10. Spatial outings of lesbian desire, El niño pez. *Copyright Historias Cinematográficas Cinemania.*

the borders of Paraguay and Brazil. While ephemeral, the image is potent in situating or overlaying the eroticism of the narrative onto a real referent of outing, suggesting that their lesbian desire can truly be liberated only away from the urban/Buenos Aires.

The figure of the *niño pez* appears in a diachronic sequence of images that mixes the past and the present, the real and the magical in a montage that decenters notions of truth and accuracy in the narrative. Ailín and Lala rest languidly in a bathtub as the former recounts a dream she had where both characters lived by the lake years before the locals erected the shrine. As night falls, Ailín continues, the water rises and covers the whole world until the Mitay Pyra comes and takes her away. The audio track overlays a separate visual narrative where Lala, presumably now in the future, after she has fled from the reality of her father's death, walks during daylight toward the pier and the shrine marking Ailín's baby's grave. These visual cues sever the images of Lala walking from the audio track, pushing the film across semantic fields of being, that is, between the dream state and the narrative and a parallel reality. Lala submerges herself in the water, and the camera follows her as she sees an underwater shrine to the *niño pez* and then a shadow moving deftly through the darkened waters of the lake. The shadow is none other than the mythical Fish Child, who in his CGI glory makes a swift appearance that jars our sensibilities of viewership away from an ethical realism to a more "Latin American" magical terrain.

Puenzo demonstrates a candid consciousness of this shift in viewership as Lala rises to the surface for air, and the ambient music in the underwater shots (which provide a sort of ethereal wonderment at the apparition of the child) is silenced by the silence of the real world above the water. Lala submerges herself one more time in a fruitless search for the child, and the image adopts again the aesthetics of the magical. In the next scene, she lies in bed clutching a doll that earlier was shown below the surface of the lake in the underwater shrine, suggesting that her journey into the magical is real and that the Fish Child does indeed exist.

The aquatic space, as in *Contracorriente*, is charged with both the eroticism of homosexual relations and the possibilities of the magical—even if anachronistic—in outing normativity to a culturally specific narrative space. Prior to her submersion, Lala sits in the tub with Ailín. The sequence of audile and visual cues, images, symbols, and vectors in this cross-temporal and cross-phenomenological montage suggests, then, that the magical-realist mode can be an effective medium or point of entry into queer subjectivities. More than this, though, the foray into magical realism demonstrates a queer praxis, akin to the strategy deployed by Fuentes-León, of using a familiar narrative mode that is then unhinged by the doubt brought about by the film's failure to account for or bring into acceptance Lala's meeting with the child. This occurrence becomes, instead, a forgotten point that is left unexplained, as though it never fully accommodates the narrative mode yet uses its ethics of viewership to bring the viewer-reader into a terrain of normativity wherein subjects and desires of homoeroticism can come to fruition.

Puenzo's *El niño pez* possesses other visual and haptic qualities that align it with the categorization of the New, namely, the presence of facile symbols of gender difference (dolls), marine environments and sounds that encourage the

6.11. Queering narrative modes, El niño pez. *Copyright Historias Cinematográficas Cinemania.*

situating of the viewer in an intimate relationship of tactile and visceral contact, and the viability of homoerotic relations combined with open endings that suggest an embracing of gender difference and nonnormative orientations. If we combine the opening movement away from the urban, or outing, it is worthwhile to place *El niño pez* in this nascent genealogy, even though the film stops short of deepening and problematizing the representation of lesbian relations and sexualities. If anything, Puenzo sins by not going further, by taking a step back from the emancipatory politics posed in XXY that so strikingly both visualizes intersexuality and problematizes the erotics of desire posed by *bothness*.

El niño pez, then, is a timely landmark in the development of a corpus of Latin American female-female narratives but falls short of entering any sustained debate or praxis of queerness (on the global scale). That being said, however, the film deserves recognition for outing lesbianism from the shadows, silence, and veiled insinuations that have otherwise characterized its representation in Maricón films.[12]

The film ends with the two leads getting on a bus that takes them away from the urban sphere of acceptability toward an uncertainty that is, however, punctuated by their togetherness. During a close-up of them kissing, Lala states: "Now you kiss me and it ends" [Ahora me besás y se termina]. Ailín replies: "What ends?" [¿Qué se termina?]. The dialogue, when read in tandem with the camera's close reading of their faces and gazes, gestures toward the convention of the happy ending where, as the credits roll, boy and girl go on to a happy and long procreative life together. Lala's quick glance away from her lover toward the outside accentuates this possibility, as though the outside, what is being left behind by the moving bus, expects that happily ever after of heteronormativity. Their subsequent conversation affirms this, as Ailín considers that at least they have the house—a gesture toward the spatial contract. Puenzo, like Fuentes-León, stresses the possibilities of breaking the contract and its norms, as Lala quickly interjects that they also have the lake. The reference here to the aquatic as a haptic/affective and magical-realist space suggests the queer potential of this particular happily ever after. The credits roll in *El niño pez* immediately after Lala asks: "Are you going to swim with me?" [¿Vas a nadar conmigo?]. Ailín's response, though quick and almost clichéd, is, however, a poignant reference to the portrayal of lesbianism in Latin American cinema, as her assertive "Until the very end" [Hasta el fondo] establishes a point of departure for future films that capture female-female sexual and amorous relations, a legacy, if you will, that is unapologetic, not euphemistic, and definitely not oblique in its portrayal of female homosexuality.

CHAPTER SEVEN

Final Notes on Outing Latin America

THE FILMS STUDIED IN THIS SECTION DEMONSTRATE a clear aesthetic and political cohesiveness that in effect severs them from a select genealogy of homosexual-themed cinema in Latin America. They evidence an acute self-consciousness about this difference and highlight various strategies or trajectories that successfully "out" the movies produced in the region from facile, euphemistic, and, at times, demeaning representations of sexual difference. While I am not going to reiterate these points of contact here, I will suggest that this initial list is not exhaustive and that there are other films that enter into dialogue with the categorization of New. In fact, the chapters in the third part of this volume address those "Newer" films that share a structural and aesthetic basis with the films studied in the preceding parts.

With that being said, however, one other candidate, produced prior to the films studied in earlier chapters, merits consideration as a possible precursor to the New, or as a sort of political intermediary between superficial representations of homosexuality and more complex, nuanced, and affective takes. Ricardo de Montreuil's *La mujer de mi hermano* (2005), like Lombardi's *No se lo digas a nadie*, brings to the screen a novel (of the same name) by Jaime Bayly.[1]

The film describes the marital woes of a wealthy couple that are compounded by the wife (Zoe) having an affair with the husband's brother, hence the title. The brothers are a study in opposites, as one is a rich banker (Ignacio) and the other a philandering artist (Gonzalo) whose lack of ethics with regard to the women he beds plays on the archetype of the promiscuous bohemian. The film includes *telenovela*-like relationships and dialogues between the film's four principal characters (the brothers' mother is also involved) that ultimately out the husband as a sterile maricón leading a double life. It concludes with the artist impregnating his sister-in-law and then rejecting the baby. The twist in the film, the moment that one may argue brings it and us as viewers back into the closet (reminiscent of Joaquín's acquiescence to marriage and a career at the end of *No se lo digas a nadie*), is Ignacio's acceptance of the affair and his agreeing to rear the child as his own, thereby maintaining the façade of normativity in the household.

For all intents and purposes, then, we can read a strongly nonqueer politics in de Montreuil's film, taking us back to Foster's note that homosexual-themed cinema in Latin America cannot be confused with queer filmmaking. This is the case with *La mujer de mi hermano*, as it repeats several queer issues and themes but fails to critically intervene in a broader dialogue about queerness as politics. It is, therefore, located within the sphere of Latin American Maricón film but shows an evolution in the sense that it deviates from a strictly scopic approximation to sexuality and favors instead what we see in the New films, that is, a call to the senses and the circulation of affective intensities that break the subject-object barrier between homosexual character and sex and the viewing public. De Montreuil, like Fuentes-León and Puenzo after him, adroitly manages aqueous substances, images, and sounds, which play a key role in the opening and closing montages of the film in addition to situating certain critical moments of the plot and its characters in relation to bodies of water. By doing so, he inserts the film into an aesthetics of affection that draws the viewer into contact with the erotics of the narrative.

Though Ignacio returns to the closet by agreeing to raise his brother's son while maintaining the charade of the perfect marriage, he does bring to light the fact that a closet exists and that the struggle for emancipation is not only an escape from its spaces but a collective societal acknowledgment that it is present in relation to bodies that otherwise go about their business under the auspices of the spatial contract of normativity. Such a consideration—a knowing reference to identitarian gestures—sets the stage for Miguel, Mario, Álvaro, and Lala, among other characters, to push the boundaries of the normative. These characters are all charged with the task of escaping the frame (both symbolic and real within the moving image) and of moving beyond the flippant and at times stereotypical takes on homoeroticism. It comes as no surprise that many of these New films have scenes and sequences that focus on the action and process of escape, though there is still a long way to go if Latin American cinema is to accurately and productively enter into dialogue with global waves of queerness and film.

If de Montreuil's film can be tagged as an important step toward the "affective turn" in LGBT cinema in the region, it is perhaps equally useful to go a step further in our informal archaeology to unearth when or in what sequence films began to move away from the scopic and toward the empathic, especially if we are to underline affective circulations of empathy as the primary characteristic of New Maricón cinema. There are two films that I want to highlight in this transition, though their placement and study do not equate to a simple process of aesthetic and political causality but, perhaps more precisely, they are a case of ethical contagion of representations of difference.

The first of these films, Julian Schnabel's *Antes que anochezca* (2000), augurs what can be considered the temporal shift toward the New. Starring Javier Bardem, Johnny Depp, and Diego Luna, among others, the film necessarily triggers a debate about what "Latin American cinema" really is in the twenty-first century. Is it enough that the majority of the scenes were filmed in Mexico, or that the principal actors are of Hispanic origin? Perhaps most important, the story is about post-revolutionary Cuba and is an adaptation of Reinaldo Arenas's seminal novel of the same name. Are these factors not enough to label the film "Latin American"?

Critics of this inclusion are justified in pointing out that the dialogue is originally in English, the director is North American, Bardem is Spanish, and Depp, American, and the production dollars all came from the United States. These (valid) points, however, have not stopped the film from being included in studies on Latin American cinema and on course syllabi on topics ranging from "Cuban Cinema" to "Queer Latin American Literature and Cinema."[2]

For the purposes of our discussion of New Maricón cinema, I am including the film as a milestone in the shift of genealogical perception that comes with the New due to the film's overwhelming acceptance in critical and cultural interventions concerning Latin American film. It furthermore warrants inclusion if we think of the cinema as a poietic product that concludes a reflective process; that is, moviemakers are touched by aesthetic and ethical contagion within (though not always) their subfields.

While Schnabel's adaptation of the novel highlights the idiosyncrasies of difference under a culturally oppressive government and is useful in any sustained inquiry into nonnormative sexuality in Cuba, there is, for our purposes, one particular scene that merits consideration. Early in the film, immediately after Reinaldo and a group of young men engage in a wild midnight orgy with a group of police officers, we hear a narrator's commentary about the revolution and its relationship to sexuality over images of a changing Cuba: "There was also a sexual revolution going on that came along with the excitement of the official revolution." Here we are reminded of the tie-in Gutiérrez Alea makes between politics and sexuality, though for him the revolution was more political and idealistic than personal.

The montage of images and sounds here is primordial to the insertion of the subsequent erotics of the film within a genealogy of Maricón cinema in Latin America. In addition to images of Bardem driving down the streets of Havana, we see documentary footage of a young Castro juxtaposed with a close-up of Bardem typing the manuscript of *Antes que anochezca*. The assemblage of images, both documentary and fictive, locate the film within a historical and aesthetic moment that crossed issues of nation in Latin America, moving instead toward a transnationalism of revolution and the Left. This detail establishes or roots the film within a specific politico-cultural matrix, even if its production details suggest an exclusion from any such cultural canon. It further locates the film within one of the original parameters of the Maricón genre through its usage of (homo)sexuality to reflect on a broader theme.

The narrator ends this montage with a note on the "three wonderful things" about his life at that moment in the 1960s: "my typewriter, at which I sat like a dedicated performer sitting at his piano; the youth of those days when everyone was ready to break free; and lastly, the full discovery of the sea." This triad locates the narrative within a specific historical and literary genealogy yet goes further by including the sea as a critical vertex of self. There is some continuity here between the repetitive lyrics of Roberto Cobo's "En el mar" in *Amor libre* and the usage of the aqueous in later New Maricón films as a space for outing sexual difference and for its ability to generate positive affective intensities that engender empathy. Yet while the reference to the maritime in Hermosillo's film never goes beyond the lyrics of the street singer or the metaphor of the fish tank in the apartment, it plays a vital role in the way we *perceive* but do not *see* Reinaldo's desire and self in *Antes que anochezca*.

In fact, the final image of this nondiegetic narrative montage underlines my hypothesis that we are explicitly instructed to stop simply seeing homosexuality and instead to intimately approximate ourselves to the subject of difference, what I argue to be the principal ethico-erotic purpose and product of New Maricón cinema. In this final image, we see Reinaldo behind a set of glass-louvered windows, his penetrating eyes strategically visible while the rest of his face is obscured by the smoky tones of the glass. His eyes, centered in the frame, glance to the right of the viewer, suggesting that we follow his gaze to see what lies beyond our immediate scope. This directionality involves the viewer in an almost unconscious but corporeal maneuvering, which is the first step in going beyond superficial scopic practices. This suggestion is made explicit just as the narrator mentions the sea and the louvers fully close, leaving us with the blurred outline of Reinaldo behind the glass. More important in this at first mechanical action is the "cutting" of the gaze as the hinges sever Reinaldo's eyes, harkening back to Buñuel's archetypical image. The film's message here is crystal clear: sight is no longer viable as the principal medium of perception and must be substituted with something else, especially if we are to relocate to the space alluded to by his now-cut gaze.

The image that immediately follows this cutting suggests just what that substitute should be, as the camera brings us below the surface of the sea. Analogous to the aural-visual hapticity of the aquatic that de Montreuil, Fuentes-

7.1. Cutting gestures and the severing of the scopic, Antes que anochezca. *Copyright El Mar.*

León, and Puenzo mint in their later films, the submarine shot in *Antes que anochezca* establishes a different way of perceiving Reinaldo *and* homoerotic desire. Almost in reaction to and reiterating this, a snorkeling Bardem floats into the frame, but unlike in the earlier image behind louvers, he now looks directly at the camera, thereby establishing an intimacy with the viewer that was absent in the above-water shots.

The establishing shot then cuts to a close-up of a male groin in a tight bathing suit. This sequence, aside from providing comic relief in the person of the underwater voyeur, does two things. First, it places the viewer, through the oppositional geometry of the shot-reverse angle, in the place of the penis, as though the camera is occupying the contoured bulges of the male's bathing suit. This positionality decenters the pillars of Maricón films, which struggled with creating an intimacy between the viewer and the representation of male homoeroticism. Second, the juxtapositional nature of the sequence suggests an acknowledgment of the heteronormativity and phallogocentrism of the camera (and, by extension, the cinema in all its acceptations) in focusing and framing sexual and gender difference. For these reasons, this specific sequence is both highly self-reflexive and critical of how films interact with nonnormative desires.

While this initial dyad of images can be mined for its self-reflexive theoretical richness, the dyad that follows is even more stimulating in its use of the gaze and directionality, all within the hapticity of the aqueous as a different medium and approach to perception. We see again a floating Reinaldo in a shot-reverse shot assemblage, but what follows, instead, is a nude male groin. While the initial apparition of the clothed penis posed a problematization vis-à-vis viewership, the camera, and heterosexism in the cinema, the second image of the second dyad is even more thought provoking, as the viewer is now placed in the position of the exposed and flaccid penis, a point of desire for the picaresque writer. The inversion of objectivity here (we are no longer in a privileged position of viewing homosexuality but are now strategically placed, through a calculated montage, within the spatial parameters of the desired body) makes possible a reversal of roles, encouraging an almost unconscious approximation to homosexual desire in the form of Reinaldo's gaze. The viewer is caught looking at the penis, but Schnabel's tactic of montage in the first dyad suggests that we are to understand the image as a representation of us; the camera is simply considering us, like the clothed groin, as a point of viewership.

Such a theorization, however, is quickly proven false as the camera zooms out slightly and shows a floating Reinaldo gazing at the same penis from the left side of the frame. This ostensibly minor detail is provocative in that the initial possibility suggested in the first dyad, that is, that the viewer occupies the position of the desired object through the shot dynamic, is cancelled out. Instead, we are left with the realization that the second dyad does not repeat the geometric coordinates of the first and that we have been caught in flagrante, joining Reinaldo in this act of sexual voyeurism. The viewer is thus also guilty of stalking fresh young meat in the waters off the Cuban coast, joining the protagonist in an act of homoeroticism that is quietly and seamlessly eased into the viewing of *Antes que anochezca*. The image, then, does not solely foster a viewing and alienation of homoerotic desire; it encourages, by a slippery visual and geometric game, the embracing, albeit momentary, of Reinaldo's desire.[3]

This set of images emphasizes a particular ethics of the cinema that breaks with its thematic antecedents in Latin America, though, again, I am not explicitly affirming any real causality. The shift toward inclusion, that is, toward inserting the viewer into the erotics of the narrative and not solely as a privileged, voyeuristic, external entity, is reaffirmed in Alfonso Cuarón's *Y tu mamá también* (2001). Cuarón's film is easier to locate in a sustained inquiry into homoeroticism in Latin American film. In fact, it is the only Latin American feature to appear in Eduardo Nabal Aragón's *El marica, la bruja y el armario*. While Cuarón's film has often been given credit for a boom in Latin American cinema and Gael García Bernal's reputation as a go-to actor for producers wanting international success, it also merits special study when traced as a precursor to the recent boom in New Maricón films.

The film is a sort of *bildungsroman* about the adulthood of two friends from different backgrounds: Julio (García Bernal), a middle-class youth from a family with strong leftist political leanings; and Tenoch (Diego Luna), a rich brat from a politically connected family. The youths meet Luisa (Maribel Verdú), a Spanish expatriate and the wife of Tenoch's writer cousin, and take a trip to a fic-

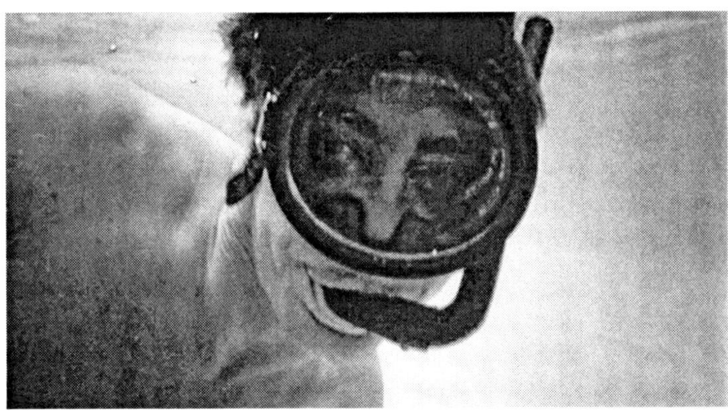

7.2. *Visual and affective experiments as Reinaldo moves toward a New Maricón aesthetic,* Antes que anochezca. *Copyright El Mar.*

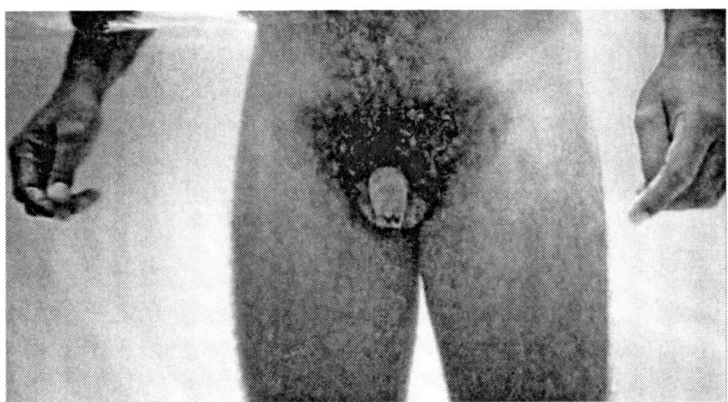

7.3. *The dislocation and repositioning of the viewer,* Antes que anochezca. *Copyright El Mar.*

tional beach on the coast after her husband drunkenly confesses that he has cheated on her (again). Unknown to the boys and the viewer at the start of the trip is the fact that Luisa is terminally ill with cancer and is making the trip as a sort of final pilgrimage. During the ride, we are privy to the fact that both Julio and Tenoch had at one point bedded the other's partner.

Given these sexual tensions, the trio, predictably, has sex with each other, culminating in a final scene where the three bodies entangle in what can be assumed is a free-for-all threesome as Julio and Tenoch drunkenly kiss while Luisa fellates them in turn, though she might have held both their members in her mouth at once, adding a new erotic level to the in-frame kiss between the men.

While Cuarón's reliance on characteristics typical of the road movie are at times clichéd, the fact is that this *is* a road movie but one that shifts the narrative away from the streets of Mexico City toward the coast and portends later films such as *Contracorriente*. In their quest to find the beach, the trio inadvertently allows the viewer into the realities of Mexican life at the start of the twenty-first century, where the drug trade, abuses by the state, and rampant economic disparity are visually though silently dramatized by the old station wagon making its way to the coast.

While the use of through-the-window shots are central to the road movie and to this film's exploration of socioeconomic issues plaguing turn-of-the-century Mexico, they also succeed in outing the narrative and its erotics from the urban referent—an important first step in any New Maricón film.[4] In essence, Julio and Tenoch and their homosocial relationship (which has more than its share of homoerotic ties) are deterritorialized, following Deleuze and Guattari's terminology in *A Thousand Plateaus*.[5]

We can thus read their first and only kiss in the beachside cabin, where, as a sort of reterritorialization of homosociality and severed from the territory and systems of the urban, homoerotic desire makes its appearance. Of note in this condition of Newness permitted by the movement away from the systems and spaces of Maricón cinema or the outing of desire is the shift in the condition of homosociality, as it no longer subscribes to the tenets of its original territorialization. It is important to note that "reterritorialization does not mean returning to the original territory but rather refers to the ways in which deterritorialized elements recombine and enter into new relations in the constitution of a new assemblage or modification of the old" (Patton, *Deleuzian Concepts*, 52). *Y tu mamá también* thus can be viewed as a step in the reterritorialization of the Maricón in the coast/nonurban setting, where the aural and visual reminders of the aqueous are ubiquitous.

In addition to the spatiality of desire in the film, we can unearth further ties to a genealogy of the Maricón in the images immediately preceding the threesome. Here we again see the connection I drew earlier to Schnabel's feature, where the viewer is directly involved in the erotics of the moving image. The scene that is of interest to us occurs almost at the end of the film, as the trio sits drinking beer and shots of mezcal in an outdoor cantina by the sea. It is here that Julio says "y tu mamá también" as a joke, or *albur*, in reference to his having seduced Tenoch's mother (in addition to his girlfriend). The statement emphasizes the strained ties that are keeping their homosocial relationship in place, as their female partners become a sort of proxy of their own desires. Coinciding with the phrase is Luisa's drunken stumble toward the back of the cantina and the jukebox. The camera follows her, unsteady as though also inebriated and walking in the sand, and zooms in on her as she decides which song to play.

A wooden pole, the trunk of a tree used to prop the cantina up, is a critical framing tool in this image, as it bisects the composition. On the left we see Luisa fiddling with the machine, and on the right, almost as if in a different metaphysical plane, a group of men drinking and playing dominoes. The binary drawn together by the foregrounded pole emphasizes the recombination or reconstitution of the homosocial dynamic on the left side of the image as a calque of the men on the right. The representation of the homosocial is a trope repeated in Fuentes-León's film, where Santiago's ghostly presence dissolves some of the tensions present in the group.

The camera moves closer to Luisa as she selects Marco Antonio Solis's "Si no te hubieras ido" and raises her glass to the men to her right (now out of frame). This gesture evokes a consciousness of the pole's sectioning of the space into a binary image, that is, a juxtaposition of territorialized and reterritorialized homosociality.

The camera centers Luisa, with her back to us, in a medium shot as she begins to move seductively to the music. She then turns around to face the camera and locks eyes with the lens. The composition of this image is primal to the camera's earlier creation of intimacy in the scene through unsteady movements, as we are included, through her gaze, in the syntax and erotics of the film's particular reterritorialization of gender. We, too, are present on this side of the pole, away from the structured hegemony of patriarchy and instead in some other outed space.

Luisa dances toward the retreating camera and back to the table with Julio and Tenoch. She never breaks eye contact with the viewer, akin to what happens during Reinaldo's underwater adventures in *Antes que anochezca,* which breaks the barrier between the virtual and the actual. Yet unlike in Schnabel's film, which tricks the viewer into occupying the position of desire vis-à-vis homoeroticism, the meeting of the gaze in Cuarón's film serves to include the viewer in a particular metaphysics of desire where the rules and regulations of the territory, that is, of the urban patriarchy left behind in the narrative, are no longer valid.

The minutiae of her gestures and the intensity of her gaze seduce the viewer, the last entity on this side of the spatial binary that she has yet to conquer. There is an explicit acknowledgment of this intention, as on her way back to the table, she suggestively grasps and then swings from the separating pole, as though highlighting for the enchanted viewers the fact that they, too, are now bidden to partake of the mezcal and the luscious curves that her dress reveals.

Luisa leaves her glass on the table and beckons the two men to dance with her. The camera moves back behind a seated Julio's head and stays at the table as the three revelers suggestively dance to the music. The intoxicating lyricism of the music coupled with the ambient potential of the bar openly suggest that the men's once individual episodes with Luisa are now going to be a shared fantasy.

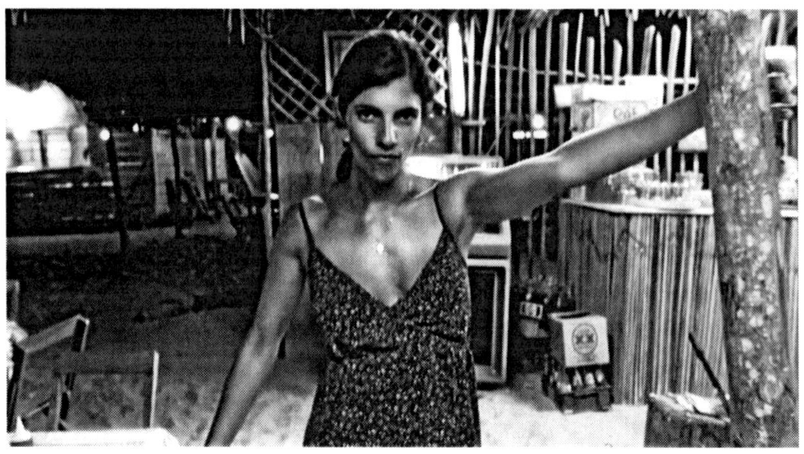

7.4. Maribel Verdú seduces the viewer, Y tu mamá también. *The pole in effect frames desire vis-à-vis the spatial contract of the homosocial. Copyright Anhelo.*

The scene, however, suddenly cuts to a longer shot of the cantina contextualized within the mountains behind it and fishing boats in front of it as we hear the sounds of the ocean. The aural cut to the aqueous is sharp, as it is quieter and noticeably less rhythmic than the cantina, thereby increasing the sensorial intensity of the waves. This pause, a figurative checking of the image's pulse, brings us back to Barker's theorization of viscera and how self-conscious techniques trigger a deeper-than-tactile relationship with the image.

Though perhaps solely a contextual shot of the nonurban, we can equally argue that this image is a vector of the New in New Maricón cinema as it emphasizes the reterritorialization of desire and gender along with the aural-haptic cues of the water to establish an empathic, or "touched," praxis of viewing. Instead of breaking directly to the subsequent action in a more private sphere, that is, a hotel room, Cuarón unambiguously directs us to consider the spatiality of the erotics of the film and how its semantic referents portend a challenge to the norms of the homosocial.

The cutting image of the landscape directly implicates the outed nature of *Y tu mamá también* as a primal prerequisite for any exercise in filmic gender and sexual negotiation, or as José Amicola affirms, it is only in "that no man's land that seems to be a leitmotiv of construction" [esa tierra de nadie que parece ser un leitmotiv de la construcción] that any systematic intervention into desire and body can occur. The shift that the image suggests bears directly on the ensuing action where Julio, Tenoch, and Luisa are shown in the confines of a room in the beach hostel. The preliminary geometry of this image shows Luisa and a seated Julio on one plane while Tenoch lingers between and beyond them, aligned in a vertical angle to the camera and thereby creating a rough diamond shape of the entities present. Remember that the previous seduction by Luisa includes us as viewers, as another body to be molded by the erotics of the narrative, and therefore includes us in the system of the room. This is made clear when a naked Luisa drops out of the frame to fellate the two men, the camera inching closer to their excited and mildly orgasmic faces. The slight zoom suggests that Luisa's earlier seduction in the cantina is culminating off camera and out of frame, as the lens (and the viewer) zooms in on the two men lost in pleasure. When Julio and Tenoch kiss, in an action that again is permitted only by their bodies being reterritorialized (albeit momentarily) vis-à-vis the territory embodied by the domino-playing homosocial, the viewer—disoriented by the sucking and licking mouth of Luisa off camera and the naked, drunken heat of the two friends discovering silenced facets of their desire—physically and metaphorically partakes of this slippage from acceptability. The eroticism of this scene is charged, provocative, and moves us into the unwatchable. We engage this scene not as distanced observers privileged by the scopic vantage of Maricón cinema, we share saliva and caress the tongues and lips of Julio and Tenoch (again, albeit momentarily) as (homo)erotically *involved* and complicit subjects, just as Luisa culminates the earlier seduction by including us in her off-camera oral stimulations.

The inclusive gesture of these two scenes situates *Y tu mamá también* in an ethical continuum with *Antes que anochezca* that, in turn, roots the later New films I analyze above. Importantly, *Y tu mamá también* ends with neither protagonist claiming any ownership of their actions at the beach; they lose con-

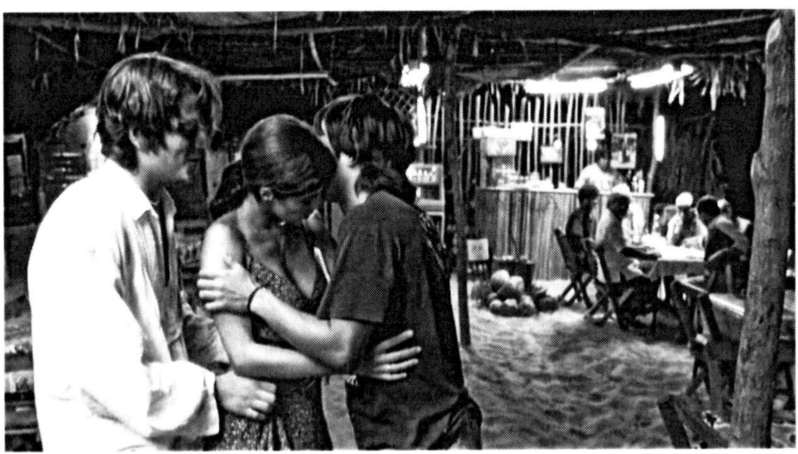

7.5. The viewer is brought in as the homosocial looks on, Y tu mamá también. *Copyright Anhelo.*

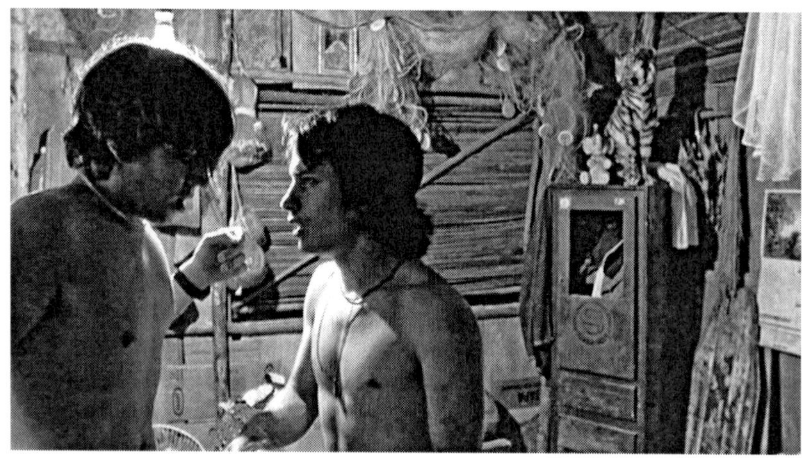

7.6. Sharing the flesh as the film climaxes, Y tu mamá también. *Copyright Anhelo.*

tact with each other and go about their lives back in the city as though the drunken kiss never occurred. The ending, therefore, does not shape any persistent inquiry into homoeroticism or "out" either Julio or Tenoch as closeted homosexuals; it does underline the unequivocal position of same-sex desire in strongly homosocial masculine gender systems.[6] For our purposes in establishing a lineage of Maricón cinema in Latin America, however, the film hints at the shift in viewership and the start of a circulation of positive affective intensities that lie as a substrate of the filming, screening, and critical and popular reception of such films as *Contracorriente* and XXY. The image is no longer meant to be abstractedly and callously seen as a static representation of gendered and sexual difference, but more provocatively as a haptic and polysensorial point of entry into experiencing and empathizing with positions that challenge notions and practices of normativity.

Part III

REMATERIALIZING BODIES AND THE URBAN SPACE

IN THIS SECTION I WANT TO HIGHLIGHT A SEPARATE trajectory of films that, while not completely congruent with the audiovisual praxes and corresponding aesthetics of New Maricón cinema, do engage in certain strategies that engender affective economies that circulate a positive empathic charge in relation to gender difference and the wider consciousness of a gay identity. These, arguably, may be seen as a sign of Anglo "contagion," using this term, of course, in its most positive, albeit imperialist, sense. The omnipresence of nature and the natural (in their capacity to house and generate varying affective intensities) is a key element in the aesthetic and phenomenological break with Maricón films. A separate strand of films highlighted by productions from Argentina and Mexico and films from countries with nascent industries, such as Venezuela are, however, increasingly producing positive narratives that encourage viewer alignment with difference in urban settings.

These films are very much part of a New Maricón cinema, but resist complete physical deterritorializations. Instead, they promote similar tactics and strategies of alignment and empathy within the urban, but through the use of specific natural vectors. Important in this schema is the idea that we cannot view New Maricón cinema as a complete or finite genre; it is, rather, an evolving schema of the audiovisual. Thus we must mitigate any description of a Newness as being an aesthetic movement in process.[1] These urban films can be seen, instead, as a parallel vein that feeds on some of the images and conventions popularized in early New Maricón films such as XXY and *Contracorriente* but engaging an altogether more complex process of viewership and identification.

The films I identify in this tangential move are characterized by positive depictions of queerness in urban settings; they bring, so to speak, the bodies of gender and sexual difference back to the spatial referents that once regimented the heterosexist gaze and social structure behind cinematic narrative.[2] While New Maricón films benefitted from "outing" these bodies and desires to nonurban spaces, and thus were able to interrogate and provoke the circulation of positive affective intensities, the films I will discuss in this section deploy similar economies within the urban, thereby permitting the exercise of normativity or the potential of resemanticizing "normal" topological sites. These films, furthermore, are circulating after the relatively popular and critical success of some of the films identified as New Maricón and thus benefit from the economies of circulation already in place (though, as mentioned, these economies are still evolving).

I want to bring us back to Sara Ahmed's theory of economies of affect here, particularly when she argues that "affective economies need to be seen as social and material . . . In other words, the accumulation of affective value shapes the surfaces of bodies and worlds" ("Affective Economies," 121). Imperative for these economies is an understanding that, in terms of bodies, those associated with strong intensities of positive affect (or an alignment or empathy with) become more accepted and legitimizing. When read, then, in terms of space and movement, this association creates an environment wherein specific bodies are restricted and others are allowed freer movement. The circulation of affect linked to New Maricón cinema has created certain bodies that, while allowed to freely circulate within the nonspecific topologies of the natural, are now being allowed to move back into very specific cities, undoubtedly as an effect of or practice corollary to real social movements.[3]

In other words, New Maricón cinema and its accompanying and productive economy have shaped the social and material planes of cinema production and consumption, permitting thus the evolution or normativization of gender difference back into the spaces occupied by Maricón films. Intrinsic to this line of thinking is a reconsideration of public space, something Néstor García Canclini develops in the concluding passages of *Consumers and Citizens*. Debating the critical relationship between the state and civil society (and here he includes the dialectic between citizen and consumer) as we move into late-capitalist modernity, García Canclini notes that what is "at the heart of this reformulation . . . is an attempt to reconceptualize the public sphere" (*Consumers and Citizens*, 154). My study of the return of the maricón to these urban referents—filmic settings of an identifiable public sphere—can be read in line with García Canclini's broader hermeneutic push. By focusing on affect, however, I reiterate Lauren Berlant's affirmation that "public spheres are always affect worlds, worlds to which people are bound, when they are, by affective projections of a constantly negotiated common interestedness" (*Cruel Optimism*, 226).

By portraying difference in nuanced and sensitive techniques that encourage viewer alignment and empathy, New films shape a particular symbolic urban terrain open to consumption and reflection.[4] In other words, Fuentes-León's urban audience took part—through a positive and intimate approximation to homoeroticism—in the creation of a new symbolic urban terrain and communal body mediated by acceptance and openness. But did that change occur purely at the symbolic level? Can such acceptance and commercial popularity translate into real ethical shifts in how gender difference is treated?[5]

I believe this is the case, creating what Valerie Walkerdine terms an "affective community" ("Communal Beingness," 113), since, as Margaret Wetherell argues, "the flow of affect is located in the body but it is located, too, within the flow of ordinary life. It becomes part of social interaction, caught up in social business" (*Affect and Emotion*, 77–78). The ethical project of aligning behind the aesthetics of New Maricón cinema makes possible real social resurfacings (reflective of Shaviro's productive cinema) that craft the communal body into a political orientation or, to use Ahmed's lexicon, "collective direction" (*Queer Phenomenology*, 15) wherein repeated alignments with a group direction along a particular "line" result, through repetition, in the line's disappearance. In other words, group alignments can potentially, though often inevitably, readjust the politics of said group, this of course being an in-process observation of a present very much in flux.[6]

In a vein of inquiry separate from Wetherell's and Walkerdine's interest in social practice, Nigel Thrift theorizes about the relationship between affect and space, arguing that we cannot "assume that the transmission of affect is from individual to individual, contained within one skin and being moved to another. Rather, that transmission is a property of particular spaces soaked with one or a combination of affects to the point where space and affect are often coincident" (*Non-Representational Theory*, 222). Thrift's esteem for space is primordial, then, to a conception of affect as a communal and interactive phenomenon, which Ahmed emphasizes in her attempts at tracing a queer phenomenology.

This dialectic is plainly evident in the changing semantics of space in Latin American film, from early periods through the *fichera*, Maricón, and New Maricón genres. The studied use of space and an analysis of its effects provide us with a point of entry into how cinematic narratives of gender difference can create lasting and tangible ethical ties to the viewing public. I am interested in how these films engage in affective economies that then shape and materialize real collective entities and surfaces.

I find Edward Soja's theoretical framework to be useful in understanding how space is crafted and the role of language and symbols in real spatializations both of structures and of bodies. Working in a vein that relies heavily on semiotics, Soja develops a theory of spaces that interpolates plural semantic and material valences. He articulates a triadic understanding of spatiality beginning with firstspace, defined as "a set of materialized 'spatial practices' that work together to produce and reproduce the concrete forms and specific patternings of urbanism as a way of life" (*Postmetropolis*, 10), followed by secondspace, which occupies a dialectical position where cityspace becomes "more of a mental or ideational field, conceptualized in imagery, reflexive thought, and symbolic representation, a *conceived* space of the imagination" (11). This second notion is the realm of an "urban epistemology, a formal framework and method for obtaining knowledge about cityspace and explaining its specific geography" (11). The combination of both spaces, a hypothesized thirdspace, conversely, occupies a third axis where the urban is "a simultaneously real-and-imagined, actual-and-virtual, locus of structured individual and collective experience and agency" (11).

In terms of spatiality, the New and its linked affective economies and the natural in *Contracorriente*, *El último verano de la Boyita*, and *XXY* manage—through empathic bodies, practices, and narrative points that reflect Ahmed's notion of a sticky surface—to resemanticize the urban (understood here in its symbolic and social qualities), even though the narrative action in these films often takes place in a spatial antonym. In fact, certain scenes, such as when the protagonist in *El último verano* plays in the river with a virtual cityscape in the background, gesture toward this remapping of the urban in a sly indication that what is being seen over *here* by outing gender difference from its traditional loci of representation can impact the ideational fields of over *there*.[7] (Conversely, we see at times the nonurban as a virtual relational point that dialogues directly with identitarian work in the urban, as is the case in several scenes of Marco Berger's *Plan B*, though the urban remains very much the tableau of the tableau vivant of gender difference.) My argument, then (and I believe Ahmed suggests this also, though in other terms), is that any ethical work being done to shape this secondspace invariably impacts thirdspace, which can be understood as a hypertextual reading of real space as sign and signified of deeper sociocultural and historical processes.

What we see in these post-New or, more accurately, urban-New films is a self-conscious linkage between a specific affective economy and a representational thirdspace, understood here as the settings and portrayal of the urban and its components in the image. Such a trajectory invites a cognitive evaluation of the materiality of this particular urban place and a subsequent resemanticization of the extrafilmic space (a thirdspace related but not equivalent to the representational space) as then being accepting to this specific economy. I am not arguing that the urban places of these films represent a corollary urban acceptance of lesbigay lifestyles; rather, these representations permit a wider approximation to these specific bodies and lifestyles within the comfort zone, so to speak, of a largely urban audience.[8] Such a viewing experience and alignment, this time not only with specific bodies but also with their surroundings and contextual cues, provoke the circulation of positive affective signs within a real firstspace, thereby modifying and shaping the actual lived thirdspace that is symbolically evoked in the representational-urban space. If New Maricón films outed the homosexual (to the rural space), these films bring him or her back to the spaces of homophobia and gender violence so prevalent in earlier and Maricón periods.

In essence, such a move reflects Ahmed's inquiry into the positionality of signs of affect.[9] In other words, the urban-New genre works through similar problematics tackled in New films but pushes the envelope, so to speak, by bringing these queer issues and erotics into recognizable representations of real spaces familiar to a Latin American and global audience.

Returning to my dyadic division of recent Latin American cinema, these films are intensely local even if they situate their narratives in seemingly globalized spaces that foster, tangentially, transnational actions and entities. In a certain regard, I am exploring here a similar problematic planted by Bill Nichols in his seminal *Representing Reality*, though my focus, of course, is not on the documentary as a medium. The issue at hand, and Nichols develops this thoroughly in regard to the genre he is studying, is an adaptation of what he terms "axiographics," or "an attempt to explore the implantation of values in the configuration of space, in the constitution of a gaze, and in the relation of observer to observed" (*Representing Reality*, 78).[10] I will modify his analytical tool in the following pages by working with fictive narratives (as opposed to the real that documentary fictionalizes) and affective signs and intensities in an attempt to examine how New Maricón films can be brought back in to representational social-urban spaces. This move is informed by Thrift's suggestion that space is "a series of conditioning environments that both prime and 'cook' affect [and] depend upon pre-discursive ways of proceeding which both produce and allow changes in bodily state to occur" (*Non-Representational Theory*, 236). My take on axiographics thus triangulates affect with space and values, emphasizing an analysis beyond the visual in the "relation of observer to observed" (*Representing Reality*, 78) wherein the sensorial (in its plural capacities) seeks linkages beyond the purely visual.

CHAPTER EIGHT

Plan B

LET'S GO BACK TO THE CITY

Unlike Argentine contemporaries such as Puenzo and Solomonoff, who have funded their films with help from national and international foundations and grants, Marco Berger has taken a slightly different route, using popular Internet and social media platforms to underwrite and disseminate early trailers and clips of his projects.[1] His catalogue also breaks with the films of his contemporaries because of his use and development of urbanized characters and plot points. Like his contemporaries, however, he has cultivated a calculated examination of desire and related vicissitudes in several films, but he has cautiously stayed at the margins of any true identity politics, preferring to place homoeroticism and homoerotic desiring bodies at critical axes over a broader, dynamic plateau of human interaction.

Plan B (screened in 2009 at the Buenos Aires Film Festival, in popular release in 2011) has a relatively simple plot: boy 1 (Bruno) loses his girlfriend (Laura) to boy 2 (Pablo); boy 1 turns to Plan B—to seduce boy 2 and thereby win back the affection of the girlfriend. Adding to the developing dynamic between the two men is the fact that Laura continues to sleep with both of them, complicating further the institution of monogamy within compulsory heterosexuality. Predictably, Bruno and Pablo begin to realize that they have more than enough in common and a burgeoning though unnamed desire that leads to the inevitable final scene of the two men rushing to the bedroom as the credits fall.

Set in working-class Buenos Aires, the film explores nascent homoeroticism without falling into the facile polemics of identity politics so prevalent in LGBTQ cinema. In fact, the film barely mentions the words "gay," "maricón," and so on, focusing instead on the intricate intimacies that develop between the two principal male characters. *Plan B* succeeds in "naturalizing" same-sex desire, which emerges in the everyday practice and texture of these men's lives, situating itself thus at a point of escape from any overt lesbigay politics.[2]

This process, though, is contingent on there being a receptive community, that is, various secondary characters who do not balk at Bruno and Pablo's increasing attraction to each other. These characters are metonyms of a seeming friendliness toward same-sex relations in contemporary Buenos Aires; this real space reflects, in turn, a virtual affective community shaped by the circulation of signs set in place, arguably, by films such as XXY. This community, as I argue earlier, is a positive one open to nonheteronormative expressions and desires, shaped through the strategies of alignment pervasive in nonurban New Maricón films. The plot in *Plan B* is a direct reflection of this positive circulation and shaping as it portrays as "normal," whatever that may mean, and "natural" the burgeoning feelings between the two men in a recognizable Buenos Aires.

This last detail is fundamental in identifying the impact and reflective semiotics behind the film as a resemanticization of the Maricón genre by means of detailed renegotiations of spatial and technical facets of the moving image. This process, however, is not vacuous but progressive when read within the trajectory of cinema I have already identified. *Plan B* cultivates new surfaces and refashions older, stickier surfaces that New Maricón cinema managed to negotiate via the circulation of positive affective signs and intensities. It thus mobilizes an affective community open to narrative and spatial representations that successfully bring the maricón back to the city.

I am not implying that there is a direct causality between film A and film B; rather, film B is produced and received in a certain ecosystem facilitated by previous and contemporary films (among other cultural productions responsible for a certain affective economy). In this regard, and I am speculating here, *Plan B* perhaps is only a *plan* within a specific trajectory that, predictably, begins with a *Plan A*, that is, with Maricón representations of difference.

Given the film's efforts to naturalize desire in an urban setting in lieu of engaging in a drawn-out compendium of stereotypes or reinforcing positive associations with a historical precedent, it is problematic to label *Plan B* as an LGBT or Q film; it is almost disingenuous to call it a New Maricón film, as there are no crises of identity, affirmations of sexuality, or a broader politics of desire. This lack or absence—a defining aesthetic and poetic characteristic of *Plan B*, and reflected in the title of Berger's *Ausente* [Absent], (2011)—however, is a facet of New Maricón cinema that I failed to properly stress in part II. Though New films at times strategically interrogate gender and desire vis-à-vis identity (*Contracorriente* perhaps being the most obvious), they also engage in a separate trajectory not held together by identitarian impulses or tactics. This can be noted in XXY's inconclusiveness in regard to Alex's and Jorgelina's final reflections on self and desire in *El último verano*. This obviation of a particular Anglo politics, though, actually reinforces the terminology Berger uses, as the maricón is not easily located in Anglo gender dichotomies but placed in a continuum of the sociosexual fabric of Latin America. The New, however, goes beyond the static labeling of the maricón but provokes plural manifestations and points of entry into its ontology.

I want to focus on how *Plan B* contextualizes some of the impulses and gestures seen in the New Maricón crop of films but within a starkly different narrative space and amid a particular economy of affect. These factors are immediately evident in the first images of the film, a panning close shot of a kitten being exchanged among children, an older woman, and, finally, Bruno. The camera then rests on a foregrounded Bruno cuddling another kitten with undifferentiated and out-of-focus buildings in the background. This image is within the framing of the film in terms of spatiality (they are in a park in a city) and of identifying the affective intensities that we are to glean from the male body. His playing with the fragile animal contrasts with the overpoweringly masculine aesthetic promoted by his hirsuteness and soccer jersey in a juxtaposition that emphasizes a sentimental layer beneath the macho façade. We also see in this shot how the cat's claws stick to the fabric of his shirt. In a purely metaphorical sense, it is easy to read the stickiness of this figure as a body shaped by a particular circulation. The hapticity of the image in this case is ontoformative to the represented body, this being, of course, an assemblage of virtual signs and intensities that generate our perception of Bruno. The subtle tactility of Bruno's body also suggests that the viewer is to feel a positive alignment with him, akin to the representational postsex dynamics of the two naked men in *Contracorriente*. This "feeling," or contagion, of a strong positive affect is emphasized by calming, instrumental nondiegetic music, which monopolizes the soundtrack.

In fact, the strong intensities generated by the cat's claws sticking to Bruno's shirt are produced by an audial-tactile image that provokes alignment and empathy, or at least an instruction to *touch* his image-body, to orient us in proximity to his sticky shirt. This is a subtle but concerted early effort to create positive endearments that follows the axiographics of New Maricón films.

The camera then pans outward and follows the two children away from Bruno, breaking abruptly to track Laura as she greets and kisses Pablo. The use of a long take in this opening sequence suggests a certain spontaneity in the action and a splicing of visuals to sound, especially if we consider this spontaneity as provoking a phenomenological decentering in the viewer, who is piqued by the multiple possibilities and lines of movement and flows within the image. The break to track Laura toward Pablo highlights this reading as the viewer is left to wonder who the couple is and when or if the camera will break again to track a different body in motion (and what this body's story will be).

8.1. The tactility of the body, Plan B. *Copyright Rendez-Vous.*

The image then cuts to a close shot of Bruno gazing at the couple; his carefree expression and playfulness with the cat is replaced by an almost sinister glance, his lips pursed and eyebrows furrowed as the kitten rests on his shoulder. This image and its accompanying gaze enter into direct contention with the viewer and alignment produced by the hapticity of the earlier contextual shot of the character. The latter image of a disapproving Bruno is reinforced through a long take that cuts to a close-up of Laura and Pablo chatting and creates a narrative continuity between the two seemingly disparate sets of bodies and relations. We can thus intuit from the cut and close-up an invisible plot line that ties the characters together, one that the narrative will reveal.

The film then cuts to an image of Pablo's crotch. He is holding an SLR camera in such a way that we can easily interpret the camera's extended lens to be a metaphor for his penis. The music at this point takes on a sinister tone and cadence, and the camera moves upward toward Laura's and Pablo' faces, their lips locked in a kiss. Movement here can be interpreted as linear with Bruno's gaze; that is, he is focused on the sexual ties (as evidenced by the camera) between these two spied-on subjects. We can thus deduce that the visual interchange between Bruno and Pablo and Laura is preempted by a backstory—a narrative that situates not only the characters' presence in the park but also how these bodies align or reject the viewer's position.

The image abruptly cuts to a medium shot of Bruno leaning on the balcony of a verandah and looking into the distance at what can be discerned as a city, here a virtual semiotic space evocative of Jean-Clet Martin's city-image. There is a causality to this shot in relation to the previous interchange in the park, as Bruno is wearing the same shirt. The idea here that his current existentialism is provoked by what transpired between Laura and Pablo. The cityspace as a background to this contextual shot is thought-provoking in that the film not only spatializes the erotics of the narrative within a defined topology, but also explicitly invites the viewer to consider this spatial act within the development of the narrative's erotics. Like other films in the New genre, *Plan B* situates specific virtual spaces as centerpieces in perception-images that then set the tone of action and affection-images that relay a particular point of entry into desire—and here I am thinking particularly of the use of static shots foregrounding the rural in XXY and *Contracorriente*. This shot in *Plan B* invites a similar process, though the city here is the axiographic plane.

This thesis is reaffirmed by the subsequent image, an elevated static shot that captures fragments of several buildings in addition to the upper third of a group of trees. The nondiegetic music of the previous montage is replaced by a rumbling, undifferentiated noise, more appropriately described as a nonsound, that reverberates unassumingly throughout the take. The image then cuts to Bruno in conversation with Víctor in a nonlinear time event from the earlier montage, as evidenced by his wearing a different jersey. It is in this conversation that he reveals the details of the backstory that is suggested in the tensions of viewership produced in the first scene in the park.

The cutting image of the city in this montage is contextual in that it situates the story and backstory within a specific urban landscape; it also further emphasizes the spatialization of this narrative. The image is composed of four plain buildings cut in different shapes and shown from varying angles amid a contrasting phallic structure, most likely a chimney, in their midst. (Again, the image presents a simple association that stresses the phallus or its envy.)

8.2. Bringing New Maricón bodies back to the urban, Plan B. *Copyright Rendez-Vous.*

8.3. Perception images placing desire within the audile-tactile space of the city, Plan B. *Copyright Rendez-Vous.*

The audial characteristics of the shot jar us as viewers of the temporal and spatial present through affective intensities that place us within any urban setting. We can thus interpret this image to be analogous to the perception-images of the natural—which really double as affection-images in their aim of creating a positive alignment with homoeroticism—that are littered throughout and ontoformative of New Maricón films. It is not a narrative filler or visual transition between particular plot points, but an axiographical exercise that codes for a particular heuristic experience. That experience, in turn, impinges on the viewer's relationship to certain affective intensities developed later in the erotics of the narrative.

Of note in the film, and in Berger's later *Ausente,* is the use of the gym-space as a site of masculine becoming and reaffirmation. Long a "safe" place for the homosocial to freely cavort in the nude, the gym's showers and changing room are the site of Bruno's initial contact with Pablo. He approaches him with the pretense of getting together to watch a television show, and the two decide to meet up later at Pablo's apartment. The gym adopts characterizational traits of the brothel in pre- and Maricón cinema, where men go to peacock signs of virility in an environment that does not necessarily adhere to the visible/invisible codes that permit the homosocial to thrive. But unlike the brothel, the gym space is a purely autoreferential locus where mirrors constantly reflect the subject an autoerotic gaze, conversely permitting a homoerotic gaze, though the latter is frowned on, even in the shower. It has become an open and public space for cruising by gay and bicurious men, and *Plan B* uses this trait as a scaffolding to lend credibility to Bruno's attempts at chatting up Pablo and their watching television together later.

The film cuts abruptly to a shot that is disjointed from the wider narrative—

a transitional perception-affection image of the city, this time at dusk. Instead of fragmented buildings we are shown the cityscape as an outline, the viewer placed within this space, not spying on it from a distance. In other words, the viewer is relationally situated within the urban and asked to stop and ponder its ontology and spatiality, which is essential to an axiographics of the film and the development of a detailed erotics. Like the earlier cutting image of the urban, the image is divided by a phallic structure, this time likely a radio antenna, that breaks the plane of sight. The shot also repeats an affective intensity through the undistinguished bass rumbling of city life, emphasizing that the transitional image is both a perception shot and an affection-image that engenders a linkage between the subject and the terrain.

After a short sequence with the men meeting to watch another episode of the television series, presumably a week later, the film abruptly cuts to a shot of them leaning on a concrete wall with the cityscape around and behind them. Bruno relates in medias res an almost absurd experience to Pablo while we hear a constant but subdued humming in the background, reminiscent of the earlier cutting perception–affection images of the city between narrative sequences. This scene is thus an evolution of the former image and its arrangement, this time with human bodies interacting in an already set up space that transmits affective intensities that encourage a whole-body experience and inclusion of the viewer in the urban space of the narrative. It is almost as if these three shots operate in a separate narratological plot line told through static setting shots and interspersed dialogue-rich scenes that tell a story separate from the broader narrative of Bruno attempting to seduce Pablo to get in the good graces of Laura. The scenes focus on establishing a plurisensorial relationship between the viewer and the film, between the viewer and the heuristics of the developing relationship between the two men.

The placement of bodies and, more important, images of the body within a framing in this shot follow José Gil's Deleuzian understanding of the body and space. In *Metamorphoses of the Body,* he argues that the body inhabits "space, but not like a sphere with a closed continuous surface . . . its movements, limbs and organs determine that it has regular relations with things in space, relations that are individually integrated for the decoder" (127). In a sense, we are circling back to Elena del Río's "bits and pieces" theory of the body-image, though Gil ties this in specifically to a relationship with spatiality and inanimate spatial objects that channel or assemble confluences and trajectories of force. The body thus is viewed in bits and pieces that are then each, as movements, limbs, and organs, integrated into or co-related to specific spatial relations. The fact that the two men leave the frame at the end of their conversation and the shot continues to focus on the (urban) setting and its sounds reaffirms both this relationship between the body and space and the supposition of a separate narra-

8.4. Evading facile metaphors for identity, Plan B. *Copyright Rendez-Vous.*

tive trajectory, a focus on the affective intensities of the urban, and, importantly, the relationship initiated between body-images and spatiality. This separate trajectory underlines the presence of spatiality in the developing (homo)erotics of the film and the location of nuanced and humane representations of gender difference in representational spaces of the real loci of particular economies of affect.[3]

The disjointedness of this scene and its potential for sensorial intensities is stressed when Bruno asks Pablo what time it is, obliquely, in a sense, asking the viewer the same question to make us aware that Berger's film is not operating in a linear time scheme. Bruno's question and the realization that the natural light is quite striking leads Pablo to take a picture of Bruno. The scene recycles the eroticism of the diegetic camera lens that was central to the establishing images of the opening sequence. Bruno shyly protests, "I'm embarrassed" [Me da vergüenza], when Pablo aims the camera at him. Like Hermosillo in *Doña Herlinda,* though, Berger is quick to dispel any facile connotations that would lead to an *activo* and *pasivo* labeling by having Bruno also press the shutter after pointing the lens at Pablo. If the camera and its large prosthetic lens are metonyms of or prostheses for the organic penis, then both men get their turn to point and click the other, so to speak.

The erotic overtones in this particular sequence leak into the perception of the audial and visual snippets of cityspace backgrounded by the shot, enabling what Gil calls the "exfoliations of the space of the body" or "the essential way the body 'turns onto' things, onto objective space, onto living things" (*Metamorphoses,* 127).[4] The relation between space and the body, though, is contingent on this body being segmented, disjointed, rendered in bits and pieces; as Gil outlines:

> If we are granted that the space of the body is composed of a multiplicity of exfoliations that compose volumes, polymorphous spaces, leaves, loops; and if, in addition, each of these leaves presupposes a set of relations to things, integrated relations, that is, ones that are decoded in and through the body, it follows from this that the unity of the multiplicity of spaces of the body must be defined by its activity as a decoder. If one wishes to speak of the unity of the body or the presence of "wholeness" in each of its parts, then the "whole" must be understood simply as the action of the decoder-body in each of its organs. (Gil, *Metamorphoses*, 128)

Thus, the bodies in *Plan B*, and all New Maricón film for that matter, are dependent on their piecemeal nature in establishing lines, flows, and habituation of space(s).

In the present scene, this exfoliation allows for a correlative exercise between the point-and-click metaphor of the body that the subjects' actions evoke and its relationship to the undifferentiated image of the city behind them; a framing of the body within a frame, leading then to first a touching then a peeling of layers akin to Miguel's coming out scene in *Contracorriente*. The image thus foregrounds the linkage between desire and space, begging a critical reflection on the role of space (urbanity, in this case) within the syntax of sexuality that the film probes.

This scene, part of what can be considered a Track B of images (absurdist conversations severed from the broader narrative accompanied by strongly audile-tactile setting images of the urban that attempt to draw the viewer in to the spatial topologies of the film), is then collated with the film's Track A (where the thicker details of the narrative develop with secondary characters and the viewer adopts a more disaffected posture). It is somewhat appropriate that Berger creates such a division, given the film's title and the logic that behind every Plan B is a Plan A. By switching off between tracks, though not always in a particular order, that is, without allowing the narrative montage primacy over the affective, *Plan B* provokes an audile-tactile relationship with the image (and not an urban scopic one).

Central to Track A are scenes where Bruno and Pablo negotiate their nascent attraction and friendship/relationship within the social milieu of a young urban class in Buenos Aires. At a rooftop party frequented by their peers, for example, Bruno jokes that Pablo is his boyfriend. Of note in this track is the public nature of these interactions, as the film naturalizes the bond and attraction between the two men through social relations and bodies that conform to the surface and fabric of the community that the film addresses and, tangentially, shapes through its tying of specific affective intensities (in Track B) to an exploration of homoeroticism (in Track A). The film cuts to a long shot perception-image (Track B) after the party scene where Bruno and Pablo share a first tentative kiss to prove to the other partygoers that they are a "couple" (Track A), the view most likely the coastline between the Aeroparque Jorge Newberry and Quilmes.[5] The image is the first in the film's Track B (and Track A, for that matter) that foregrounds the natural and the aqueous, a key characterizational and affective sign of New Maricón cinema. We are met with the water undulating onto the shore and hear the monotonous white noise of the sea. The image is visually stimulating, but richer in audile-tactile qualities that, like all images from Track B, succeed in transplanting the viewer as observer into the spatial dynamics of Track A. The image thus permits an opening gesture toward Nichols's notion of axiographics and how the observer is related to the observed within a specific framed space.

Thrift's theorization of affect and spatiality allows a point of entry here that goes beyond the scopic limitations of axiographics. In discussing the experience of nature and the natural, he notes that they form an "'embodied unconscious' . . . through which nature is constructed, planes of affect attuned to particular body parts (and senses) and corresponding elements of nature" (*Non-Representational Theory*, 67). Part of this process diverges from a posturing or positionality of the subject in relation to the natural; the body and embodiment materialize through a specific and dimensional relationship to space. In axiographical terms, the observer is tenuously placed through the technicalities of the camera. I do not want to delve into apparatus theory but must acknowledge that its placement and framing within a representation of the real establishes the axioms by which Nichols constructs axiographics as a framework. In fictive narratives such as *Plan B*, though, I part from the premise that the pictured does not pose a mimesis of the real but is instead a representation of spaces and possible subjectivities (and their narrative trajectories). As such, it bears paying attention to other cues that place or situate the observer in a Cartesian relationship with the observed.

I want to draw the reader's attention here to the particularities of sound-cum-space-cum-affective economies in this sequence. Berger highlights the importance of sound to the reception dialectics of axiographics throughout Track B, though perhaps not more so than in the extreme long shot of the coastline. What jumps to the viewer's attention is the vagueness of the cityscape in the background—reminiscent of a similar image in *El último verano*—and the continuity of the sounds emanating from the water. The image then cuts to a closer medium shot of Pablo contemplating the water, a sort of affective two shot that relays two subjective bodies in flowing states of motion: Pablo decoding the libidinous connection to Bruno after the kiss in Track A; and the water encouraging a tactile relationship between the observer (through the lens) and the image.

Of note in the jump between these two shots is the unchanging volume and tone of the water sound. Writing on the role of sound in relation to representation and space, James Lastra notes that there are two distinct models of cinematic sound reproduction that fall along the dividing lines of "representation-as-(legible)-inscription" and "representation-as-sensory-simulation" (*Sound Technology*, 126).[6] The former, which follows a critical trajectory highlighted by Christian Metz's well-known theories, cultivates a "sonic space whose principal goal is the intelligibility of some sounds at the expense of others" (Lastra, *Sound Technology*, 141). Such a space, in topographical and topological terms, is favored in Track A of the film. These sequences focus on narrative cohesion, where the viewer becomes a reader, so to speak, of the dialogues and bodies in the image.

The latter, representation-as-sensory-stimulation, though, is "constructed in order to represent a particular real act of audition" (Lastra, *Sound Technology*, 141), where the point of audition shapes the sonar mapping of the spatial image. This technique positions the viewer in a particular coordinate of acoustic space which then intersects with visual space to "locate" the observer in relation to the actions and bodies of the image. In the opening shot in this sequence of the coast, it seems that Berger favors this second model; the persistence of natural sound both heightens the tactility of the sand and wind and places the viewer, through a point-of-audition shot, within the space. The sound of the waves and wind is not silenced but allowed to filter into the experience of the film, even if it does not provide any tangible signs within a "narrative." In essence, then, and as Lastra notes, "the *spectator* is the 'character' whose presence within the space is represented by the use of perspective and who is, implicitly, *within* the 'diegetic' space" (*Sound Technology*, 214, emphasis in the original). Such a gesture makes evident the embodiment of the viewer within the diegetic space and thus provokes an ethical exercise of relationality vis-à-vis the values (and, in this case, the erotics) of the narrative.

The cut to the second shot in this scene, however, reveals a self-consciousness on the part of the filmmaker of the power of sound in instilling the ethical posture of the viewer. Captured from a shorter distance, the intensity and tone of the audio track do not change as they should in a point-of-audition technique and thus draw our attention to the haptic experience of the previous image. In other words, we are made explicitly aware of the implicit materialization of the spectator in this sequence; Pablo's lack of movement in the first seconds of this establishing shot allow for that realization to sink in.

Berger adds to this heuristic gesture by then overlaying the same musical track from the opening sequence on the water sounds. The meshing of different audial tracks and narratives in this image reveals a cognitive awareness of sound in shaping the relationship (and surfaces) of the observer to the observed. Even as Pablo moves across the nonurban space, we revert back to the opening shots of the urban park and the immediately preceding image of the water. The film therefore promotes a meshing of two semiotic surfaces—the urban and the aqueous—to form a hybrid surface where alternative affective economies can circulate and "stick."

In crafting an analytics of sound in the cinema, Edward Branigan notes that sound makes possible a critical point of entry into visual space through the "interplay of epistemological boundaries created *within* a text" ("Sound," 319, emphasis in the original). Branigan examines the relationship between sound and space in crafting narrative, or what he terms a "story world," and explains that "by juxtaposing sound and image drawn from different levels of the narration (e.g., a subjective sound with an objective image; a diegetic sound with a nondiegetic image), one may complicate and delay the matching of sound to a source which is to be made visible" (319).

In *Plan B*, this interplay, or breaking, of the "story world" is evident in the montage and exposes several layers of narrative, essentially a Track A and a Track B, suggesting then that the viewer's relation to visual space and its values is not purely scopic. Therein we find a clear break between the film and previous urban Maricón features. This is heightened through the establishing images in Track B that use sound to place the viewer within a particular space, as the film encourages a spatial-corporeal relationship that breaks down the layers of the image just as it exfoliates the body through varying haptic and affective forces and intensities. The images in Track B provoke a spatial and sensorial placement of the viewer that then extrapolates the affective intensities within the diegesis to external circulative economies.[7]

The cognitive duality of the visual image in the shot of Pablo in front of the water foregrounds the sensorial emphasis in Track B. He moves toward the right of the frame, the camera tracking him, as he nervously waits for Bruno to arrive. The lack of diegetic audio (remember: we hear the water and the music, neither of which occupies a point of audition in the visual space) places a subtle emphasis on the kinesthetics of the scene, creating a separate, nonverbal narrative through motion. Several signs of nervousness announce Bruno's impending arrival and the libidinous motivations behind their meeting in this separate space.

Upon arriving, Bruno acknowledges the spatiality of the sequence, pointing

8.5. The aqueous as vector of difference is central to Plan B *and urban New Maricón film. Copyright Rendez-Vous.*

in a semicircle away from their location, his finger finally resting on where the water was visible in the establishing shot of Pablo. His motion draws the viewer back to the coast, reminding us again of the parallel affective narrative made possible by the spatial placement of the viewer as a character in the diegesis, thus permitting a receptive site for affective circulations. The coast in the preceding image and the corresponding sound of the water, for all intents and purposes, join the locus of reception with the spaces of representation, or as Lastra argues, place "the auditor as literally as possible *in* the profilmic space" (*Sound Technology*, 182, emphasis in the original).

In axiographical terms, then, this scene is phenomenological and heuristic, though it foregrounds presence over legibility (of the ethics and erotics of the narrative). By pointing toward the water, Bruno instructs us to rewind the image to the opening extreme long shot and to engage in the subsequent actions between Pablo and him through this privileged space of perception. In effect, the film questions which exactly is the profilmic space. Is it what we see, that is, the interactions between the men, or, as I argue, the spatiality, hapticity, and coded cultural semiotics of the water as a site of nonnormativity? In this fashion, *Plan B* taps into a specific affective economy put into circulation by other films that rely on the hapticity of the aqueous as a semiotic coding for gender difference and a correlative empathic reaction in the viewer. I am not arguing here in favor of causality—that Berger made *Plan B* in reaction to the seminal early works of New Maricón cinema, which is highly unlikely given the film's production dates—but that the film taps into the affective signs of a particular economy (generated partially through a collective cultural consciousness) that in turn shapes its aesthetic codes.

8.6. Gestures toward the sea: guiding affective circulations and orientations as Plan B *takes shape. Copyright Rendez-Vous.*

By setting in motion these two parallel narrative planes (the visual and the haptic) and by tracing their respective epistemological boundaries, the actions that unfold between the two men take on a subtly homoerotic tone. The sight of them sitting together against a concrete wall and smoking is nothing more, at face value, than two *pibes* (dudes) enjoying a smoke and conversation. Reading their actions through the parallel optic, however, it is easy to revert to the previous scene of the two men in front of a concrete wall and the sly symbolism of Bruno's camera lens. We can even interpret Bruno's casual stretching of his arms over his head as a giveaway of his desire for something more than friendship with Pablo: he pauses awkwardly half-stretch and self-consciously scratches his head with both hands, nixing the usual modus operandi of the seducing male who uses the arm stretch as an excuse to corral the seated female. The awkwardness continues the focus on nonverbal language (as seen in Pablo's nervous tics prior to Bruno's arrival) to produce a separate narrative thread that is woven into the sensorial, not-necessarily-linguistic fabric of Track B.[8] The juxtaposition between a sensorial and a legible narrative reflects on the two traditions of sound in the cinema, which is a detail that the film calls to our attention through the seamless continuation of point-of-audition dynamics into a scene with nondiegetic music and sounds.

This same self-conscious technique is deployed in a second dyad of images. Berger repeats the pattern of using a static situational shot followed by a medium shot of bodies interacting or performing in this same space, though the frame this time moves slightly away from the spatial referent in the original image. The first image in the set shows two buildings under construction on the urban skyline. They are towering apartment buildings or office blocks set against a third, completed, building and "bits and pieces" of several other buildings below them. Note here my appropriation of Elena del Río's concept of the urban space, as in a similar fashion (and if we are to treat building images akin to body images in that they are representational and polylayered as assemblages of varying forces and intensities), the urban here does not result from a bygone unity or aim for a future restoration. It is, instead, a curated fragmentation that in its fragments makes possible variable reconfigurations and varying affective intensities and their subsequent transference; it is a body present through its virtuality.

In this particular shot, we are met with the nonsounds of the urban, though in a higher intensity than previous images in Track B. The first thing that strikes us is that the undifferentiated rumblings evoke a sense of verticality in the image that is already suggested by the towers, which logically emanates from the roads below the camera's point of view. The viewer, therefore, is placed within the spatial coordinates of the image through this sense of height created by sound.[9] Once they are physically placed within the shot, the presence and condition of the towers prove to be a facile metaphor for the two male protagonists: two buildings/bodies under construction within a specific cityspace.

This reading is underscored in the second image of the dyad: Pablo and Bruno on one side of the image and a heterosexual couple on the other, all casually chatting and drinking beer on a rooftop. We can in fact see the two buildings under construction in the background immediately behind Pablo and Bruno. By correlating the visual angles between the two shots, it is likely that the first was captured from this same roof, placing the viewer within the cartography of the image and its erotics. We are thus not casual observers—voyeurs allowed a means *in* through the lens—but materialized entities that are actively plotted against the bodies in the image. As such, the film compromises the body of the observer into an ethical viewing practice that encourages an affective transference. That transference, in turn, makes possible the shaping of not only the observer but also the space of viewing. In other words, the dyad gestures toward a contouring of real bodies and places through representational stand-ins or bits and pieces.

From a narrative standpoint, this second image is quite rudimentary in its suggestion of equity; the two men are contrasted with the heterosexual couple engaged in a public display of affection. She is leaning into him while his arm, beer in hand, cradles her. The casual normalness of their body language reflects the public and private (spatial) aspects of desire that Hermosillo so deftly illustrates in *Doña Herlinda* and the cultural double standard concerning the visibility of same-sex relations. In this scene, I do not think the film is explicitly contrasting homosexual and heterosexual desire in relation to acceptability (as Bruno and Pablo are not a couple yet) but showing instead what the two men—

8.7. Normalizing difference with the city as backdrop, Plan B. *Copyright Rendez-Vous.*

currently "under construction" like the buildings behind them—can aspire to. In regard to the viewer, there is an invitation to normalize the potentially erotic and amorous relationship between Pablo and Bruno through the example of the heterosexual pair. That is, the juxtaposition asks the observer to not differentiate between the possible linkages between the couples.

As the scene ends, Pablo pours Bruno more beer, and we can easily discern a geometry to the desiring bodies. Bruno, with beer in hand, stands on the same horizontal plane as the heterosexual male whereas Pablo is slightly closer to the camera, suggesting that they could adopt the physical relationship of the heterosexual pair.

The movie then moves back into Track A as the two couples move inside to a narratologically and sociologically apical scene. The heterosexual male lies asleep in a bed while the other three sit on the floor remembering Pablo and Bruno's brief kiss during the party. The woman cajoles them to kiss again, calling Bruno a *puto* for not kissing Pablo more passionately during the party: "You don't become gay just by kissing a dude" [No te hacés gay por darle un beso a un pibe].

We might ask, then, what does make someone gay? Her statement suggests that homoeroticism is not synonymous with gayness, this latter understood as a transnational phenomenon of identity politics: there is a cognitive dissonance between the coding *gay* and actual expressions of desire. Recourse to the word "gay" inserts the dialogue into a broader conversation on LGBT-ness in Latin America and its viability as essentially a transplanted politics. The brief interchange reminds the viewer that Latin American sexuality does not follow the strict identitarian connotations of gender, something José Quiroga thoroughly argues in *Tropics of Desire*. If we are to take her argument at face value, homoeroticism within the spatial context (evoked in Track B) is allowed to tentatively enter the public realm of acceptability, even if proidentity postures are disqualified as being *gay*. This is, in a sense, a counterdiscursive exercise in reaction to Manrique's resemanticization of the maricón: gayness is still negative in *Plan B*'s Buenos Aires, but same-sex desire is permissible as long as it goes unlabeled.

The two men themselves are hesitant to put any marker on their feelings. In a later scene, Bruno asks Pablo to help him practice kissing for a supposed casting opportunity. They both reaffirm their developing attachment and intimacy as a sign of friendship and of not being *putos*. Even after sharing a deeper, sober kiss, they show discomfort, Bruno thinking aloud: "I can't believe I kissed a guy" [No puedo creer le besé a un chaval]. Later, Bruno vomits a sandwich after his friend, Victor, asks him if he now likes men. Such scenes reaffirm the film's commitment to escaping identitarianism in favor of intimate, nonpolitical explorations of desire, same-sex or not.

The image of Bruno heaving over a toilet cuts to a studied shot of the inner courtyard of a house. Like images in Track B, the shot forces a coming to terms with space. In this image (repeated in several iterations in the last quarter of the film), domesticity and its social semiotics are brought under the microscope, recalling the spatial contract of heteronormativity I theorize in the discussion of *Contracorriente*. Like the directors of other New Maricón films, Berger is aware of the spatiality of normativity and strives to communicate this to the viewer through establishing shots of the domestic space.

Bruno and Pablo's relationship expectedly develops beyond the boundaries of the homosocial as there are several shots of the men lying half-naked in bed together, at times conversing and at others sleeping. This narrative leads to a scene in Track B that uses a pseudo–reverse angle shot dynamic to home in on the nonlinguistic communication patterns between the two men. They are again shown on a rooftop space surrounded by the urban, and playful music is the sole presence on the audio track.

The camera is first placed behind Pablo, who is gesticulating and seemingly telling Bruno a story. Bruno's body language and gaze communicate captivation and desire. The image then jumps to a shot of Pablo telling a story, though in an alternate temporal space as the two men are wearing different clothes. The setting, though, remains the same and thereby emphasizes the nonlinearity of Track B. It reaffirms the notion that the sensorial signs and circulations in this trajectory of images is protonarrative and must be considered through heuristic processes different from simple legibility. The director is asking us to feel their developing connection and to identify on a personal level with the emotions percolating under the surface of the body-image. He develops a language coded through affective signs and symbols that encourage in the viewer not only a sense of empathy and contact but also an active heuristic process. A later image in Track B, for example, shows the top of an apartment building from a low angle, backdropped by clouds. Note in this image the lack of other buildings or placement within a specific cityspace; instead, the camera focuses on the finished building, which can be seen as an iteration of the previously unfinished towers. The piece of this complete building suggests, correlatively, that the feelings and emotions that were previously in progress or under construction are now stabilized, though only in a partial sense, as the building is never presented as a whole. The framing of the building suggests that the completed processes of desire and construction do not necessarily equate with a collective whole or sense of unity. In other words, though the two men now can feel and uncomfortably (at first) acknowledge their mutual desire, this does not ineludibly fashion a sense of self or identity; desire is ontoformative but not ontological.

Given their increasingly intimate friendship, both men start to lose interest in the third axis of the triangle, Laura. The two men grapple with their materialized desires and Laura's departure from the unorthodox love triangle; with her gone, the artifice of seduction that preempted Bruno's initial actions in the gym are now left without a supportive scaffolding. Following Laura's exile from the triumvirate, Berger sutures together several shots into a visual collective of the different spaces of Track B. Backgrounded by the track's characteristic urban audio, the montage traces backward through static long takes, starting with an image of Pablo looking over the flowers in the earlier establishing shot of domesticity that provoked Bruno's bout of vomiting, then a close-up of Bruno gazing at the unfinished buildings from the rooftop. We then see an out-of-focus image of the park, followed by the outdoor urban setting where the two men photographed each other. This image comes in heavy contrast with a subsequent medium shot of the beach, a reframing of sorts of the original establishing image. The viewer is thus taken backward (or forward, even, given Track B's lack of linearity) through several narrative spaces of affect to a second montage of shots that focus on symbolic signs, the first an image of louvered windows not unlike those that "cut" Bardem's vision in *Antes que anochezca* prior to the film's full immersion in the haptic space of the ocean and the subsequent misdirection that leads to the viewer's identification with the homoerotic point of view shot.

While I doubt that Berger is directly referencing this particular image or sequence, I do believe that he is building on the cutting gesture permitted by this kind of window construction, as it makes visible the artifice of seeing and explicit instruction *to not see* through a simple closing mechanism: the image as sign underlines Track B's emphasis on sensory perception as the primary point

8.8. Reminders of the importance of the liquid in the poetics of nonnormativity, Plan B. *Copyright Rendez-Vous.*

of entry into the erotics of the narrative. The montage ends with a low-angled shot of a red water tower on top of a building. The brightness of the tower immediately draws our attention in a film otherwise composed of sober hues and nudges the viewer to ponder its particular placement within the sequence of affective images.

In a simple metaphorical reading, I want to suggest that this image foreshadows the possibility of a New Maricón poetics in the urban by succinctly combining within one frame the haptic potential of sexual difference, as embodied and suggested by the aqueous (as sign and affective charge), within a real urban spatial referent. The montage in fact sets up the step-by-step instructions for such a reading by tracing us back through the different affective spaces and textures of the film, ending with a combination of water (as the first sensorial image in the track that focuses on same-sex desire) and the urban (as the plane of circulation for a particular affective economy).

The film concludes with the two men rushing off to Pablo's bedroom to finally consummate their relationship in an act that goes unseen by the viewer. Berger thus evades the typical questions about Latin American *activos* and *pasivos,* leaving the viewer with a "happy" feeling that the two are finally together, a feeling undoubtedly shaped by the circulation of positive affect put into place by particular spatial signs located throughout the film's Track B. *Plan B,* therefore, breaks ground on discussion of the traditional problematic of public versus private that Hermosillo skillfully planted though never successfully negotiated, and provides us with a candid narrative of desire that does not "stick," so to speak, with Anglo notions of queerness. It, instead, provokes a culturally nuanced take on sexuality more in line with the real spaces of these films. This, in turn, puts in motion a correlative social surfacing that sets the stage for the normativization of same-sex relations, at least within the urban milieu.

Berger's latest film, *Hawaii* (2013), showcases the director's awareness in filming gender within the urban, as he does in *Plan B*. With Manuel Vignau (Bruno in *Plan B*) as Eugenio and Mateo Chiarino as Martín, the film, much like *Plan B*, develops the underlying sexual tensions between two men who let go of their inhibitions in the final scene. The narrative recounts the meeting of the long-lost childhood friends in Eugenio's uncle's house, which Eugenio is caretaking during the summer. Martín arrives looking for work and a place to stay, his homelessness unexplained as Berger focuses more on the affects and symbols of desire than on any true narrative development of the characters.

The title stems from an old View-Master reel of Hawaii that Eugenio finds among the boxes stored in the house. The reel and the View-Master are at the center of the film's concluding visual narrative as Eugenio repeatedly looks at the 3-D images of Hawaii, taking the reels with him to different spaces that are traced throughout the film's trajectory.[10]

What sets the film apart from its predecessor, though, is an engagement of the nonurban, or natural, and a minting of its affective intensities, in addition to a careful exploration of its semiotic potential in coding for gender. This is brought to our attention in the opening sequence, where a behind-the-shoulder shot shows Eugenio driving through a city. As in *Plan B*, Berger uses nondiegetic sound in this sequence and throughout the film, used later to also place the viewer within a particular space when the two men sit by a swimming pool, and the symphony is overlaid on natural sounds such as birdcalls.

In the opening sequence, Eugenio is constantly shown looking, almost in an exaggerated manner that seems to indicate that the audience, too, should take into account where the car he is riding in is; his motions are predicated on knowing from where he is coming, a strategy seen in the long perception shots of *El último verano*. His constant, almost neurotic looking around is an indication that we must identify the spatiality of the narrative.

The image then cuts to an establishing shot of foliage and trees in the background, foregrounded by an in-focus barbed wire fence. Explicit in this image is a sense of separation between the lens and the setting, placing us, in axiographical terms, in a liminal paradigm. In other words, the image highlights the shifting nature of setting between the *here* and the *there* (separated by the wire) and how these visual spaces can house particular affective *and* semiotic coda that then reframe viewership and its eventual surfaces (the viewer, the broader social body, the circulation of cinema, etc.). Like Solomonoff, who uses the long shot to underline a narrative and ethical movement from city to not-city and vice versa, Berger underlines this shift initially in purely personal terms by not directly showing the movement of diegetic characters between paradigms. The film instead focuses on the viewer's relationality to space and thus engenders a more personal relationship between the ins and outs of sexuality on the Latin American screen.

The image then pans to the left and tracks Eugenio as he makes his way down a path into the woods and the wire goes out of focus, suggesting that we are to follow him into this new space. It cuts to an extended black screen that implies, I argue, a need to refocus what was perceived immediately prior, that is, a spatial-semiotic-affective move to the natural as a dialoguing agent of self. *Hawaii,* therefore, is a much more traditional New Maricón film — if we can at this stage talk about a "traditional" variant of a very new genre — exposing how the natural permits a way out of the hegemony of representation.[11]

The film, in fact, shares many points of contact with the corpus of New Maricón films I analyze in the previous section, including a spatial outing from the urban to the natural. There is also an authorial awareness of the spatial contract of heteronormativity that Fuentes-León exposes in *Contracorriente,* seen in *Hawaii* through establishing shots of Martín against a house in ruins. The film is not rich in dialogue but manages to develop other interactions between the viewer and the image through strongly audile-tactile images; the hapticity of Martín washing a peach, for example, engages a polysensorial relationship with the film that is a hallmark of New Maricón cinema. The aqueous is also ubiquitous in this film, appearing either as a narrative device (the swimming pool or river as a setting for the interactions between the two men) or as an affective sign that engages the viewer. This occurs in tandem with a preference for the "bits and pieces" technique in portraying the male body, which is also the case in *Plan B* and *Ausente.*[12] Berger even recycles some of the simple intratextual metaphors used for interrogating gender systems that can be seen in *XXY* and *El último verano* — Eugenio is writing a novel about a six-year-old girl who questions her father and his ways in a strongly patriarchal family, metonymic, no doubt, of the director's ideological engagement with heteronormativity throughout the breadth of his work.

In genealogical terms, then, it is easy to locate *Hawaii* within the broader New Maricón genre, though it is important that Berger makes this film after *Plan B,* which is strongly urban. I qualify this statement, though, by arguing that *Plan B*'s success is largely allowed by a particular circulation of positive affect that was only put in place by the forerunners of a transnational Latin American genre that created positive ties between the viewing audience and sexual difference; that is, Berger's earlier work was not produced or consumed in an ideological vacuum, but in a space that was increasingly open to these kinds of films in a regional industry that had, historically, in commercial and critical terms, not given visibility to particular gender difference topics.

On a final note, there is one shot in *Hawaii* that captures the relationship between the body-erotic and the spatial, an intrinsic relationship for any theorization of the erotics of Latin American cinema. About halfway through the film, Eugenio and Martín challenge each other to a race in the wilderness immediately after a scene in which the two men are shown floating in the river, not unlike Jorgelina and Mario in the concluding montage of *El último verano* and Alex in XXY. Berger chooses a static shot and lens over a tracking technique to show the movement of the men as they race each other—undoubtedly a reference to the games that establish hierarchies of masculinity that Solomonoff uses to backdrop Mario's becoming. In this particular image in *Hawaii*, the static shot is focused on overhanging foliage, not unlike that present in the establishing image that predicated Eugenio's (and the film's) abandonment of the urban. The men are perceived in the background as out-of-focus bodies quickly moving toward the vegetation and finally reaching the focal plane that the camera established earlier. This plane is centered on the natural, not on the narrative event of the racing men, thereby placing (natural) space at the apex of the film's schema of representation. The running men quickly come into focus as they approach this topographic referent, come into focus and *materialize*, so to speak, as defined bodies within the chosen space. The shot therefore underlines the relationship between space and the body, the former as a primordial axis of characterization and representation, the latter as a materialized assemblage of both impending and captured forces and intensities that explains, in part, the New Maricón preference for bits and pieces (over the Maricón genre's pervasive scopic regime of the whole). This shot of materializing bodies in *Hawaii*, in addition to the cutting gesture of the window in *Antes que anochezca* and the postcoital studied close up of Miguel and Santiago in *Contracorriente*, is the vignette par excellence of the poetics of New Maricón film.

CHAPTER NINE

On Children and Neoliberal Structures of Feeling

As noted in the opening lines of this book, there is a decided boom in films produced or set in Latin America that deal with homosexuality, intersexuality, and other LGBT issues and bodies. I have attempted, by theorizing a New Maricón cinema, to create an understanding of how these films sever themselves from previous referents while maintaining a visual-audial language that entices, through multiple positive affective ties, a linkage to and then a resurfacing of the viewing public. If Maricón films succeeded in finally bringing difference to the screen, then New Maricón films succeed in actively renegotiating the popular consensus on difference.

That being said, however, there are several films produced since 2005 that do not adhere to the aesthetics or poetics of the New Maricón genre but that *were* made with an emancipatory and empathic politics in mind. Though they are not specifically scopic in their interrelation of the observed (queer) and the observer (a multidemographic audience, mostly heterosexual) and they essentially lack a true consciousness of representation but favor instead a visual style geared toward narrative, they promote in a jocular tone the normality of being "gay" today in an urban setting. I allude to this in the opening lines of the introduction, where the protagonist of the *Qué pena tu vida* series first comes to terms with and then accepts his homosexual buddy in the heart of downtown Santiago.

These films are aware of local idiosyncrasies of gender, notably, the *activo-pasivo* balance in the case of *Qué pena*, but also are open to transnational understandings of sexuality, including the gaylib movement.[1] These films are decidedly more mass market, eluding the stylized, often sparsely dialogued films of the New genre. They delve instead, using comedy, romantic comedy, and light melodrama, into gay issues and everyday gay lives, examining how subjects who identify with gayness negotiate their identity within a strongly conservative telos; they unravel the presuppositions of traditional normativity that, throughout Latin America, have provided the nuclear and metonymic foundation for the nation-state.

Latin American commercial cinema, coinciding with what is popularly known as the neoliberal turn across the region, has taken on some of the topics approached in Maricón films such as *Doña Herlinda* but through careful trajectories that detail what Ignacio Sánchez Prado refers to as the neoliberal structure of feeling.[2] Central to Sánchez Prado's thesis is a historicization of recent romantic comedies in Mexico (though he specifies that this can be generalized across the neoliberal states) and how they align with the aesthetics of the neoliberal paradigm, including the state, space, and subjective bodies. Working with Raymond Williams's well-known concept of structures of feeling, Sánchez Prado affirms that "the unequal access to the structures of representation and consumption of feelings create distinct regimes of affect that replicate rather than question existing ideological, racial, and class separations," and that the structures of feeling that these films generate are "based on the aspirations of the middle and upper classes to achieve the promise of individual success brought forward by neoliberalism" ("Regimes of Affect"). He notes how spatiality is key in framing a narrative that focuses exclusively on this particular urban class, which then segments both demographics in terms of viewership and representation.

While I strongly agree with Sánchez Prado's understanding of this neoliberal cinema (something I allude to in my initial dyadic division of recent Latin American films), it must be noted that he does not immediately address separations or structures of gender. Though the neoliberal agenda has promoted economic and racial inequities, leading naturally from ideological divides, it has, ironically, helped in promoting an awareness of gender difference, though I know that any "awareness" is ontologically vacuous without proper action. In the case of the gay agenda, the neoliberal turn has facilitated its export as political ideology and cultural prepackaged product, as a primal social regulator of cultural imperialism: being "gay," understood in Anglo terms, or open to gayness is a sign of social and economic modernity and advancement. As such, an acceptance and definition of gayness (as opposed to local notions of the *joto, mayate, cochón* [synonyms for homosexual used mostly in Central America], etc.) falls under Sánchez Prado's identification of what the middle and upper classes aspire to. Ironically again, this particular aspirational goal breaks with the initial characterization of the neoliberal structure of feeling, one that specifies existing separations. If anything, we see an ostracizing of traditional machismo and homophobic sentiment that runs parallel to a reappraisal of the individual and her or his "inalienable" identity, again an import from the Anglo North.

Here, though, Sánchez Prado is spot on, as the acceptance and empathy of gayness is seen as a characteristic of the middle and upper echelons of society, particularly what Richard Florida calls the "creative class" (*The Rise of the Creative Class*), and homophobia is often portrayed as a sentiment of the backward and provincial lower economic and racial classes. If anything, we must remember that Florida's creative class—central to Sánchez Prado's cultivation of a neoliberal thesis of feeling—is stereotypically a professional hotbed for fictional and real homosexual bodies. We have seen this stereotype repeated in the *fichera* genre, the films of Hermosillo, and *Contracorriente*. It is no surprise, then, that this regime of feeling is open to lesbigayness and encourages a materialization of these bodies within an urban matrix, rechristened as "gays," from the original "maricón."

Sánchez Prado's optic into recent commercial Latin American cinematic production is a keen analytical tool for understanding and contextualizing some of the "lighter" fare often uncommented on in cinema and cultural criticism. It explains in no uncertain terms the aesthetics and affective coda behind such films as the *Qué pena* series and other commercially successful features, such as the Mexican *No sé si cortarme las venas o dejármelas largas* (I don't know whether to slit my wrists or leave them, 2013), that, in some cases, have a gay character or that actively affirm a progay agenda over the homophobic lay attitude. I would thus modify his thesis to include, at least as a footnote, this positive (if we assume individual equity in this regard) outcome of the neoliberal turn in cinema, even if it regiments and reiterates an overall regime of plural inequities.

In an essay on neoliberalism and Mexican cinema, Sánchez Prado explores the "use of sexuality as a threshold between the innocence of childhood and adults as citizens" ("Innocence," 117). Parting from Cuarón's *Y tu mamá también*, he argues that sexuality or sexual becoming marks a point of severance between childhood and the "inescapable fate of middle-class adulthood in neoliberal times" (118).[3]

While I agree with his reading—though my point of entry into *Y tu mamá también* is more axiographic than narrative—I want to focus instead on child and youth characters that do not themselves undergo a critical sexual-developmental event. In other words, I am less interested in characters such as Cuarón's Tenoch or even Jorgelina in *El último verano* (though this film falls outside of the neoliberal turn) than in children who serve as mediators within the structure of feeling engendered by the cinema. That is, while children who come to terms with their sexuality and identity provide a fruitful site of inquiry, I am more interested in how childhood characters provide a narrative and axiographic approximation to sexual difference in adults.[4]

Below I study two films: one Chilean (*Lokas*, Queens, 2008) and the other

Mexican (*La otra familia*, The other family, 2011). These depart from Carolina Rocha and Georgia Seminet's affirmation that children are "usually objectified as vehicles of adult anxieties over the nature of civic society" and that "beyond simply representing adult anxieties, [children] may actually attempt to produce, play with, or reshape these anxieties" (*Representing History*, 3). I read this, however, in tandem with Sánchez Prado's thesis on neoliberal film and thus do not view the child figure or childhood as politically sympathetic mediums that formally engage with these anxieties (in this case, gender difference); rather, they are narrative elements that further a particular agenda. Children in these films do not represent an inherent innocence that dismantles societal prejudices and constructs; they are, instead, a carefully woven together assemblage of varying discourses present in the neoliberal episteme.[5] They thus facilitate the creation of a structure of feeling open to gayness. These films repeatedly emphasize that being gay is okay, even if the children themselves do not undergo a sexual-developmental crisis.

I find this line of inquiry apropos at this stage in developing a thesis on New Maricón film as I consciously neglected examining the childhood facet of several characters in films such as *El último verano* and *El niño pez* in favor of analyzing sensorial coda of affect. I want to further propose that some of the narratological elements identified in *Lokas* and *La otra familia* may prove useful in shedding light on different readings of the New films studied previously. These films, furthermore, out the themes and tropes of sexual and gender difference from the aesthetically vivid mode of films from the festival and art house circuit to more commercially appealing and popular features, which tend to go unnoticed by film scholars.

Gonzalo Justiniano's *Lokas* has attracted little critical attention, likely due to its low technical quality and unabashed recycling of previous gay-themed features. The film follows Charly (Rodrigo Bastidas), a newly widowed Chilean living in Mexico City. After one too many brushes with the law, he is sent back to Chile with his young and impressionable son, Pedro (Raimundo Bastidas). In Viña del Mar he finds his estranged father, Mario (Coco Legrand), whom he hasn't seen in thirty years, shacking up with Flavio (Rodrigo Murray). Homophobic Charly thus must reconcile his father's sexuality with his previously held beliefs of what a man should be. The film throws in for comedic effect the fact that Charly cannot find employment and must work in a gay club run by an acquaintance of Flavio's. The usual gender-bending antics of the *fichera* genre are recycled here, as Charly must convince others of his gayness.

The film subtly reutilizes several tropes and narrative points from well-known gay-themed films. Perhaps the most obvious is the interage relationship between gay father and young lover, seen in *The Birdcage* (Mike Nichols, 1996), itself a remake of the Franco-Italian *La cage aux folles* (Édouard Moli-

9.1. A sly wink toward stepping-stones in the genealogy of Maricón cinema, Lokas. *Copyright Banco Estado.*

naro, 1978). The offspring of said couple must first hide and then come to terms with the father's difference, the principal shock being that the mediating character is a biological product of the gay man.

Lokas further alludes to the film by Mike Nichols when Pedro first comes to his grandfather's house and observes a canary in a cage, this being, of course, an explicit reference to *The Birdcage*. The scene ends with Mario looking slyly past the camera in an acknowledgment of the film's cultural heritage.

In a later scene, Justiniano alludes to another gay favorite of international audiences and a classic of Maricón film—*Fresa y chocolate*. Pedro and Charly join the couple for an outdoor breakfast one morning, and Flavio provocatively eats strawberries, evoking Diego's iconic opening actions and dialogue in the Cuban feature. *Lokas* recycles the gastronomic metaphor of sexuality by then contrasting the strawberry with Charly's choice of toasted bread, the understanding being that the bread is more masculine than the fleshy strawberry, metaphor for all things feminine.

Aside from inserting the film into a broader corpus of gay-themed cinema, the characters manage to engage in what can be considered didactic conversations where their rehearsed interactions are aimed less at forwarding the narrative and more at instructing the audience on the terms of social acceptability. We see this early, when Pedro tells his father he is taking cooking classes, to which Charly replies that said classes will only turn the boys into "homosexuals . . . perverts . . . those degenerates that like men" [Maracos . . . pervertidos . . . esos degenerados a que le gustan los hombres]. Pedro, the smartly dressed child being educated during the neoliberal episteme, and as such a model for citizenship, retorts that they are not to be called "maracos" but "gays," to which Charly responds, quite appropriately: "We're not in the United States" [No estamos en Estados Unidos].

This seemingly innocuous dialogue, coming very early in the film, sets several parameters within which Justiniano will undertake a progay agenda: first, there is a geopolitical understanding of culture, where the older generation avows cultural difference whereas the younger neoliberal-educated citizen argues for transnationality; second, the preference for Anglo terminology exemplifies an exportation of identity politics beyond the cultural episteme and academic halls of the global North into contexts that hold their own sets of beliefs; and last, an emphasis on the child as a cultural mediator in the film, shown as the voice of reason and the base model for future modernity—a tantalizing prospect for the segmented audience the film addresses as Sánchez Prado's neoliberal structures of feeling.

Pedro furthers his claim to being a purveyor of modernity to the audience upon their arrival in Chile after Charly's antics, which landed him in prison (a space that Justiniano mines for its homophobic potential).[6] Seeing a male airline pilot lock lips with his partner who comes to the airport to greet him, he exclaims: "Look, Dad! Those guys are gays!" [¡Mira papá! Ésos son gays!]. There is a carefully threaded connection between sexuality and modernity, read loosely as inclusion within the global North, no matter how geographically disparate Chile may seem from such a simplistic spatial binary.[7] The pilot (whether hetero or homosexual), as is the case in Hermosillo's *Amor libre*, portends sexual liberation as a symptom of seeing the world, a world that Latin America(ns) must aspire to. Homophobia and the usage of the traditional lexicon of gender difference are thus seen as backward. This is highlighted by Charly's correction that they are not gays but Russians, the disconnect with a contemporary audience being that Charly is still living under the political episteme of the Cold War, a condition now extinct as polar ideology is secondary to capital accumulation. In other words, this scene sets the trajectory for the film's exploration of space as making possible an Anglo episteme (in terms of modernity, economics, and erotics); after all, by calling them "gays," Pedro asserts that *we could*, or more accurately, *we ought to be* in the United States.

Pedro's surprise at seeing the two lovers in the airport furthers another thesis that *Lokas* brings to bear, even if the film lacks the aesthetic and sensorial qualities of some of the more critically acclaimed fare coming from Latin America. The scene normalizes homosexual relations in the space of the airport, seen as the first impression and thus a cultural microcosm of the nationspace, though one can easily argue the contrary, that what we usually see in airports is what the neoliberal state *wants* us to see in terms of actual marketing, placement, and semiotics, or in the representation of airports in mass media outlets.

9.2. An argument at the airport for emulating the North, Lokas. *Copyright Banco Estado.*

In fact, the film goes to great lengths to plot out a mapping of Latin America through its diegetic settings and specific topologies. In the early scenes in Mexico, for example, the dialogue spoken by several secondary characters (including the two police caricatures that lock Charly up for fraud) is an exaggeration of the local lexicon. Another example is Mario's house, a veritable catalogue of stereotypical gay kitsch and Latin American cultural artifacts and curiosities.

The nationspace then attempts to go beyond the artificial borders of a "Chilean" film on gay issues—even if such national labels are extinct in an age where production dollars, actors, technical staff, and narratives are better labeled as "Spanish-language" or "Latin American"—forging Pedro's mediation of gay identity as a transnational process. This is reinforced by the club that Charly ultimately works for, a chain by the name of Lokas located all over Latin America and the United States (Viña del Mar, Miami, Cancún, Punta del Este, Rio de Janeiro). The club, like the house, posits a spatial agglomeration of transnational nodes that are interchangeable; that is, Lokas is more than a diegetic club where Charly confronts his homophobia: it channels the film's agenda in aligning Latin America with a global ethics of identity where the local is only an iteration of the international. The real places implicated in this process, though, underline the film's espousal of the neoliberal paradigm—a facet Sánchez Prado develops in approaching this praxis of recent Latin American cinema—as Viña is said to be like other places favored by the wealthy global upper class. That group really is nationless, held together more by first-class airline tickets, flutes of champagne, and brand recognition than any passport or anthem (and, for that matter, the legislative control they harbor over the individual). This is no place for the homophobic Charly and his fears of *maracos*.

Lokas (the club), then, is a neoliberal space, or a transpositional yet defined site that serves as a point of capture for some of the intrinsic problems behind the neoliberal project, where modernity is proclaimed while its rejects are visible only to an analytical eye that is adept at reading between the lines.[8] Flavio, in fact, proudly proclaims that Lokas will see that Bolívar's dream becomes a reality—a mighty aspiration indeed—though, sadly, only in terms of a cultural homogenization where Anglo terms and identitarian systems are taken as axiomatic and progressive.[9] But that is enough for the likes of Flavio, metonym of an audience the film targets, where belonging to the neoliberal order and its benefits overshadows the rampant inequity left on the outside, or all those spaces that *Lokas* glosses over in the tradition of the neoliberal genre.

Charly, in fact, becomes a changed man through contact with this neoliberal space, for the better, if "better" refers to an orientation toward Anglo ideals. He defends the rights of homosexuals to partake in traditionally masculine pastimes such as watching football and even explains, at his son's prodding, toward the conclusion of the film, that "we shouldn't applaud homosexuals but, rather, respect them" [a los homosexuales no hay que aplaudirlos, hay que respetarlos].

The film thus can be seen as an evolution of Charly's struggles with homosexuality and homosexuals, a feel-good narrative that underlines the positive change that comes about when one becomes a modern global citizen from a provincial and backward locale. Charly's proclamation after enlightenment, furthermore, adds to the film's didactic tone, which is shrouded in comedy, though it is easy to unearth the message behind the familiar antics of man dressed as a homosexual, "homosexual" being here, of course, a stereotyped trope. That and the film's early exaggerated Mexicanness reveal a further intertext to a knowing audience: the *fichera* genre, though in this modern take, the male as queer comedic trope relates a positive message of understanding and respect, even if we are not to "aplaudirlos."

Perhaps the most obvious strategy in framing a didactic attitude toward difference comes from the film's choice of using Pedro as a narrator who provides off-diegetic commentary and who serves as an axis of focalization in several point-of-view shots. The latter mostly focus on Charly's love interest's (Liliana) cleavage. The film is unapologetic in exploiting the child's point of view to further two ends: to draw attention to the female's curves, a symptom of the neoliberal aesthetic of the body, which objectifies the flesh (both female *and* male) as (sculpted, silicone-injected) consumer products that appease libidinal desire within a system of production; and to keep the film within certain bounds of acceptability as Pedro, for all his culinary adventures and openness to his grandfather's identity and lifestyle, is decidedly *not* gay.

The film plays with this ambiguity near the conclusion as Charly pairs up with Liliana and Pedro invites his new *amor* to a family dinner. We first see a boy (much to Charly's visible disgust), but then realize that Pedro is in love with said boy's sister. The point-of-view shots then forward the notion that being open to homosexuality does not imply "contagion" but modernity, as Pedro is the seed of an upstanding (educated, white) neoliberal citizen, a (heterosexual) model for the future, and not the symbolic offspring of the ethically suspect father past. This concluding sequence emphasizes the position of the image of the child as a mediator for neoliberal politics and not simply as a purveyor of gender acceptance per presocial innocence; the child does not play out the unveiling of the socialization of homophobia per se. He is (and I say "he," as the male is privileged in this regard), instead, a key component of the political, or as Lee Edelman emphasizes in his psychoanalytical probing of a communal death drive and the limits of queer theory, "the image of the Child invariably shapes the logic within which the political itself must be thought" (*No Future*, 2). You see, the image of the Child (perhaps Edelman's capitalization is appropriate here, as we are not talking about any lived experience) is a key cog in the political, and thus in the shaping of the cinema as a productive discursive and affective site of the neoliberal agenda, as the image "serves to regulate political discourse—to prescribe what will *count* as political discourse—by compelling such discourse to accede in advance to the reality of a collective future" (*No Future*, 11). María del Carmen Caña Jiménez furthers not only that the Child serves a political, narratological purpose, but that childhood as a construct is also an affective locus that operates as an "epistemological crib of political discourse" [cuna epistemológica del discurso político] ("The Writing of Childhood," 150). In *Lokas* and other such features, the Child denominates the boundaries of acceptability in terms of gender acceptance, as he (Pedro in this case) "embodies the citizen as an ideal, entitled to claim full rights to its future share in the nation's good, though always at the cost of limiting the rights 'real' citizens are allowed" (*No Future*, 11). Thus Pedro is given sole authority to negate his father's homophobia under the guise of an imminent futurity, one inhabited no doubt by those who look and think like the young Pedro.

The child character in *Lokas* follows Rocha and Seminet's observation that children often are both the focalized and the focalizers of filmic narratives; that is, they are an object of fixation and the visual and ethical site of enunciation. This dual nature is explored in a vignette that breaks from the greater narrative. We see Pedro, dressed as "Flyman," wearing a mask and playing with his now-deceased mother. The film in fact opens with Pedro watching the Flyman cartoon and donning the mask, an action he repeats in a later scene set in Viña. Filtered through sepia tones, we not only see a masked Pedro interacting with his mother (as a focalized position), but we are also presented with several point-of-view shots (making him the focalizer). This visual interplay coincides with an audial overlap of strongly haptic sounds that are common in the New

Maricón genre—amplified sounds of crashing waves that are drawn out in bass and treble, thus provoking an image of water gliding over sand and of aquatic fauna—and is the only moment that the film breaks from standard narrative techniques. The vignette is a memory that washes over Pedro when he wears the mask, linking perhaps several dispersed memories of his early youth. The montage of third- and first-person images, furthermore, creates a sense of embodiment and identification with the child, wherein the viewer seamlessly assimilates his position. This subtle and ephemeral recasting of viewership, combined with the explicit audial-visual cues of the haptic, generate a positive affective intensity that I recount in the discussion of true New Maricón films. In the case of *Lokas,* though, the technique enmeshes us with the child not only as a character but also as an intersection of multiple discourses, including those of the neoliberal paradigm and the gay agenda.

The positioning of the viewer at the cue of putting on the mask proves useful to the plot's climax, when Pedro puts on the mask to escape his father and grandfather's arguing, code here, of course, for their metonymization of radically divergent postures toward modernity. They argue because Charly is accused of stealing from the club, and Mario and Flavio don't believe in his innocence. By putting on the mask, Pedro not only escapes momentarily from their argument but also provokes a realignment in the viewing experience that places the viewer within the framework of childhood, which, in this case, is within the matrices of the neoliberal subject. Remember that the child implicates a narrative tonal didacticism; as such, we are caught up in the film not only through the affective potential of the mask and its gesture toward escape but also as subjects to be lectured to on the importance of tolerance. Pedro leaves the house and goes back to the harbor, the site of the earlier vignette, and the audio goes back to the amplified sounds of the water while Pedro narrates in an off-diegetic voice a hypothetical dialogue between Flyman and his mother. He sits on a pier as cutting shots show his relatives futilely searching for him; the camera closes in on the child backgrounded by the bright water, evoking in visual and audial terms the spaces and sensations of queerness (so expertly generated in the genealogy of New Maricón film). His inexplicable jump into the water temporarily throws a kink in the film's reliance on crass humor and stereotypical characters as we are met with the seriousness of the existentialist exercise. Mario, of course, saves him in an action that provides a judgment of the previous debate between clashing discourses: only a progay, transnational, and socially enlightened (read: Western) future is viable to ensure that the youth of today will thrive.

The child and his (imaginary) world, therefore, provoke the ideological denouement of the film, which explicitly encourages and forwards a particular

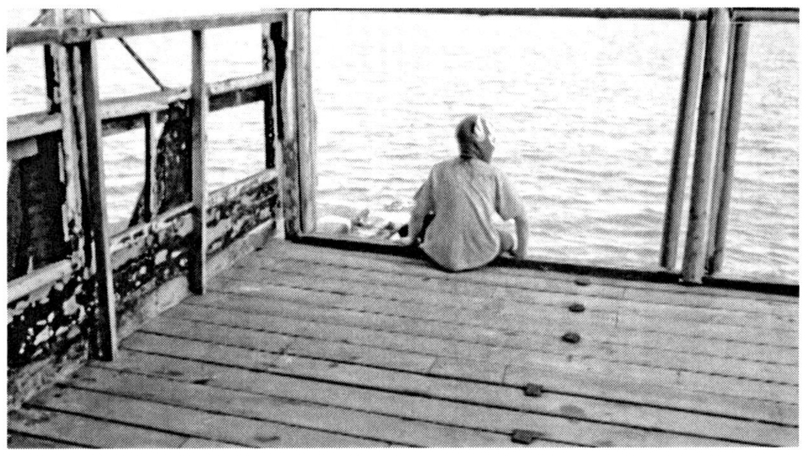

9.3. The child as focalizer and focalized in the neoliberal structure of feeling engendered in Lokas. *Copyright Banco Estado.*

neoliberal ideology and erotics where acceptance and Anglo identities overtake traditional denominators such as the maricón and the *maraco*.

A similar dynamic is fostered in Gustavo Loza's *La otra familia*, a Mexican film about the contemporary politics of sexuality and family structures that is exportable to other contexts. As in true neoliberal cinema, the core narrative plot does not have to take place within a defined national-cultural space but can be reappropriated to different contexts.

In broad terms, the film is about Hendrix, the son of the drug-addicted girlfriend of a low-level *narco* (drug trafficker) who is informally adopted by Chema (Luis Roberto Guzmán) and Jean Paul (Jorge Salinas), a gay yuppie couple that hesitantly agrees to foster the child at the behest of lesbian friends. While on the surface this story could take place in Los Angeles or London, in practice, Loza includes a separate though not mutually exclusive plot line involving the boy's mother, Nina, and the drug trade and violence in contemporary Mexico. The film, therefore, stitches two divergent cinematic tropes into a narrative that is really two films in one. As such, it shares a point of contact with several films in the Maricón corpus that treat sexual difference as a subplot within a broader interrogation of specific societal issues.[10]

The gay narrative follows in the line of Sánchez Prado's neoliberal lineage of films (mostly comedies, though I would also include light drama) that engender specific structures of feeling, and one could argue that the *narco* track furthers a separate critical inquiry as it panders to academics and cultural critics who are hell-bent on theorizing about *la violencia* and the border (sometimes

9.4. The normalization of gay marriage within traditional institutions, La otra familia. *Copyright Río Negro.*

9.5. The child as symbol of the neoliberal future, La otra familia. *Copyright Río Negro.*

rightfully so, and other times, not so much). The gay track conforms to the specifics I reviewed earlier. It begins with an almost over-the-top marriage ceremony complete with beautiful people of the creative class engaged in libidinal tactics that underline the neoliberal as ontoformative.

While at face value this scene is a portrait of the wonders of wealth and social progressivism (the concluding thesis in *Lokas*), Loza throws a wrench into the power structure that the film shows by introducing a priest who unites the two men in holy matrimony. You see, in *La otra familia,* one can be "un gay" but must also believe in (a Catholic) God. It is easy at this juncture to introduce the well-known critique of proponents of gay marriage—a discourse that the film inserts itself in and addresses at length in that it posits marriage as *the* unifying social stitch.

La otra familia takes this facet of the agenda even further by portraying this particular gay marriage as church sanctioned, thereby replicating a model of patriarchy that could otherwise be challenged in a truly queer praxis.[11] Jean Paul later even admits to being "pretty conservative" [bien conservador]. As such, marriage in the film is solely another vehicle to perpetuate extant social thought systems, perhaps keeping in mind Fuentes-León's Latin American audience, as even the priest is uncharacteristically progressive and progay.[12] Reviews of the film further note that it "does not attempt to be a pro gay adoption pamphlet" [no intenta ser un panfleto sobre la adopción gay] (Molina, "Pantalla grande"), showing instead that a loving family as a structure is what is most important for the future of a child.

This future builds the primacy of the Child in these films, as the promise of a better tomorrow (in neoliberal terms, of course) panders to an audience open to and mimetic of the patterns of consumption played out in the narratives. Marriage—even of gay god-fearing men—is the nucleus par excellence of this politics and thus positions the film at a rather conservative point of enunciation, imposing, as Edelman outlines, "an ideological limit . . . preserving in the process the absolute privilege of heteronormativity by rendering unthinkable, by casting outside the political domain, the possibility of a queer resistance to this organizing principle of communal relations" (*No Future*, 2). The film therefore does not decenter marriage or systemically unstitch the social fabric of normativity (thus making possible an explicit queer drive), but instead sticks to a script wherein the sanctity and viability of the Child (as discursive axis, cultural sign toward the [neoliberal] future) is left untouched.[13]

Returning to Sánchez Prado's thesis, this film (like *Lokas*) is both reflective of and didactic toward several audiences and engages in relaying and portraying multiple discourses that categorically fall under the umbrella of the neoliberal state, understood as a condition of being and not as a political entity. In other words, the audience is or aspires to be the very public present at the nuptial ceremony: an educated, urban, wealthy class that is more comfortable around gays than around characters like Charly and that does not subscribe to the official church line on gender identity (see note 11), even if religiosity remains a key descriptor of the communal body. Homosexuality and its acceptance are normalized through this affective dynamic of viewership and are presented as a characteristic of belonging, as the sequence cycles through a series of stereotypical wedding scenarios typical of the romantic comedy, with the difference being that it is two *novios* taking part in the shenanigans.

While the yuppie couple provides the narrative raw material for a discussion of gayness in contemporary Latin America (much like Mario and Flavio in *Lokas*), it is the child, Hendrix, who makes possible a critical point of entry into the diegesis. Instead of relying on images and sounds that generate an affective closeness, usually through the haptic, as is the case with *Lokas*, the child character here is aligned with the viewer through the empathic ties that are generated in melodrama, as melodrama characterizes the tone and plot of the *narco* track in the film. Not only are we to empathize with the child's state of affairs—the panning establishing shot in the opening of the film shows a decrepit space that nobody would want to inhabit—but he is also our narratological mediator between worlds/tracks. Like Pedro, Hendrix is a point of empathy and a go-between for the cultural discourses that intersect the film, being both teacher and representation of the viewer as student of the film's overall message. In this latter regard, in fact, one can almost confuse the boy for an adult as Loza dresses him and poses his body in the opening scene as though he were a middle-aged man depressed and alone in squalid surroundings.

Hendrix is a mediator between competing discourses of Anglo modernity and provincial backwardness, the latter represented by the couple's domestic help: Gabino the gardener, the prototypical Mexican *machito* (or traditional masculine figure), dark-skinned and mustachioed; and Doña Chuy, the maternal house servant who takes care of the traditionally feminine domestic tasks that the two male leads neglect. There is a clear discursive divide along class and racial lines, where modernity is decidedly not for or of the layperson. After all, doesn't neoliberalism promise and isn't it substrated by such invisible bodies? Gabino and Chuy, however, are very visible in the plot development of *La otra familia*, at least as foils to the otherwise modern characters, including the priest. Like Charly in *Lokas*, they and their coded discourses are introduced to the narrative through the focalized child that must ingest and negotiate their point of view and, ultimately, educate them in the ways of a progressive society. Gabino, for example, constantly suspects the protagonists' intentions in fostering the young child. He repeatedly insinuates that they are pedophiles, even in scenes where the montage emphasizes their increasingly paternal interactions with Hendrix. His interjections—often in the form of insinuations or double entendres—accentuate the absurdity of his entrenched values with regard to gender roles and behaviors almost to the point of being comical to a viewer who can simply dismiss him and Doña Chuy as country bumpkins. This is particularly true when Gabino warns Hendrix to not spend too much time with the couple, as "that is contagious" [eso se pega], "eso" being, of course, homosexuality as disease.

Doña Chuy adds to these efforts by equating national identity to heterosexism (a strategy clearly seen in cultural artifacts from the colony onward in Latin America) and by explaining to Hendrix that Chema and Jean Paul kiss each other because they are foreigners (*extranjeros*), not *mexicanos* like her and the child. It is of note that her banishment of homosexuality to the foreign is something that Hermosillo does not suggest in *Doña Herlinda*, a film that similarly probes the structures of family and communal identity in Mexico. By doing so, however, Doña Chuy is seen to be just as ridiculous as Gabino in his quackery and fear that homosexuality will infect the young and impressionable boy, no doubt—like Pedro—a symbol of a communal and viable future. If anything, Doña Chuy's suggestion calls into question the very thought of national essentialism, a line of thinking that is increasingly foreign to the neoliberal subject.

This is highlighted in another caper, when Gabino takes Hendrix to a wrestling match [*lucha libre*]. The scene is a microcosm of the aesthetic codes of gender in which men are expected to be muscled and tough (though not as sculpted as recent neoliberal idealizations of the male anatomy that follow the classical Grecian mold, as seen by the figure cut by Chema tanning by the pool) and women are skimpily dressed adornments to the main event. His efforts to instill a spirit of *mexicanidad* in the boy are seen for what they are: ridiculous attempts emanating from a theory of social conditioning that hypothetically impacts gender orientation, a belief known for some time to be patently false and misguided.

Hendrix, furthermore, is used, albeit briefly, as a focalizer for same-sex relations. He walks in on a naked Chema and Jean Paul kissing in their bed and is angrily asked by the former to leave. This scene occurs early in the film, upon the child's arrival at the mansion, and opens with a medium shot of the two men kissing in bed, their nudity strategically hidden in the interests of not "losing" a susceptible audience. The child's unannounced entrance into the room unveils the viewer's position as a voyeur vis-à-vis homoeroticism (a trait of Maricón film). In the ephemeral moment of panic when the men, Hendrix, and the viewer realize that the unseeable has become visible, we are affectively aligned with the child as intruders who have violated their privacy.

This dynamic is emphasized throughout the film (as it is in *Lokas*) as the viewer is expected to take the position of the child as recipient of the film's dogmatism or subjective position as neoliberal citizen. If anything, the brief scene exemplifies Michele Aaron's notion that spectatorship is "not simply a speculative or default site for ideological endorsement or multicultural multiplicity, but as a live venue for testing out the limits and resonance of public and private, good and bad taste, conformity and subversion . . . In other words, it becomes easy to see how spectatorship is ethically loaded" (*Spectatorship*, 88). This manifesto is twofold in *La otra familia*, where alignment with the child as subject and point of view introduces an ethics of social equity, even if it is only a masquerade of northern cultural imperialism.[14]

Aside from serving as a cultural mediator between competing discourses, the child character also enables scenes that employ a didactic tone wherein the audience is also infantilized as recipients of the film's explicit agenda to educate. The viewer stands in with Hendrix as Chema and Jean Paul take turns instructing him on the benefits of gender equity and gay acceptance. First we find ourselves with Hendrix in a same-sex take on the prototypical parents-reading-to-a-child scene where the two men, with an age-appropriate book titled *Está bien ser diferente* (the Spanish edition of Todd Parr's popular *It's Okay to Be Different*), instruct Hendrix—and the viewer—that different types of families are acceptable. Again, the film fails to actually decenter or question the very notion of the nuclear family, placing it therefore within a (neoliberal) gay corpus and not a truly queer body of work. Of note in this scene is the fact that the adults mediate the relationship between (age-appropriate) literature and the child subject, which comes into strong contrast with the scenes of Jorgelina perusing clandestine materials on anatomy and sexual differentiation in *El último verano*: the child in Solomonoff's film is less a stand-in for the viewer within a structured didactic dynamic. In other words, Jorgelina escapes the facile and transparent ideological traps that plague *La otra familia* and *Lokas*; she is, instead, a truly decentering point of view and entry point into a broader exploration of body, gender, and sexual pluralities.

Returning to Loza's film, it is apparent that there is little effort made to mine the potential of the child as an epistemological narrative point into gendered structures. Even when Hendrix makes an attempt to go against the script—in one scene, he almost opens a coffee table book about the penis—Chema or Jean Paul is quick to step in as teacher figure to carefully shape his education. They are, as Jean Paul says early in the film, his (and the viewer's) "guardian angel" (*angelito de la guarda*). They continue in this role when Chema goes to Hendrix's school for a sort of meet-and-greet activity and outs himself to the young, impressionable students as a highly successful gay father. The viewer, again, is infantilized and invited to share a seat in the classroom and to be indoctrinated, that is, if he or she is aspiring to the creative class. To the viewer already sharing the film's sensibilities, Chema's dialogue is nothing more than preaching to the choir and a reiteration of how archaic nonidentitarian and homophobic views can be.

Furthering not only the neoliberal structure of feeling but also its specific cultural agenda, *La otra familia* specifies that homosexuals are to be known by the Anglo word "gay." They are no longer to be portrayed as or called "*jotos*," the ubiquitous trope of the *fichera* and early Maricón films. In the same classroom scene, one of Hendrix's classmates volunteers that his father calls homosexuals "gays," to which Chema promptly—again playing the pedagogical role—provides a bare-bones but informative explanation that the term is a descriptor for all same-sex relations. In addition to defining the term for a possibly ignorant audience, his explanation furthers the word's usage in everyday parlance as a modern and appropriate substitute for the plethora of slurs and idiomatic expressions so popular in the Mexican lexicon. The pedagogical value of this scene recycles Charly's slow conversion in *Lokas*, from calling homosexuals *maracos* to accepting his father as a *gay*.

Hendrix's school, furthermore, is an important site, or thirdspace, of this process of cultural osmosis: it is a bilingual school for the wealthy youth of Acapulco; the children have Caucasian features and come from economically successful homes; and perhaps most important, they are less citizens under the Mexican flag and more of the neoliberal paradigm in which transnationality, capital accumulation, and cultural hegemony are the values of patriotism. Hendrix, in fact, emphasizes this facet of the school space when he asks at matriculation: "Why are they speaking English if we're in Mexico?" [¿Por qué hablan en inglés si estamos en México?].

It is evident, then, that the film uses the child not as a focalizer in the erotics of same-sex relations but as a pawn within a specific pedagogical space cultivated to imbue the film with the ability to dictate cultural norms. We are, in fact, no longer in Mexico but in a slippery space that is permeable to discourses of Western modernity, including the gay agenda.

That being said, however, Loza's conservative gays are not necessarily the flag bearers of an Anglo LGBTQ movement but, more precisely and quite ironically, of a local iteration that maintains distinct cultural structures such as the church in place. The film, then, is not a transnational gay-movement manifesto but a Latin American stepping-stone (like Fuentes-León's feature) to true sociocultural emancipation.

CHAPTER TEN

Closing Notes on a Very Open Field

TO CLOSE, I WANT TO OFFER THAT THE BOOM IN homosexual-themed cinema in Latin America is just getting started. We will continue to see mainstream and festival-circuit films that portray and challenge established gender norms. There are, in fact, several films that I do not discuss in these pages that merit future consideration, including the 2014 winner of the Goya for best Latin American film, *Azul y no tan rosa, Un año sin amor* [A year without love] by Argentine director Anahí Berneri, and the films of the Mexican Julián Hernández, a modern-day Hermosillo, who has made a slew of gay-themed films that are provocative in their aesthetic craft.[1] His films are stylized works of art that trace and interrogate contemporary Mexican gay lives.

Of further note in this boom is the production of films, both Maricón and New Maricón, by film industries and contexts that have lagged behind in the region's cinematic output. *Azul*, for example, comes from Venezuela, as does Eduardo Barberena's *Cheila: Una casa pa' Maíta* [Cheila: A house for Maíta], while Diego Araujo's *Feriado* is a recent Ecuadorian offering that outs homosexual desire to the natural and aqueous, following the trajectory planted by Fuentes León, Puenzo, and Berger.

Araujo's *Feriado* (2014) shares several points of contact with the corpus of films I analyze in part II. The opening black-screen credits, for example, are overlaid with palpitant and undifferentiated sounds of the natural world that seemingly emphasize the idea of the image as skin to touch, squeeze, and penetrate, as a tactile body that is symbiotic to that of the viewer. The juxtaposition between the natural (and often aqueous) and the urban is highlighted in the first set of images, where the camera goes from an out-of-focus framing of the city at night to several cutting long shots of the urban. The out-of-focus shot

10.1. The city as invertida *[literally, inverted; figuratively, homosexual],* Feriado. *Copyright Lunafilms.*

harkens to the urban as a virtuality or assemblage of the heteronormative in *El último verano de la Boyita,* whereas the images of streets and buildings remind us of the scopic space of the Maricón. Araujo, however, adds a layer to this reading by then inverting the images of the urban; that is, we are presented with upside-down shots of the city. These shots are later explained as the protagonist (Juanpi) looks at the city while lying upside down supine on a roof, but their initial presence suggests a severing of the autonomy and authority bestowed upon the visual and the exercise of seeing.

A final upside-down urban image pans downward into the clouds and releases the film into the narrative diegesis of the rural. The film clearly suggests a spatial outing akin to the tactics and techniques evidenced in *Contracorriente* and XXY. Here we see a gravel road and a car meandering down it, hinting at an (epistemic and erotic) movement away from the urban and toward the natural and aqueous, again as spaces of outing and becoming. Of note in this image is the fact that Araujo is not entering into dialogue with any specific Ecuadorian antecedents but with a corpus of earlier Latin American Maricón films that situate difference at an ethico-aesthetically safe distance in earlier films.

His desire to seek ties with a transnational lineage is further evidenced in the protagonist's first intimate scene with a girl. She asks him where he is from as he looks Argentine and not from around the sierra in which much of the action takes place—perhaps a knowing wink to the boom in New Maricón films in Argentina (Puenzo, Solomonoff, Berger, etc.).

A second example can be found in a scene between Juanpi and Juano, his love interest from a different socioeconomic and racial background. The two men cavort in a nearby river in their underwear, and the camera adopts a POV angle to follow Juanpi's gaze toward the other's penis. Viewers familiar with Maricón films will no doubt see the linkage to Lombardi's *No se lo digas a nadie,*

10.2. Diego Araujo re-creates a classic scene from Maricón cinema, Feriado. *Copyright Lunafilms.*

where a similar interaction takes place between Joaquín and a young attendant at the hunting lodge; in *Feriado,* however, we are not presented with homosexual panic and violence.

The river scene is one of many that highlight a possible self-reflexivity concerning the strategies of a New to represent difference. Prior to their submerging in the water, Juano tells Juanpi (and the viewer) to listen. He closes his eyes, as does Juanpi, and the soundtrack is overtaken by a soft and then more persistent rumbling of water. The scene, though short and perhaps irrelevant to the plot, tacitly acknowledges a regime of the affective over the scopic, as though the film itself orders us to move laterally into the film and to come into contact with its audile tactility. Juano's short instruction to listen (and then feel) instead of to look underlines a structure of experience where the fluid movement and seduction of the aqueous is deployed to decenter viewership, to fragment the wholeness of the assemblage that is the viewer apparatus, and to then allow lateral, polydirectional movements and contact with libidinal desires now freed by the liquid. Unlike in Lombardi's similar scene, the sounds of the water and its accompanying textures override the narrative, so much so that we feel the embodiment of desire between the two men more than establish ourselves on the outside looking in. We, like Juanpi, are instead invited to intimately feel, to come into contact, and to emerge. As the director notes: "In the mise en scene, the colors become warmer, the mountains give way to a more lush vegetation, full of life, till we arrive at a waterfall where the light is warm, the sun intense, and the images slightly overexposed. There, Juan Pablo experiences a symbolic rebirth when he performs a physical and emotional dive, and something changes when he emerges from the water" [En la puesta en escena, los colores se tornan más cálidos, las montañas dan paso a una vegetación más frondoso, lleno de vida, hasta llegar a la cascada donde la luz es cálida, el sol intenso y las imágenes ligeramente sobre expuestas. Ahí Juan Pablo experimenta un renacer simbólico cuando da un salto, físico y emocional y, al salir del agua, algo en él cambió] (Araujo). What Araujo hints at here is the power of New films to put into circulation empathic conditions so that we, too, emerge from the water changed.

Again perhaps in a moment of reflexivity, the director explains the opening shots of the urban when the two men lie on a roof during a night of drunken revelry. Gazing upside down at the virtual urban—a pastime of the young protagonist, who is unsure of himself and his burgeoning desires—Juanpi wonders: "Am I the one who's upside down or is it the city? [Soy yo el que está al revés o es la ciudad?]. There is a tongue-in-cheek play with the idea of inversion or to invert, *invertir*, where the inverted city is sutured to the idea of the homosexual in Latin America as an *invertido*. By placing the metonym of the normative on its head, the film thus suggests that what is inverted and needs to be righted is the social body and not the body of difference.

But like other films in the New genre, *Feriado* makes no attempt to simplify or homogenize same-sex desire. When Juanpi is asked at the very end if he likes men, a sheepish "I don't know, I think so" [No sé, creo que si] reminds the viewer to not apply facile labels and identities.

There is also a separate and very young corpus of films that investigate the potential for gender subversion and the exploration of desire in the virtual world, that is, in the spaces and bodies that circulate on the World Wide Web. Enrique Buchichio's *El cuarto de Leo* [Leo's room] (2009, Uruguay) is a fascinating though slow portal into the protagonist's (Leo) grappling with sexuality. In the vein of Gustavo Taretto's *Medianeras* (Sidewalls, 2011, Argentina), which focuses intently on the intimacies of one or two characters and their rela-

10.3. Coming to terms with the maricón, No se lo digas a nadie. *Copyright Lola Films.*

tive anonymity within the urban milieu, *El cuarto de Leo* demonstrates how the Internet has become a new spatial outlet for desire, where anything and everything is available.[2] These films seemingly sidestep the spatial considerations of the urban and nonurban by outing the body and desire to cyberspace, though one can equally argue that cyberspace is nothing more than a reiteration and replication of extant gender structures. Buchichio's film, however, merits further consideration, as the ending sequence explicitly outs the protagonist to an unidentified natural-aqueous space, following, then, the aesthetic and haptic trajectory of New Maricón film.

That being said, the New and Maricón genres are still open to negotiation and cannot be seen as finite and closed categories. Rather, it is more accurate to consider this tracing of recent Latin American cinema to be a snapshot of an incomplete evolution.

This is perhaps most clear in a trio of Venezuelan films that I collocate in relation to each other given their chronology and national origin, but whose aesthetics and their resulting ethics diverge convincingly along the bifurcating paths already traced. Ferrari's *Azul y no tan rosa* is, for all intents and purposes, a very Maricón film, even if its production date of 2012 would suggest a shift to the New instead. There is an acute emphasis on seeing and placing gendered bodies as the object of the lens; this is perhaps most evident in the opening credits, which are punctuated by the protagonist (Diego) shown behind a lens, feverishly snapping pictures of topless male and female dancers. First we must consider that we cannot escape the fact that he belongs to the creative class and that these opening images may be taking place in Caracas or any other global nonspace. The film and its characters all subscribe to the neoliberal universe and its structures of feeling, which I outline in the previous chapter. This is highlighted in the movement of the dancers in relation to Diego's lens, as the framing of their bodies affirms the ethical distances between the viewer and the film; that is, there is no exercise in affective orientation or an engendering of the empathic through such subcutaneous and muscular movements. There is, furthermore, a certain didactic angle to the whole film, which can be viewed as more a characteristic of recent neoliberal Maricón features than of New films, which leave as ambiguous the bodies and conclusions we may draw from the narrative.

A trans character, Delirio, concludes the movie by having garnered her own television show, which aims to spread the message of acceptance and difference, akin to the message in *La otra familia* and *Lokas*. Acceptance is equated with modernity, and subscribing to Anglo orders and erotics over any possible local differences is taken as axiomatic.

The narrative, in fact, is situated within the juridical and legislative shifts currently taking place in Latin America, as a television reporter comments on the legalization of same-sex marriage.[3] This moment serves as a cementing substrate that conditions the film's broader aim of partaking in the political process; that is, *Azul* aims to be as productive as possible, taking, of course, Shaviro's definition of the term.

Of note in the film's cultivation of a neoliberal structure of feeling is the place accorded the son: he comes from Spain (indicating a real circulation of ideas from the North to the South in the present day—contemporaneity being important as Diego's father is also Spanish but a vestige of the Francoist regime in his machismo and homophobia), accepts his father's homosexuality (this being a condition, of course, of the son's being seen as the model of the neoliberal future), and spends a great part of the movie looking for a girlfriend. The second half of the film thus almost completely evades the question of gender difference, focusing instead on the boy's search for and inclusion within the heteronormative and mimicking the concluding sequence of *Lokas*. The viewer, then, is given the message that acceptance and plurality are intrinsic to the neoliberal episteme without necessarily jarring her or his sensibilities or reorienting the foci of desire (albeit ephemerally), which is the case in New Maricón films.

Mariana Rondón's *Pelo malo* (2013) is a welcome break from Ferrari's yuppie-gay blandness. Also locating her film in the Venezuelan urban space, Rondón chooses instead to center the film on the coming of age of Junior, the young biracial son of a single mother living in one of the poor high-rise residential complexes that dot the vertical landscape of Caracas. Junior is quite unlike his classmates and friends: lanky and almost fragile, with a sensibility for dance and music that separates him from the accepted types of the masculine.

Several aspects of New Maricón cinema are manifested in this feature. First, the viewer is introduced to Junior in the opening scene, where he lies floating in a full bathtub, going against his mom's orders while she cleans the house of a richer family. He tells his mother he will clean the tub but strips down instead and submerges himself in the water. The camera lingers on his skin as it makes contact with the water, and the audio track is overtaken by the hapticity of the liquid and its rhythms coming into contact with Junior's eardrums. The effect in this opening sequence is clear, as the audile tactility of the image alienates the viewer and orients him or her to the protagonist's body and subject position within the narrative and sets the tone for an affective transmission that poses an ethical approximation to difference.

A second strategy is evidenced in the film's usage of dolls or doll-like toys (clearly seen in *XXY*) to juxtapose notions of desire, the body, and identity. There is an effort made to complicate and problematize rather than to sermonize (as is the case in recent neoliberal Maricón films).

Instead of lingering on images and sounds that point toward an emergence or coming into being of the viewer vis-à-vis the body, *Pelo malo* chooses instead to situate the narrative in relation to intensely audile-tactile urban images

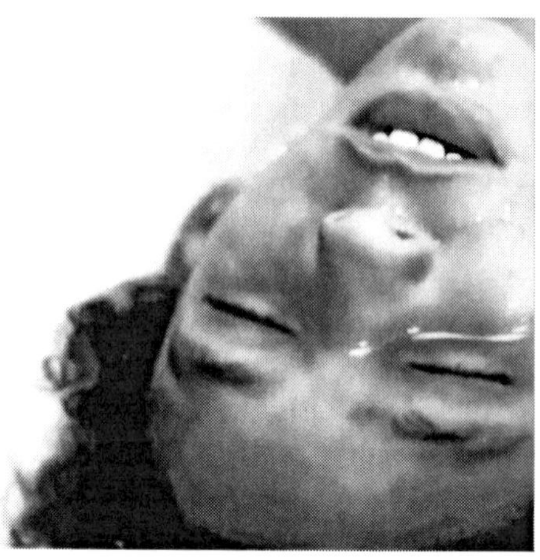

10.4. Rondón's protagonist in Pelo malo *in an archetypal image that provokes a sensation of floating in New Maricón film.*

that situate the viewer in the milieu of Caracas. That is, we are asked to weave cognitive threads between the initial orientation to Junior and the polysensorial space in which the narrative takes place. Unlike strictly New films such as *Contracorriente,* which rely on the metaphor of urbanity to underline any possibility of a circulation, Rondón's film is intensely local and engages the audience to confront gender and sex difference within a very real space.

Unlike those of *Azul y no tan rosa,* the characters and spaces of *Pelo malo* show the other side of the neoliberal agenda, which is more often than not invisible. Of note in this switch is the use of the child or adolescent as the point of entry. Junior is not meant to play a didactic role or to model modernity but to amply critique the very strategy that serves as a platform for other films that rely on a neoliberal structure of feeling. His character has no pretensions of harboring a "new" or "better" Latin America; rather, he simply and brutally shows how homophobia and hegemonic masculinity regiment expressions of difference.

It is important here to remember that the film offers no clear thesis about difference—we do not know if Junior is gay, trans, or what have you—but that Junior has been forced to conform to the aesthetic expectations and strategies of the normative. Herein lies the film's greatest contribution to the corpus studied here, as it, like several of the New films mentioned above, forces questions and deep reflection from the viewer rather than providing simplistic (and often homogenizing) answers. Returning to Russo's framing of *how* difference is shown, *Pelo malo* seeks a heuristic viewership predicated on a positive orientation that engages plural audiences to seek plural conversations and dialogue rather than simply accepting Anglo norms in the Latin American scene and on the screen.

Javier van de Couter's *Mía* (2011) is another feature in this informal Venezuelan corpus that merits study, as it, quite unlike *Azul*, follows the ethico-aesthetic tactics plotted out in New cinema. The narrative documents the contact between Ale, a transgender woman, a *cartonera* (recycler of cardboard), living in a shantytown inhabited by other gender and sex outcasts on the outskirts of Buenos Aires, and a recently widowed man, Manuel (Rodrigo de la Serna), and his daughter, Julia, in the city. During her nightly collections, Ale finds Manuel's wife's (Mía) journal and slowly enters into contact with the city folk, even after Manuel's initial homophobic rejection of her. The film ends with Julia's being sent away and the shantytown destroyed. The concluding image is of a visibly hopeful Ale holding a baby and accompanied by her abject peers, who are potentially restarting their lives in the city. Slow-motion shots of the burning shantytown and a dissolve cut to the walking outcasts accentuate the possibilities that the film poses of reterritorializing the maricón to the city.[4] Starring Camila Sosa Villada, a trans actress who has made inroads into the Argentine theater scene, the film is a curious capstone of some of the trajectories I plot in *New Maricón Cinema*, including the structured usage of space as a coding for gender, the possibilities of materialization in specific topographies, and the presence of the aqueous as a polysensorial image surface that in its hapticity breaks the regime of the scopic. (Rigoberto Perezcano's *Carmín tropical* [Tropical lipstick] can be fruitfully studied in connection with *Mía*, though I do not do so here).

The first of these characteristics is evident in the film's geographic spaces. Van de Couter carefully juxtaposes tower structures with images, sounds, and textures of the natural early in the film as the camera pans from the urban to the spaces occupied by the inhabitants of the shantytown in almost the immediate vicinity of the capital. The first semantic agglomeration in this dyad is evocative of Jean-Clet Martin's conceptualization of the urban image as a virtuality, wherein the dialectic benefits by contrasting this with its antonymic natural. In fact, the film emphasizes in several scenes the spatial characteristics that separate the queer periphery from the urban heteronormative order, wherein the former is characterized by audile-tactile images that slowly demythify the hegemony of the latter. The shantytown itself is a curious demythifier of the spatial contract, an alternative structure wherein difference is allowed to operate as analogous to the images and practices of the normative order. This is a characteristic scene in several New Maricón films, where impromptu and just-put-together spaces reenact the spatial contract, both interrogating its power and suggesting an alternative.

Second, the shantytown demystifies the semiotic hegemony of the neoliberal order and its corresponding structures of feeling, as, unlike *Lokas* and *La otra familia*, the space (and its bodies) materializes the subjectivities often left unseen in the interstitial fluids that neoliberalism glosses over. The fact that a child serves as an intermediary between the queer and the urban-neoliberal class is important in that Van de Couter evades the facile tactics of the Child as informant/teacher/model citizen in favor of the child as point of entry to the queer body. Therein perhaps lies a third demythification of the neoliberal episteme in the film, sourced no doubt from the structured juxtaposition of spatial difference.

The second factor—the possibilities of materialization—lies at the center of the film's portrayal of difference. Unlike Maricón films, which separated and almost took for granted the representation and existence of the sissy-butch homosexual, *Mía* (like other New Maricón features) explicitly calls our attention to the materiality of these bodies, not solely as representative stand-ins but as bits and pieces of real and virtual forces and affects that then evoke an empathic relationship with difference. This aesthetic preoccupation is underlined in the first sequence of the film as the image of normativity (a stereotyped family celebrating a birthday, all factors of the normative [gender, age, race, temporality]), materializes behind a restaurant window as the lens comes into focus after initially lingering on a closer plane occupied by a bird model affixed to Ale's cart.[5]

The panning camera then comes to rest behind Ale in the initial plane, equating her thus with the sign of the bird in flight versus the performance of normativity inside the restaurant. Of note in this sequence is the nature of the body coming into being, into focus, as the stylistics emphasize a sort of congealing of the undefined into a specific assemblage, thus materializing bodies within the specific space of the urban. Ale's coming into being is similarly constructed, the camera lingering first on her masculine, manicured hands absentmindedly twirling her hair; the bits and pieces of her, in this case, her hands, channel a performance of difference, of a transgender body, the strongly masculine appendages moving sinuously in sensual vibrations. She then materializes in the frame as a reflection as she steps closer to the window. The viewer thus "meets" the protagonist not through a simple exercise of viewership but through a complex, polysensorial, and multilayered process with several bits and exfoliations that channel potent affective intensities that are then developed in the dénouement.

The third factor builds on the others identified above, namely, the "materiality" of the body as an ephemeral confluence of forces and the emphasis on bits and pieces in the performativity of gender. The visual language in *Mía* is decidedly audile-tactile and imposes—through several repeated techniques, specific cuts, and transitions—a materiality on the image and engages the body (Barker's skin, musculature, and viscera) in decoding it. The aqueous enters our systems of feeling in a particular scene that contrasts the trans body with

10.5. Affective orientations between the normative and difference in Mía *put into motion through the audile tactility of the aqueous. Copyright* INCAA.

a pregnant woman; after all, maternity is at the core of the narrative's development as Ale begins to substitute for Mía in the lives of both the daughter and the husband. In a long take of different shanty folk by the water, characterized by powerful diegetic aquatic sounds and interlaced symphonic music — akin to several scenes in Berger's oeuvre — the camera cuts between Ale and a pregnant woman sitting by the water. We see Ale looking at and are directed by her gaze toward an unnamed woman who is captured in a spotlight that emphasizes her pregnancy. When this shot is compared with the previous image of a looking Ale, it is clear that Ale not only covets but also deifies maternity. Her slow progression into becoming the mother figure brings her and transness (in its plural acceptations) inside the boundaries of acceptability as maternity and the family nucleus are never questioned or decentered; instead, the maternal drive softens the muscled tones of her arms and the squareness of her jaw for Fuentes-León's Latin American audience.

The sequence is striking in that we are oriented toward the pregnant body through the position of Ale; that is, we are initially oriented in a proximal way to her subject position, arguably through the strong audile-tactile qualities of the scene. Therefore, the trans figure is in a position of empathy that not only draws us affectively toward it but also slowly positions the viewer within a trans body wherein we understand the maternal urge. This exercise in orientation, after all, structured the film's opening establishing shot of the trans body on the other side of the window from the performance of normativity in the restaurant; the viewer was also caught looking in and not looking *at* the maricón.

This affective shaping (within the specific economy propelled by New Maricón cinema) informs the male lead in Rodrigo de la Serna's take on art forms that capture difference. In an interview conducted around the time of the film's release, he argued: "If a work of art does not change something in the spectator, then it isn't doing its job" [Si una obra artística no modifica en algo al espectador, no funciona] (Respighi, "Rodrigo de la Serna"). It is easy to glean facets of Ahmed's circulations and surfacings here, though the quotation perhaps gains special force when connected to an earlier statement he made in the same interview: "The rejection of difference, in the majority of cases, is more a visceral reaction than an intellectual one. And that is a social problem that we have to change to be able to grow as a community" [El rechazo al diferente, en la mayoría de los casos, es más una reacción visceral que intelectual. Y ése es un problema social que debemos modificar para poder crecer en comunidad]. Films such as *Mía* and this small but growing corpus of New Maricón cinema not only galvanize and reterritorialize the "visceral" (through the affective as opposed to the scopic) as a point of entry into orienting the individual viewer toward difference but also modify, shape, and *reorient* communal understandings of and approximations to difference.

Films Discussed

CHAPTER 1: *FICHERAS* AND *JOTOS* IN MEXICAN CINEMA

Qué pena tu vida. Dir. Nicolás López. Sin Perdón de Dios, 2010.
El día del compadre. Dir. Carlos Vasallo. Alianza Cinematográfica Mexicana, Esme, 1983.
El lugar sin límites. Dir. Arturo Ripstein. Conacite Dos, 1978.

CHAPTER 2: THE MARICÓN

Doña Herlinda y su hijo. Dir. Jaime Humberto Hermosillo. Clasa Films, 1985.
No se lo digas a nadie. Dir. Francisco Lombardi. Lola Films, 1998.

CHAPTER 3: FINAL NOTES ON A MARICÓN GENRE

Fresa y chocolate. Dir. Tomás Gutiérrez Alea, Juan Carlos Tabío. ICAIC, IMCINE, Miramax, 1993.
Amor libre. Dir. Jaime Humberto Hermosillo. Conacine, 1979.

CHAPTER 4: OUTING *CONTRACORRIENTE*

Contracorriente. Dir. Javier Fuentes-León. Elcalvo, Dynamo, La Cinéfacture, Neue Cameo, 2009.

CHAPTER 5: OUTING *EL ÚLTIMO VERANO DE LA BOYITA*

El último verano de la Boyita. Dir. Julia Solomonoff. Travesía, Domenica, El Deseo, Epicentre, 2009.

CHAPTER 6: XX-

XXY. Dir. Lucía Puenzo. Historias Cinematográficas Cinemania, Wanda Visión, Pyramide, 2007.
El niño pez. Dir. Lucía Puenzo. Historias Cinematográficas Cinemania, Wanda Vision, MK2, 2009.

CHAPTER 7: FINAL NOTES ON OUTING LATIN AMERICA

Antes que anochezca. Dir. Julian Schnabel. El Mar, Grandview, 2000.
Y tu mamá también. Dir. Alfonso Cuarón. Anhelo, Bésame Mucho, 2001.
La mujer de mi hermano. Dir. Ricardo de Montreuil. Cinefarm, Panamax, Pen, Shallow Entertainment, Well Done Ventures, 2005.

CHAPTER 8: *PLAN B*

Plan B. Dir. Marco Berger. Rendez-Vous, Oh My Gómez!, Brainjus, 2009.
Ausente. Dir. Marco Berger. INCAA, Oh My Gómez!, 2011.
Hawaii. Dir. Marco Berger. La Noria Cine, Universidad del Cine, 2013.

CHAPTER 9: ON CHILDREN AND NEOLIBERAL STRUCTURES OF FEELING

Lokas. Dir. Gonzalo Justiniano. Banco Estado, Corfo, Sáhara, 2008.
La otra familia. Dir. Gustavo Loza. Río Negro, 2011.

CHAPTER 10: CLOSING NOTES ON A VERY OPEN FIELD

Mía. Dir. Javier van de Couter. INCAA, 2011.
Azul y no tan rosa. Dir. Miguel Ferrari. Plenilunio, CNAC, Factor RH, Ibermedia, 2012.
Pelo malo. Dir. Mariana Rondón. Artefactos, Hanfgarn & Ufer, Sudaca, 2013.
Feriado. Dir. Diego Araujo. Lunafilms, CEPA, Abaca, 2014.

Notes

INTRODUCTION

1. All translations are mine unless otherwise noted.

2. All were distributed through DVD sales and streaming services on popular Web sites such as Netflix. The Netflix phenomenon in relation to Latin American cinema merits its own study as the site suggests films based on viewing habits. As such, the system's algorithm constantly generates new bodies of films that go beyond film criticism's informal groupings. The influence of Netflix within the distribution, circulation, production, and reception ecosystem of film or, more important, world cinemas is of interest and merits future study.

3. I address these issues in similar films in chapter 9.

4. In situating this early scene in the diner, López points to several episodes from Alberto Fuguet's classic *Mala onda*. The local iteration of McDonald's is a space and assemblage that the novel's protagonist, Matías Vicuña, repeatedly critiques. Other allusions to Fuguet's novel are scattered throughout the three films, including Javier's nocturnal bike ride through Santiago in the first film.

5. Locating these scenes in the fast food restaurant is not fortuitous; instead, it demonstrates the circulation of sex and gender ontologies from the outside in, that is, from Anglo/Euro contexts to Latin America. This idea of a circulation of (civic, juridical) ideas is seen even more clearly in Ferrari's *Azul y no tan rosa* (2012), where it is the protagonist's contact with the foreign that makes homosexuality acceptable (even if there is a staunch critique of Spain as a cultural antecessor that is responsible for the machismo that oppresses nonnormative bodies).

6. Also see Sifuentes-Jáuregui's discussion of Quiroga in *The Avowal of Difference* (11).

7. This statement, though, is tempered by Ruffinelli's insistence that the majority of these films are not *cine gay* but movies *about* gays ("Dime tu sexo," 68). He furthermore includes several documentary films in his corpus that tend to be left at the margins of critical interventions (including my own).

8. I am conscious of the drawbacks of using "Latin American" to describe a cine-

matic corpus that is not necessarily bound together by any underlying ethos, but I follow Deborah Shaw's argument that "*Latin American cinema* is a generalized term . . . clearly used and useful to discuss films from Latin America" (*Contemporary Latin American Cinema*, 3). Alberto Elena and Marina Díaz López add that the terminology should not be viewed as "fossilized and immutable" (*The Cinema*, 10) but as a fluid entity that is useful in framing and situating critical interventions. Also see the works of Paul Schroeder Rodríguez, Dolores Tierney, and Deborah Shaw.

9. The Internet and Web forums have, undoubtedly, participated in this circulation and boom. Websites such as www.cinegay.org are now fundamental to any serious inquiry into the production and reception of homosexual-themed cinema in Latin America. *Azul y no tan rosa* continues to win prizes, including special mention at the 2014 Miami Gay and Lesbian Film Festival.

10. Further analysis of these films is warranted, perhaps framed by the neoliberal structures of feeling that Ignacio Sánchez Prado coins and which I develop in chapter 9.

11. The term "*fichera*" comes from the depiction of women in these films. Related to "sexy comedies" that made their rounds in Europe, plots revolve around so-called easy women. The term "*fichera*" is used to describe women who work in certain bars and clubs as entertainers and company for the male clientele.

12. See Sifuentes-Jáuregui, *The Avowal of Difference* (201).

13. Note my exclusion of the word "queer" in the title of this book, as I believe that none of these films are necessarily Queer (as understood in the Anglo academy and lib movements) but are localized approximations to how gender and body variations permeate otherwise hegemonizing discourses of difference. I am not interested in inserting Latin America within a global queer movement or an academic compartmentalization; neither am I interested in tacking on the modifier "queer" to the title of this book to then explicate and apologize to readers in the know of how the term is a mislabeling of the examined films. Conversely, though, it would be foolish and almost arrogant on my part to suggest that the pages that come are not inflected by Queer studies and theorists, to whom I owe a great debt in informing the language and structures around which I conceive of a New Maricón genre.

14. Important here is the distinction between the new and the original regarding viewership: Maricón films were admittedly powerful to a queer audience, which saw in their characters a position of identification; New films, however, push this drive onto a wider audience as affective cues and contacts provoke identification across orientations.

15. One could also consult Adrián Pérez-Melgosa's *Cinema and Inter-American Relations*, or Ignacio Sánchez Prado's *Screening Neoliberalism* as well. We also cannot forget the anthology *El lenguaje de las emociones*, edited by Mabel Moraña and Ignacio Sánchez Prado, as a foundational text in posing an affective analysis in our field.

16. Aaron, like others I mention below, is inspired by Deleuzian angles into the cinema, which, as Elena del Río affirms, lead us to "reconsider the film image from a non-representational angle" (*Deleuze*, 3). Del Río's study, which I lean on heavily in my development of a theory of New Maricón film, follows Steven Shaviro's underlining of the importance of affect and its circulations, as, he warns, we cannot think of cinema solely in objective terms (*The Cinematic Body*, 10).

17. As Sobchack declares, "When we watch a film, all our senses are mobilized, and often, depending on the particular solicitations of a given film or filmic movement, our naturalized sensory hierarchy and habitual sensual economy are altered and rearranged" (*Carnal Thoughts*, 80).

18. See Elena del Río (*Deleuze*) for differentiation between affect and emotion.

19. As Ahmed argues, "feelings become a form of social presence rather than self-presence . . . emotions create the very effect of the surfaces and boundaries that allow us to distinguish an inside and an outside" (*The Cultural Politics*, 10).

20. As Ahmed reminds us, "emotions work as a form of capital: affect does not reside positively in the sign or commodity, but is produced only as an affect of its circulation" ("Affective Economies," 120).

21. Pedwell (*Affective Relations*, chap. 4) discusses the problematics and nuances of "affective translation" and empathy in a transnational context and continues that critique must take into account the liberal and neoliberal strategy of posing empathy as an "affective balm" to conflict. This warning and its considerations fuel, to some extent, my hesitancy to include Brazilian filmic production in the economy I pose around New Maricón cinema.

22. Such a positioning takes into account the historical precedent of a break with Lusophone genealogies, due simply to earlier channels of distribution favoring common-language features. Whereas the *sexi-comedias* of the *fichera* genre, or the films by the maestros of voluptuousness such as Armando Bó, were easily exportable, moving the borders of the industry beyond the national and into the regional, similar Brazilian features that marketed the nudity of the body in lieu of any aesthetic depth failed to capture a panlinguistic audience. Even today, in an age of torrents, MegaUpload, and other illegal repositories of "ripped" DVDs—a channel we cannot ignore in terms of diffusion—Portuguese-language films are still at a premium on download sites and forums in Latin America. Second, Brazilian cinema enjoyed a relative opening, or *abertura*, in the 1980s that coincided with the onset of political liberalization, akin perhaps to the *destape* and its aftershocks in the Peninsular Spanish context. While sexual variance and libidinal excesses were no strangers to the Brazilian screen (namely, during the era of the *pornochanchadas*, or sexploitation films), the 1980s saw the proliferation of cinema that was graphic and explicit in its handling of sex. Some films were forthright in developing themes that ran counter to any gender-based tropes or projects of normativity and nationalism. A similar stylistic revolution was also energized, where auteurs such as Walter Hugo Khouri, known for their work in the 1960s and 1970s of a cinema that broke social and cultural norms, engaged in an increasingly experimental and intimate aesthetic. As such, the cinema of Brazil has been no stranger to visual and thematic transgression vis-à-vis sex and gender normativity. This, in a parallel line, begs an inquiry into why this cinema was not more influential in restructuring the matrices of heterosexism that gave rise to a Maricón cinema only after having spent years behind the predictable politics of excluding or ostracizing difference. Perhaps this lack of influence is, too, linked to the linguistic limitations of the market and its circulations, compounding itself, then, with my first reason for working solely around Hispanic features and genealogies.

23. Of note, though, is that I am explicitly not building on Deleuzian theories of the cinema but applying his terms and concepts to the analysis of the moving image. This methodology, then, is not congruent with similar studies on Deleuze and Queer cinema, such as Nick Davis's *The Desiring-Image*, that suggest the term "the desiring-image" as a logical follow-up to Deleuze's time-image.

24. The idea of repetition and circulation underlines a primary tenet of Ahmed's economy: "Affect does not reside in an object or sign, but is an effect of the circulation between objects and signs (=the accumulation of affective value). Signs increase in affective value as an effect of the movement between signs: the more signs circulate, the more affective they become" (*The Cultural Politics*, 45). In the case of New Maricón cinema, and the films transitioning toward a proper genre, we can make a case for the aqueous becoming "stickier," gaining affective value as newer films continue to circulate its hapticity as a sign of difference.

25. Miriam Ross's piece on de Montreuil's *La mujer de mi hermano* and *Máncora* furthers this (difficult) dichotomy in two films by the same director that traverse distinct trajectories of the national versus the postnational; see "Latin American Transnational Film."

PART I: MARICÓN CINEMA

1. That is not to say, however, that there are no affective generations or connections made in these films, as all cinema operates on three distinct though at times intertwined coda: the visual, the auditive, and the affective.

2. My theorizing of the Maricón genre builds on Ahmed's understanding of how compulsory heteronormativity shapes bodies. She notes that it also "shapes which bodies one 'can' legitimately approach as would-be lovers and which one cannot. In shaping one's approach to others, compulsory heteronormativity also shapes one's body, *as a congealed history of past approaches*" (*The Cultural Politics*, 145). Of note here are two things. First, the Maricón genre through its stylistics dictates whom the viewer is meant to approach and be attracted to, again taking into consideration a generalized viewership that I account for in the introductory remarks. The genre thus *shapes* the viewer. Second, the historicization of Maricón films and my attempts to delineate a genealogy into the New address the stickiness, or "congealed" nature, of *how* sexual difference is represented. By tracing this path, I aim to concretely demonstrate how a particular aesthetics and praxis of cinema can (re)shape previously fossilized "histories."

3. Ward E. Jones provides a useful point of entry into cinema and ethics, thoughtfully arguing that "a spectator's confrontation with a narrative is ethically significant because the narrative (1) manifests an evaluative *attitude* toward its own characters, events, and context, and (2) encourages the spectator . . . to adopt a similar attitude" (Jones and Vice, *Ethics*, 4, emphasis in the original). In essence, Maricón films posit an almost aloof attitude toward gender difference, engaging the seer through several technical and sensorial techniques that emphasize disconnection. As Jones argues, "attitudes have an *evaluative* component; one's attitude toward something can be said to embody,

in part, one's evaluation of it" (4, original emphasis). This, in part, underlies my thesis vis-à-vis Maricón and New Maricón films, as I argue that the latter evoke in the viewer a quite different evaluation of sex and gender difference from that of their predecessors.

4. By ethics, I am referring to Lisa Downing and Libby Saxton's definition of the term in *Film and Ethics*. Condensing several philosophical strains, they argue that ethics "can perhaps most profitably be seen as a process of questioning rather than as a positivistic exercise of morality . . . It is productive to think about what ethics might *do* and where it may be located, rather than what it *is*" (3, emphasis in the original).

5. Caution, however, must be exercised in making such broad affirmations, as a more holistic approximation to homosexual-themed cinema in Latin America can divide films into two subsets: queer films that actively undertake an Anglo problematization of gender and queerness (most notably in independent Mexican art house films from the 1980s and contemporary cinema from Brazil); and Maricón cinema, which is a featured popular brand of film that does not substantially insert itself within a global sexual politics of emancipation and destabilization, choosing instead to focus on the representation in the public sphere of homosexual characters, stereotypes, and issues.

6. Martínez Expósito uses Mexican cinema as a model for this outline. I develop these categorizations throughout this project, with the first two divisions being located in the *fichera* genre and Maricón cinema, and the final tier more visible in the transition between Maricón and New Maricón films, though the bulk of these are affined with the former category.

7. Lisa Downing warns against such replacement, suggesting that "we might want to be suspicious of the idea that replacing 'negative' with 'positive' representations impacts in any way upon the realities of social attitudes; and be aware that such a sanitizing move can risk further erasing the visibility of deleterious cultural attitudes towards certain groups" (Downing and Saxton, *Film and Ethics*, 37).

8. See Judith Halberstam's discussion of metronormativity and narrative, *In a Queer Time and Place* (36).

9. See Foster's warning against such practices and his reference to Roger Lancaster in regards to accurate polysemantics of sexuality in Latin America (*El ambiente nuestro*, 45).

10. A similar strategy is seen in literary texts by authors such as Pedro Lemebel and Jaime Bayly that sarcastically "categorize" maricones according to their social and libidinal status. Arenas does the same in *Antes que anochezca*—a detail that Schnabel includes in the adaptation when a young Reinaldo screams "¡Maricón!" at a swimmer who refuses his advances. A similar moment of despair and anger in *Fresa y chocolate* (Strawberry and chocolate) triggers Diego to use the slur as an insult.

11. La necesidad de apropiarse, para resemantizar, reciclar, "refuncionar", ciertos conceptos, que en su origen fueron utilizados como medios para separar y condenar, define el dilema que enfrenta todo grupo minoritario al constatar que las nociones que le sirven como elemento cohesivo están permeadas por un saber marcado por la exclusión y el desprecio. La ausencia de términos incontaminados de la red opresora del saber-poder conduce a la apropiación de algunas de estas nociones que se convierten en emblemas de lucha y reconocimiento.

12. See Holly Cashman's study of homophobic slurs and public apologies ("Homophobic Slurs"). She specifically looks at the word "maricón" and the negotiation of its public meaning, referencing El Movimiento de Integración y Liberación Homosexual (Homosexual Integration and Liberation Movement), a Chilean gay rights group.

13. David William Foster's reading of Manrique's *Eminent Maricones* in *El ambiente nuestro* is illuminative and forthright in acknowledging the lack of engagement in any theorizing that is oblivious to local acts of labeling and their corollary notions of self and sexuality. Foster argues that Manrique's reflections portend a dynamic that, though empowering, acquiesces to a specific sociocultural labeling: "The liberal effort to ignore labels of social discrimination and hatred, simply to suspend the process if that somehow were enough to suspend its dreadful effects, cannot, by any victim of the process, be an acceptable strategy" (*El ambiente nuestro*, 47).

CHAPTER 1: *FICHERAS* AND *JOTOS* IN MEXICAN CINEMA

1. Like my usage of the derogatory term "maricón" in my description of LGBT-themed cinema, de la Mora emphasizes that, "although *joto* is a derogatory term, I appropriate it here as a form of what Michel Foucault calls 'reverse' discourse that challenges the oppressive effects of homophobic discourse, emphasizing instead how the category *joto* also enables the production of knowledge of male homosexuality in Mexico" (*Cinemachismo*, 5).

2. See de la Mora, *Cinemachismo* (110).

3. De la Mora theorizes the inclusion of homosexual men in these films as a double edge: "on the one hand, it [the inclusion of homosexual men] makes male homosexuality visible; on the other, this visibility is only possible at the price of stereotyping gay men with negatively coded characteristics, including weakness, frivolity, and narcissism, attributed to 'femininity' by misogynist discourse" (*Cinemachismo*, 112).

4. In a broad study on the representation of homosexuality in Mexican cinema, Michael Schuessler draws connections to European and American genealogies and affirms that the "transformation of the caricaturized and very secondary 'sissy' into a character with truly human dimensions" ("Vestidas," 133) is also the case in Mexican films. His argument bridges our discussion of the *fichera* as a touchstone for the development of more complex representations of difference in Ripstein's *El lugar sin límites*, which will only gain more nuances in New Maricón cinema.

5. I am focusing on this one film, but the reader is invited to apply the analysis to other features within the genre. There are several characteristics that *El día del compadre* shares with its peers, including the use of aerial urban setting shots, closed domestic spaces where gender relations and masculine construction take place, the presence of *jotos* and transvestites as foils for virile masculinity, and the ubiquity of breasts and buttocks, which riles up the characters on and off screen, that is, the public that sat through these films in packed cinema houses.

6. For further reading on the aesthetics and impact of the *científicos* in Mexico, see Robert Mckee Irwin, *Mexican Masculinities*, and my "Rewriting Mexican Masculinity."

Stephen Silverstein's analysis of the same novel ("Ragpickers") also furthers the creation of types, albeit not through a gender optic.

7. Jorge Ruffinelli's notes on the film's making are useful for scholars interested in the relationship between film and text ("Dime tu sexo," 59). He also notes that there was a collective rejection of the film by popular audiences, a detail that gives some historical perspective to the current boom in homosexual-themed films.

8. See Ben Sifuentes-Jáuregui, "Gender without Limits," for an analysis of the erotics of heterosexism and the phenomenology of transvestitism in Donoso's novel.

9. De la Mora's reading of the film in *Cinemachismo* is spot-on and contributes brilliantly to a broader discussion of masculinity in Mexican film. His interpretation of the objectification of the male and his genitalia is illuminative and fundamental to any critical study of masculinities in Mexican film.

10. See Foster's analysis of the erotics of Pancho's relationship with La Manuela and her murder in *Queer Issues* (27–30).

11. Felicity Colman's thesis on framing in relation to the composition and ideology of the image is pertinent to this discussion (*Deleuze and Cinema*, 44–54).

12. We can place Vieira's line of thought into a dialogue with Bill Nichols's study of documentary, specifically in terms of what he calls "axiographics," or "the attempt to explore the implantation of values in the configuration of space, in the constitution of a gaze, and in the relation of observer to observed" (*Representing Reality*, 78).

CHAPTER 2: THE MARICÓN

1. Daniel Balderston notes that *Doña Herlinda* is the last of what "one might call 'gay' films" in Hermosillo's oeuvre ("Excluded Middle," 197). Balderston's analysis advocates a contextualization of the film that breaks with the critiques published in Mexico and Latin America, as he stresses that it is "not a 'coming out' film but a 'bringing back in' film" (198). Such an observation, consistent with a theoretical focus on outing and based, of course, on the particular semantics of the closet, is reiterated in José Quiroga's reading (*Tropics*, 159–160). What must be underlined in these mediations from Latin America is a converse (yet not mutually exclusive of the semantics of the closet) focus on *how* Hermosillo's film differs from previous representations of homosexuality. As Martínez Expósito ("El cine gay mexicano") explicates: "This film put homosexuality in the center of the Mexican family, and not in the brothel or any other sordid space . . . the gay spectator could identify with the scenes, given the difficulty of being a *joto* in Mexican society in the 1980s" [Este film puso la homosexualidad en el centro de la familia mexicana, ya no era el burdel ni el ambiente sórdido . . . el espectador gay se podía identificar con las escenas dado lo difícil que era ser joto en la sociedad mexicana en los ochenta].

2. Foster, in fact, strongly reads against these interpretations when he discusses the film's value vis-à-vis gay liberation and the reinscription of patriarchal values. He argues instead that the film deals less with issues of reinscription or "passing" than with finding ways through the seemingly static and bulletproof fabric of heteronormativity: "Em-

bodying micropolitics at its best, Hermosillo's film constitutes a gesture of resistance that does not wait for the totally revolutionary restructuring of society in order to bring about the fulfillment of personal needs" (*Queer Issues*, 92).

3. Antoine Rodríguez provides a thorough analysis of the technical and narratological aspects of the film. Commenting on the possibility of an ideology behind *Doña Herlinda*, he argues that the film "does not explicitly defend an ideological or theoretical position on gay liberation. Its purpose is another: it exposes what the middle class's sense of decency can only accept in its silence; it shoes how heterosexual norms devour all marginal behavior and deconstructs, as we will see, the themes that unfortunately have fed—and continue to feed—the collective imaginary concerning male homosexual relations" [no reivindica explícitamente una postura ideológica o teórica acerca de la liberación *gay*. Su compromiso es otro: exhibe lo que la decencia clasemediera sólo puede aceptar silenciándolo, muestra cómo las normas heterosexuales engullen toda conducta marginal y deconstruye hábilmente, como veremos, los tópicos que desgraciadamente han nutrido—y siguen nutriendo—el imaginario colectivo acerca de las relaciones homoeróticas masculinas] ("El joto," n.p.).

4. Note here the relative inertness of the aqueous as a space of becoming or an audiovisual mechanism to be mined for its haptic intensity—a prime characteristic of New Maricón cinema which I will develop in part II.

5. A similar thought comes to mind when watching *Y tu mamá también*, as the two protagonists engage in several nude escapades as part of their homosocial relationship, but only cross the line into perceived homoeroticism when drunk and away from the urban referents of heteronormativity. See my concluding remarks in part II.

6. For an analysis of the intertextuality between the poem and the erotics of the film, see Balderston, "Excluded Middle?" (194–195).

7. In analyzing the film's dénouement, Martínez Expósito observes that the final portrait "freezes in the form of a happy family portrait" [se congela en forma de postal de la familia feliz] as a surprising answer "both to the civil ethic of Mexicanness and to the strong literary tradition of tragic endings for homosexual narratives" [tanto a la ética civil de mexicanidad como a la fuerte tradición literaria del final trágico para las historias homosexuales] ("El cine gay mexicano").

8. See Pierre Losson's comparative study of Lombardi's film and Javier Fuentes-León's *Contracorriente*, which I locate and analyze in chapter 4.

9. Joel del Río's article, in particular, is an important intertext to my theorization and development of a Maricón cinema as a distinctive genre with a particular ethical base. He argues that whenever homosexuality is dealt with in recent Latin American films (and here he is largely discussing a boom in the 1980s and the 1990s), it is almost always done from "the comfort of someone who contemplates and comments, without however much complicity, as though the values and conflicts inherent to the species were not similar to all, independent of their sexual orientation" [la comodidad del que contempla y comenta, pero sin evidenciar apenas complicidades, como si los valores y conflictos inherentes a la especie no fueran similares para todos, independientes de su inclinación sexual] ("Identidad gay," 70). This observation follows the thematic and ethical trajectory I argue as being the base of Maricón films, where what is engendered

is an affective othering and subsequent disconnection from the erotics of the image created through specific scopic techniques that situate the lens and the viewer in voyeuristic and subjective positions that inherently objectify the sexual other.

10. See my "Challenging Global Masculinities" on Bayly's *El cojo y el loco* and the dynamics of masculinity in his work.

CHAPTER 3: FINAL NOTES ON A MARICÓN GENRE

1. See Foster (*Queer Issues*, 147–162), and Quiroga ("Homosexualities"; *Tropics*, 131–144) for excellent analyses of the film.

2. Quiroga (*Tropics*) quite naturally follows the analysis of *Fresa y chocolate* with a discussion of Julian Schnabel's *Antes que anochezca*, highlighting how both films represent a tacit appropriation of the gay-lib agenda to expose breaches in the supposed impermeability of the revolutionary government. I leave Schnabel's film for a later section, where I argue that the semantics and praxis of viewing, in particular the gestures in a specific sequence in the middle of the film, locate it best as an intermediary or transitional attempt between the Maricón genre and the aesthetics of New Maricón film. See the conclusion of part II for my analysis of how *Antes que anochezca* encourages a different, more nuanced, and socially compromising ethics of viewership that goes beyond the simple scopics and stereotypes of *Fresa y chocolate*. Quiroga's arrangement of the films, furthermore, adds ammunition to my inclusion of *Antes que anochezca* in the discussion of New Maricón films, given its original language, production costs, and so on.

3. Hermosillo's *Las apariencias engañan* (1978, though not commercially screened until 1983) deserves its own study of the director's portrayal of intersexuality—much ahead of its time—and how desire and identity are deployed over a slippery continuum. This film is perhaps more avant-garde than *Amor libre* but lacks the commercial visibility that is key in developing a thesis of Maricón films, as again, there has been a decidedly more Queer trajectory in Latin American art house films (we can perhaps include *Las apariencias* here).

4. The sea will later be a fundamental sign and house an affective intensity critical to the development of New Maricón cinema. We can almost take the song in *Amor libre* to be a sort of premonition of the films to come in this informal genealogy, speaking solely in aesthetic and poetic terms, of course.

5. See Brad Epps's excellent essay on lesbianism and virtual sexuality, "Virtual Sexuality."

PART II: NEW MARICÓN CINEMA

1. See the works of Luis Zapata, for example. Though there has always been a sense of sexual difference in the cultural production of Latin America (and I am aware of how problematic it is to use such an overarching term), it is not until works by writers such

as Zapata that we see a coalescing of several social factors to create an open sense of gay identity that runs contrary to homosocial narratives.

CHAPTER 4: OUTING *CONTRACORRIENTE*

1. I am using the term "queerying" (instead of the more common "queering"), as queer cinema is both a que(e)ry of heteronormative practices (that is, it demonstrates a posture in line with Anglophone notions of queering) and a self-reflexive questioning of this same gesture toward subject/action/performance/politics. It is a culturally and sociohistorically sensitive process that takes into account the inherent imperialist tendencies of academic theory, yet it is also capable of mining its potential for alternative thought and practice. Essential to any queerying is the severing of a strictly Anglophone gaze, the acknowledgment or adoption of the local, and the axiomatic addition of the "Q" to LGBT, and not strictly as an undifferentiated synonym.

2. See Laura Marks's notes on haptic visuality in the preface to *The Skin of the Film*.

3. Several scenes in *Contracorriente* and the other New Maricón films I mention in this chapter evoke McLuhan's notions of audile-tactile cinema and Deleuze's notes on tactile space, where cinematic spatiality is a dynamic, vibrant, pluritensile, and haptic space, "constituted of resonant intervals, dynamic relationships, and kinetic pressure" (McLuhan and McLuhan, *Laws of Media*, 35).

4. See Deleuze's definition of affect, or how images may hold a specific "quality of a possible sensation, feeling or idea" (*Cinema 1*, 98). Also see Brian Massumi's discussion of affect versus emotion (*Parables*, 20–45).

5. All of this takes for granted, of course, the normalization of a hetero gaze behind the camera.

6. This disjunction between the urban and the rural will be seen in greater detail in *El último verano de la Boyita* and in the cinema of Lucía Puenzo.

7. Performativity here must be considered with the notion of spatiality, a path that José Gil follows and which I comment on in part III.

8. We can infer here a connection to Foster's reading of Marcelo Piñeyro's *Plata quemada*, where the only instances of male frontal nudity occur when El Nene makes love to Giselle, as the film "satisfies amply the conventions of heterosexist coupling" (*Queer Issues*, 137).

9. Of importance in the composition of this shot is Miguel's gaze, which meets the viewer, emphasizing Deleuze's affirmation in *Cinema 1* that "the camera does not simply give us the vision of the character and of her world; it imposes another vision in which the first is transformed and reflected" (74). This shift is primary to any theorization of the New vis-à-vis *Contracorriente*, as the scopophilia generated by Maricón cinema is now met with the queer gaze, thereby transforming the viewer's gaze and experience of the filmic image and its gendered/eroticized bodies.

10. See Alberto Fuguet's introductory remarks to the *McOndo* collection of short stories, "Presentación."

11. These postulations enter into a necessary dialogue with Halberstam's notions of queer spatiality and temporality. See *In a Queer Time* (1–21).

12. I say symbolic, as one can easily argue that the divide between urban and rural cannot be ascribed to any real, succinct spatial designation but is, instead, a broader spectrum of less urbanity.

13. It is useful here to return to José Quiroga's introduction to *Tropics of Desire*, where he examines the cultural specificities of "coming out" and the "closet."

14. Shaviro reminds us that films are "*machines for generating affect*, and for capitalizing upon, or extracting value from, this affect. As such, they are not ideological superstructures, as an older sort of Marxist criticism would have it. Rather, they lie at the very heart of social production, circulation, and distribution" (*Post Cinematic Affect*, 3, emphasis in the original).

15. On a purely subjective note, Rubio's rendition of the song reterritorializes Díaz' song through a globalized (read: popcentric fusion of grunts, synthesizers, and growls that Anglo artists such as Britney Spears and, more recently, Miley Cyrus have semanticized as uncontrollable and animal feminine desire) praxis that leaves most of her young audience unaware of the song's origins. Of note in this version is the concluding overlay of ocean sounds.

16. Even when homosexual sex is shown, we are left with framed bits and pieces.

17. During a presentation to a working group on gender studies, a member of the audience duly noted that *Contracorriente* is "not queer at all!!!" and simply a "gay film." My answer to this observation is that the film's "queerness," or at least its sense of Newness, must be discussed with Maricón cinema because what is novel is not necessarily its thematics, but *how* the nonheteronormative is screened, perceived, and empathized with, as opposed to simply being viewed as a gendered other.

CHAPTER 5: OUTING *EL ÚLTIMO VERANO DE LA BOYITA*

1. *El último verano* is not the first Latin American film to be coproduced by the Almodóvar brothers. See Lucrecia Martel's *La mujer rubia* (also screened as *La mujer sin cabeza* [The headless woman], 2008), *La niña santa* (The holy girl, 2004), and Tamara Acosta's *La fiebre del loco* (Loco fever, 2001).

2. Peidro's and Martin's exercise in locating the film in relation to a global Queer is one of many, bringing us back to Shaviro's rehashing of the Deleuzian axiom that the cinema is always political. From this angle, we can note a positioning of the film within New Argentine cinema (Peidro, "Dos casos," 70), though it breaks with some of the tenets put forth by Gonzalo Aguilar and, as Irma Vélez argues, with its thematic contemporaries (films by Puenzo and Carri). Vélez, furthermore, goes to great lengths to historically situate the diegesis, as she interpolates the events in the film, through an analysis of a background radio broadcast that mentions Ronald Reagan and Nicaragua. Vélez situates us in the 1980s, then, in a referential political period characterized by a Latin America caught up in the process of self-determination while under the Yankee

yoke. This detail, while initially superfluous, brings the film and the viewer back toward a cinema better characterized by its scopophilia; that is, the chronological shift evidenced early on necessitates a critical and aesthetic juxtaposition with filmic antecedents that ignored or refused to explicitly politicize the possibilities and conditions of difference extant in the intersexed body.

3. I reference time here in relation to Halberstam's discussion of a queer temporality that breaks with heteronormative narratives of maturity.

4. Deborah Martin analyzes this facet of change in the movie but focuses on the associations of human-animal to craft a queer reading of the plot. She accurately asserts that "the child's becoming-animal is the site of strategic, subversive reinscriptions of human-animal connections and their relationship to gender" ("Growing Sideways," 34). My reading of the film, however, is structural in the sense that I focus explicitly on Connell's notion of the moment of engagement as a marker of masculinity vis-à-vis the intersexed body.

5. For a complete understanding of the structural matrix of masculinity, see Connell, *Masculinities* (76–81).

6. The formulation stresses, then, that not desiring an approximation to the practices and aesthetics of hegemony implies a feminization of the subject (Connell, *Masculinities,* 78). In *El último verano de la Boyita,* this dynamic gains a primal importance given the young boy's *difference* in relation to the masculine gender structure. The body, as Connell notes, *does* matter, as "the physical sense of maleness and femaleness is central to the cultural interpretation of gender" (*Masculinities,* 52).

7. Deborah Martin accurately notes that "whilst today's rural Argentina cannot be simplistically equated with nineteenth-century gaucho culture, these codes still influence modern rural masculinities" ("Growing Sideways," 43).

8. The film undertakes several outings, including a movement away from the brothel as the space of engagement, which we in effect see in *Antes que anochezca* and *No se lo digas a nadie.* Unlike the action of engagement in these other films, the riding of the horse here does not imply a certain physicality of the subject in contact with the masculine; that is, a penis is not inherently prerequisite, as it is in the scopic context of the brothel, where an erection is paramount to becoming. This detail permits Solomonoff's film to engage and decenter the process of becoming through the intersexed subject who can effectively *probarse como hombre* even without a functional penis.

CHAPTER 6: XX-

1. The rape of Alex is perhaps the most brutal series of images in *XXY.* The framing and angles that Puenzo chooses transmit a boundless affective intensity that only seems to grow with each rewatching. To note in the composition of this action is the gaze of Alex, who distantly looks upwards away from her aggressors and the voyeuristic camera. It is easy to draw comparisons between this image and a similarly violent sequence in Agustí Villaronga's *Pa negre* (2010). In the Catalan film, a time-image shows the rapture and accidental castration of Pitorliua, the young homosexual lover of a local from

a wealthy family. Villaronga deftly uses a slight-of-image to morph the figure's face to that of other persecuted males. While this scene is similar to that in *XXY* in regard to the affective intensity generated, it is even more thought provoking, as the violated body makes direct eye contact with the camera, severing the scopophilic (and thus distanced and objective) gaze. By doing so, the raped queer body in *Pa negre* provokes a paradoxical process in the viewer: on the one hand, Pitorliua's gaze removes the cloak of anonymity and forces a confrontation with the ethics of seeing violence, thereby directly implicating the viewer in the events on screen; on the other, the image portends an empathic point of contact, akin to a gazing Santiago in *Contracorriente,* reorienting the viewer's positionality and subjectivity onto the bits and pieces of the castrated body so that we, too, feel the pain of persecution and the strategies of mob homosocial violence.

2. Santiago Peidro's reading of the credits montage is useful in situating the film within what others have called New Argentine cinema. In reference to the computer-generated plantlike organisms, he notes: "The allegoric presence of these plants attempt a visible portrayal of a supposed mystery, with the idea that it be understood by the majority, it is one of the points that we underlined as being different from the anti-allegoric aesthetic of *New Argentine Cinema*" [la presencia alegórica de estas plantas pretenden dar una imagen visible a un presunto misterio, a fin de que pueda ser entendido por la generalidad, es uno de los puntos que señalábamos como distantes de la estética anti-alegórica del *Nuevo Cine Argentino*] ("Dos casos," 75).

3. In a comparative study of *XXY* and *El último verano de la Boyita,* Deborah Martin argues that both films "contribute significantly to our understanding of the relationship between childhood and adolescence, queerness and intersexuality, and representation. *XXY* makes the intersex body the site of a post-gender, 'no-choice-to-make' utopianisim . . . *El último verano*'s ideal of childhood is Jorgelina's fluidity and propensity for identitarian play" ("Growing Sideways," 44). While both films undertake different trajectories to deal with body-sex-gender disjuncts, it is notable that there are several similarities, including a focus on spatiality, the hapticity of the marine, and the breaking of structures of masculinity that fix bodies into specific roles and relations of power.

4. See Janice Raymond's *The Transsexual Empire,* in which she argues that these surgical interventions are rather conservative practices that emphasize the sexed-gendered binary as the only option. Alex's reluctance to be operated on and Néstor's support of her indecision are really where the film explores aspects of intersexuality that "queery" contemporary notions of surgery as the only way out. By having Alex live as "both," the film posits a delegitimization of medico-ethical practices that affirm gender "disorders." See Sheila Jeffrey's critique of gender identity disorder in the wider spectrum of queer politics (*Unpacking Queer Politics,* 45).

5. Elena del Río's notes on performativity and affect come to mind in the composition of this image and what it triggers not only in the viewer but also in the affective intensity of the subsequent coital images: "bodily forces or affects are thoroughly creative and performative in their ceaseless activity of drawing and redrawing connections with each other through a process of self-modification or becoming. In this sense, the creative activity of bodily forces is ontologically akin to a performance, an action or event that coincides with the generative processes of existence itself. In the gestures

and movements of the performing body, incorporeal forces or affects become concrete expression-events that attest to the body's powers of action and transformation" (*Deleuze*, 3–4).

6. Of note in this line of thinking is the critique posed by Lúcia Nagib in relation to overly subjective criticism that "falls back into its reverse, that is, pure subjectivism through which the films themselves are almost entirely eclipsed" (*World Cinema*, 25). In the reading of these films, I hope to avoid this pitfall by identifying how feeling and the circulation of affect relate to the power and gender structures within the narrative. Hence, in XXY I focus less on the intensities generated by Alex and more on how viewership is linked to the queering of Álvaro vis-à-vis masculinity.

7. The subsequent image of Álvaro furiously masturbating evokes this moment of panic and eroticized tension, where the subject must reaffirm the original association of confusion and disgust when presented with the queer.

8. I am thinking particularly of the almost comedic penetration scene in Jaime Humberto Hermosillo's *Doña Herlinda*, where Ramón penetrates Rodolfo in a similarly enticing yet painful image.

9. Commenting on the vicarious allure of pop stars, Shaviro notes: "they are figures upon which, or within which, many powerful feelings converge; they *conduct* multiplicities of affective flows. At the same time, they are always more than the sum of all the forces that they attract and bring into focus; their allure points us elsewhere, and makes them strangely absent from themselves" (*Post Cinematic Affect*, 10).

10. That being said, it is erroneous to assume a homogeneous "Latin American" viewing audience, as we are well aware that a cosmopolitan theater audience in Mexico City will be different from a rural audience in Paraguay (in terms of politics, exposure to transnational identitarian movements, aesthetics, etc.).

11. I acknowledge that such an assertion vis-à-vis intersexuality is problematic and only regiments bodies within preestablished categories. This is not my intention; rather, I am relaying what the narrative seems to point to and not what we *should* consider Alex to be.

12. See David William Foster's notes on *Danzón* in *Queer Issues* and my earlier comments on Jaime Humberto Hermosillo's *Amor libre* in chapter 3. The reader may be further informed about the dynamics of silence, absence, and feminine desire by Brad Epps's excellent essay on Carme Riera in Paul Julian Smith and Emilie Bergmann's essential *¿Entiendes?*

CHAPTER 7: FINAL NOTES ON OUTING LATIN AMERICA

1. Like the earlier adaptation of *No se lo digas a nadie*, *La mujer de mi hermano* deviates in a few critical ways from the book. The primary difference, which I argue is central to collocating the film within a nascent corpus of the New, is the location of the story in Mexico City, a detail that Bayly leaves hanging for the reader. This location is of particular importance if we consider its genealogical ties to previous Maricón cinema, which has traditionally come from certain national industries (in Mexico, Cuba, and Argentina).

2. See David Gallagher's *Latin American Studies*, for example.

3. This is not the only instance in Schnabel's film that positions the viewer in the desiring node of homoeroticism. In an earlier scene, a young Reinaldo goes to a brothel with a male friend. Like other young men in these narratives of sexual becoming, he contracts the services of a prostitute as a demonstration of his macho virility. In one scene the camera pans upward, showing the two bodies on a bed, with the female fellating a seemingly bored Reinaldo, who is looking up at the ceiling. The viewfinder shifts to a point-of-view shot that zooms in on Reinaldo's young male friend standing in front of a painting of an exotic dancer. The adolescent adopts a casual pose as the camera zeroes in on his mouth and lengthy tongue emphatically gyrating. This image of (some would argue) obscene male-on-male desire has been used before to negatively characterize homosexual males, perhaps most obviously in the superficial character that is Pedro Almodóvar's pedophile dentist in *¿Qué he hecho yo para merecer esto!!* [What have I done to deserve this?]. In *Antes que anochezca*, however, the use of the point-of-view zoom decenters the convention of representation by placing the viewer within the geometry of desire, thereby including him or her intimately in the protagonist's becoming and coming of age.

4. We can go on to argue that they out these touches of Mexicanness to the global sphere. See Nuala Finnegan's "'So What's Mexico Really Like?'" where she discusses the overlaps of the global and the local in Cuarón's usage of these vignettes (29–50).

5. Paul Patton's definition of deterritorialization is illuminative: "the complex movement or process by which something escapes or departs from a given territory, where a territory can be a system of any kind, conceptual, linguistic, social, or affective" (*Deleuzian Concepts*, 52).

6. For more information on the nuances and fragility of homosociality vis-à-vis homoeroticism, see Robert Mckee Irwin's *Mexican Masculinities* and my "Androgyny, Football, and Pedophilia."

PART III: REMATERIALIZING BODIES AND THE URBAN SPACE

1. We similarly cannot assume an end to the Maricón genre. See, for example, Juan Fisher's *Buscando a Miguel* (Looking for Miguel, 2007), which uses the queer body as a secondary theme in a film that is really about contemporary violence and corruption in Colombia. I cannot help but think of Agrado in Pedro Almodóvar's *Todo sobre mi madre* (All about my mother) while watching Sol help Miguel/Raúl after his assault.

2. Though I am focusing on the politics and aesthetics of a particular thematic vein in Latin American cinema, in these pages I do enter into a dialogue with Nigel Thrift's work on affect and spatiality (*Non-Representational Theory*). Specifically, my probing into and theorization of affective economies within the spatial image of the urban address Thrift's identification of a "neglect of the affective register of cities" (171) in critical examinations of urbanity.

3. Primary in this argument is the notion that these spaces created and shaped by New Maricón films are visually characterized by a homogenized naturality, thus permit-

ting free movement from state to state and reception in each. This promotes a brand of Latin American cinema that is untethered to any real localized or national cinema. In terms of social movements, I am referring to both local and pan-national gaylib and proqueer entities and organizations.

4. I here echo Ahmed's comments on the sociality of emotions, specifically, that "emotions create the very surfaces and boundaries that allow all kinds of objects to be delineated. The objects of emotion take shape as effects of circulation" (*The Cultural Politics*, 10).

5. Fernando Blanco and John Petrus seem to agree with this statement in their analysis of Lucía Puenzo's novels and films, though their diachronic analysis treats the politics of recent cultural production in the Southern Cone and not affective intensities. In a thorough aesthetico-political historicization of her work, they argue not only that the films include queer sexualities, but also that such inclusion produces "a destabilization of both the narrative and sexual gender-culture system" [una desestabilización del sistema cultura-género, tanto narrativo como sexual] and that these films "associate themselves with a narrative-imaginary repertoire of revolutionary possibilities from the cultural trans-Andean cultural sphere, to thus access the social-real of their present" [se relacionan con un repertorio narrativo-imaginario de posibilidades revolucionarias en la escena cultural trasandina para acceder a lo real-social de su presente] ("Argentinian Queer Mater," 311).

6. Lauren Berlant underlines this position in her discussion of affect and historicity. She notes that "affective atmospheres are shared, not solitary, and that bodies are continuously busy judging their environments and responding to the atmospheres in which they find themselves" (*Cruel Optimism*, 15).

7. What occurs in this natural *here* is, after all, possible only when juxtaposed to what has been left behind over *there*.

8. I develop Ahmed's understanding of how queer bodies "gather" in spaces (*The Cultural Politics*, 165), albeit here in the representational sphere of the cinema, which translates, I argue, into real gatherings and spaces.

9. Ahmed specifically notes in "Affective Economies" (121): "we could hence ask how the circulation of signs of affect shapes the materialization of collective bodies, for example the 'body of the nation.'"

10. Celestino Deleyto proposes a similar analytics based on the focalizer and the focalized ("Focalisation"). I prefer Nichols's approximation, as it explicates the relationship between the gaze and "values" from polydirectional axes and positions; Deleyto focuses solely on ideology.

CHAPTER 8: *PLAN B*

1. Berger has used the popular North American Kickstarter portal to fund several films. In Mexico, services such as fondeadora.mx are behind his efforts to fund films such as *Velociraptor* (2014).

2. Foster argues that the film is "probably the best queer Latin American film since Jaime Humberto Hermosillo's *Doña Herlinda y su hijo*" ("Plan B," 256).

3. I use "humane" to describe a sign or practice that encourages an affective alignment between human subjects and viewers. In regard to the idea of "real loci," I am referring to both domestic and transnational economies of affect.

4. The argument here is a source for Elena del Río's later theorization of bits and pieces as separate corporeal loci of production and identification, a detail evident in the opening images of *Ausente*. Of further importance in this sequence from *Ausente* is a consciousness of the gaze and seeing, which, I argue, Berger attempts to reveal and then sever through the use of strategic audile-tactile images and montages in both films. In *Plan B*, this is evident in the final montage of establishing shots prior to Pablo and Bruno reuniting and rushing to the bedroom. Returning to Gil vis-à-vis del Río, it is pertinent to note that the former's conception of exfoliations takes as axiom the "dialectic between parts and the whole, and between container and contents, for which the referent is the image of the body proper" (*Metamorphoses*, 122). This suggests that the exfoliative process is keyed by a conditional whole, even if this comes as a particular possibility from the notion of the body as bits.

5. Another possibility is the coast of Mar del Plata in the Buenos Aires province, though that would suggest that Pablo and Bruno had driven a good 400 kilometers. I must thank my colleague and friend Paco Brignole and his various relatives, who know the region inside and out, for their keen sense of location.

6. The literature on cinematic sound theory is surprisingly scarce. Chapter 3 of Lastra's *Sound Technology and the American Cinema* provides a thorough bibliographic review. He notes that Hollywood cinema typically moved to the legible-inscription model, which favors narrative over an attempt to spatialize the viewer within the diegesis. Cinema thus can be "read" instead of "sensed," so to speak. Also see Edward Branigan's "Sound and Epistemology in Film" and Rick Altman's *Sound Theory, Sound Practice*.

7. My ideas about sound in this film (and perhaps in all New Maricón cinema) can be read in reaction to Altman's critique of sound-focused scholarship, which tends to "treat cinema as a series of self-contained texts, divorced from material existence and the three-dimensional world . . . heavily marked by semiotics" (*Sound Theory*, 1). What I aim to elucidate in the analysis of *Plan B* is that sound is intra and extra spatial, fostering a relationship that not only places the viewer within the film but also engenders extrafilmic processes, which, in the case of New Maricón films, is an economy of positive affect.

8. The scene, however, continues into an extended conversation between the two men that is similar to the absurdist dialogue in the camera scene. Using jump cuts to emphasize the lack of a linear temporality in Track B, the scene shows them talking about random hypotheticals and stories unrelated to the broader narrative in Track A.

9. Ahmed's discussion of orientation and a "queer phenomenology" may prove useful in conceptualizing the orientation of the viewer, in axiographical terms, to the erotics of the narrative and the urban in *Plan B*. Namely, "the concept of 'orientation'

allows us to rethink the phenomenality of space—that is, how space is dependent on bodily inhabitance" (*Queer Phenomenology*, 6).

10. The use of this device in the film is a sly wink at the scopic regime of gender-representation so prevalent in Latin American cinema. Though there is no explicit "cutting" of the gaze, I argue that Berger centers the View-Master as a critique of the regime of representation over affect, an important dialectic that he mints in *Plan B* and *Ausente* to focus on how the cinema can engage viewership through polysensorial techniques and mediums.

11. The title is a reference to the natural not only as a setting but also as an ideational field and semiotic topology that evokes an exotic and paradisiacal experience. The film could have been called *Bali*, *Copacabana*, or *Boracay*, all commercially exploited sites that are located in a global mapping of such places that are easily transmutable—they represent not a particular space but a generalizable experience. This, we must remember, is a key component of (traditional) New Maricón cinema's outing of gender difference, as its characters are easily assimilated and identifiable across borders.

12. *Hawaii*, however, is unlike the director's previous films in that full-frontal male nudity is shown. Formerly a taboo in Latin American and Western commercial cinema, the penis has made an appearance in several recent films, including *Contracorriente* and *Buscando a Miguel*.

CHAPTER 9: ON CHILDREN AND NEOLIBERAL STRUCTURES OF FEELING

1. Perriam (*Spanish Queer Cinema*) thoroughly goes over this facet of Spanish sexuality, which I half-jokingly reference as "to be gay or not to be gay," that is, men and women who are not exclusively heterosexual but who also refuse the labeling that comes with being "gay," undoubtedly, a friction point of identity politics.

2. Note here, of course, that not all of Latin America has become neoliberal, and that those states that have adopted said policies have done so to varying degrees.

3. Sánchez Prado channels several well-known postulates on childhood and adolescence to argue that it is "not a single trope but rather a set of clearly differentiated discourses that together interweave a network of symbolic imaginaries, which underlies the social ideology of identity formation" ("Innocence," 129).

4. Karen Lury emphasizes this point by arguing that critics should analyze children and childhood as "*being* rather than becoming" ("The Child," 309, emphasis in the original).

5. I am grateful for the many conversations I have held with María del Carmen Caña Jiménez about the "writing" of childhood in narrative. Her insights into this process and product in recent Colombian and Spanish texts inspired my probing into these child characters in these films. Her examination of childhood, memory, and the politics of the contemporary is a critical entryway into any further investigation in this area ("The Writing of Childhood," 22–88).

6. We can include here the typical prison fag, who, ironically, sexually services other inmates while also being a focal point of their homophobia. The same character sings "We're going to the beach" [Vamos a la playa] in jail, evoking the aqueous as an endpoint of liberation, akin in a sense to Roberto Cobo's minstrel in *Amor libre*.

7. A similar placement is carried out in *No sé si cortarme las venas o dejármelas largas*, where the gay protagonist's living space is decorated with a large map of Mexico overlaid with neon lighting that spells out "You are here." The English text superimposed on the Mexican topography signals this linkage between the cultural sphere of the North and the local, neoliberal practice of the diegesis.

8. See my "Malaysia *Boleh*," where I further develop this idea of neoliberal space.

9. Note here that I am *not* arguing in favor of traditional machismo and its intrinsic homophobia but of being open to local manifestations of gender expression and equity. The gay agenda, for example, in its most essentialist vein stereotypes gay behavior, undoubtedly always placing gays as members of the "creative class" that the neoliberal condition panders to.

10. The movie includes narrative forays into the drug trade, human trafficking, social violence, discourses on race, and so on. As such, the gay couple (and not homosexuality) is a mechanism for probing several facets of contemporary *mexicanidad*.

11. The film showcases several types of marriages — man-man, woman-woman, man-woman — which all go through issues related to procreation and child rearing. There is thus no questioning of marriage, or of its condition as social structure and guarantee of the sacrosanctity of sex as procreative and not libidinal.

12. The Mexican church did not view the film favorably. In an official communiqué to the press, Cardinal Francisco Robles Ortega argued: "We can see, without a doubt, a circumstance wherein a couple of men or women have the custody of a child. But to call that an alternative family, which is a different kind of family, confuses people and offends those who truly are working toward the plan for humanity" [Se puede dar el hecho, no se niega eso, se puede dar una circunstancia en donde una pareja de hombres o dos mujeres tengan la custodia de un pequeño. Pero llamar que eso es una familia alternativa, que es otro tipo de familia, eso confunde y eso también ofende a quienes verdaderamente luchan por llevar a cabo el plan de la humanidad] (Zambrano, "Crítica iglesia").

13. My framing and study of these child images follows Jyotsna Kapur and Keith B. Wagner's suggestion that "the cinema can offer a lens into both the political economy of the neoliberal project and its far-reaching implications on culture" (*Neoliberalism*, 4), the latter point underlined by the negotiation of said Child with the emancipatory politics of a cinema that accepts homoeroticism as a sign of cultural modernity and an (often neglected) axiom of the creative class.

14. My words should not be interpreted as an affront to LGBT movements and agendas but as an acknowledgment of their point of enunciation. I do not, furthermore, favor any particular local politics of sex and gender but leave the door open to heterogeneous perspectives and discourses on desire and identity.

1. See Subero's excellent analysis of Hernández' oeuvre, *Queer Masculinities*. I see these films more as art house projects than commercial or festival-circuit offerings.

2. Marialy Rivas's *Joven y alocada* (Young and wild, 2012, Chile) can be included in this grouping.

3. I would even dare to further that the film won the Goya for this reason only and not because of any aesthetic or cinematographic value.

4. The characters that populate the shantytown call themselves maricones with their husbands and boyfriends. Note the lexicon of sex and gender here and the problematization of the orientation of these husbands and boyfriends, evoking the dialectic of the *mayate*, the *joto*, and the *cochón* that Irwin, Foster, and others have identified. Such a naming emphatically locates the film within a specific sociocultural matrix and resists any calls to a global queer filmmaking by maintaining the limits and contours of the maricón.

5. Note here the use of simplistic metaphors of liberation or difference, akin to the symbols used in XXY and *El último verano*. Also note the fixation on reading as a point of entry into gender and gender becoming, problematized here and in *El último verano* and acknowledged, though in a dogmatic fashion, in *La otra familia*.

Works Cited

Aaron, Michele. "New Queer Cinema: An Introduction." *New Queer Cinema: A Critical Reader.* Ed. Michele Aaron. New Brunswick, NJ: Rutgers University Press, 2004.

———. *Spectatorship: The Power of Looking On.* London: Wallflower, 2007.

Aguilar, Gonzalo. *Otros mundos.* Buenos Aires: Santiago Arcos, 2006.

Ahmed, Sara. "Affective Economies." *Social Text* 22.2 (2004): 117–139.

———. *The Cultural Politics of Emotion.* New York: Routledge, 2004.

———. *Queer Phenomenology: Orientations, Objects, Others.* Durham, NC: Duke University Press, 2006.

Altman, Rick, ed. *Sound Theory, Sound Practice.* New York: Routledge, 1992.

Amicola, José. "Las huellas del presente y el mundo queer de XXY." *Lectures du Genre: … dans la Production Culturelle Espagnole et Hispano-Américaine* 6 (2009).

Araujo, Diego. "Nota del director." *Feriado* (2014).

Ayala Blanco, Jorge. *La búsqueda del cine mexicano.* Mexico City: Posada, 1974.

Badiou, Alain. *Cinema.* Trans. Susan Spitzer. Cambridge: Polity, 2013.

Balderston, Daniel. "Excluded Middle? Bisexuality in *Doña Herlinda y su hijo.*" *Sex and Sexuality in Latin America.* Ed. Daniel Balderston and Donna J. Guy, 190–199. New York: New York University Press, 1997.

Barker, Jennifer. *The Tactile Eye: Touch and Cinematic Experience.* Berkeley: University of California Press, 2009.

Berlant, Lauren. *Cruel Optimism.* Durham, NC: Duke University Press, 2011.

———. "Unfeeling Kerry." *Theory and Event* 8.2 (2005).

Beugnet, Martine. *Cinema and Sensation: French Film and the Art of Transgression.* Carbondale: Southern Illinois University Press, 2007.

Blanco, Fernando, and John Petrus. "*Argentinian Queer Mater.* Del *Bildungsroman* urbano a la *Road Movie* rural: Infancia y juventud post-corralito en la obra de Lucía Puenzo." *Revista de Crítica Literaria Latinoamericana* 73 (2011): 307–331.

Branigan, Edward. "Sound and Epistemology in Film." *Journal of Aesthetics and Art Criticism* 47.4 (1989): 311–324.

Brioso, Jorge, and Óscar Montero. "Apuntes para una crítica 'invertida.'" *Ciberletras* 2 (2000).

Bryce Echenique, Alfredo. *El huerto de mi amada*. Barcelona: Planeta, 2002.

Caña Jiménez, María del Carmen. "The Writing of Childhood: Between Nation and Political Discourse." PhD diss., University of North Carolina–Chapel Hill, 2011.

Cashman, Holly. "Homophobic Slurs and Public Apologies: The Discursive Struggle over Fag/*Maricón* in Public Discourse." *Multilingua* 31.1 (2012): 55–81.

Castillo, Debra, and Andrés Lema-Hincapié. *Despite All Adversities: Spanish-American Queer Cinema*. Albany: State University of New York Press, 2015.

Chow, Rey. *The Protestant Ethnic and the Spirit of Capitalism*. New York: Columbia University Press, 2002.

Clavel, Ana. *Cuerpo náufrago*. Mexico City: Alfaguara, 2005.

Colman, Felicity. *Deleuze and Cinema: The Film Concepts*. Oxford: Berg, 2011.

Connell, Raewyn. *Masculinities*. Berkeley: University of California Press, 1995.

Cristóbal, Ramiro. *La homosexualidad en el cine*. Madrid: Ediciones Irreverentes, 2010.

Davis, Nick. *The Desiring-Image: Gilles Deleuze and Contemporary Queer Cinema*. New York: Oxford University Press, 2013.

de la Mora, Sergio. *Cinemachismo: Masculinities and Sexuality in Mexican Film*. Austin: University of Texas Press, 2006.

Deleuze, Gilles. *Cinema 1: The Movement Image*. Trans. Hugh Tomlinson and Barbara Habberjam. London: Athlone, 1988.

———, and Félix Guattari. *A Thousand Plateaus: Capitalism and Schizophrenia*. Trans. Brian Massumi. Minneapolis: University of Minnesota Press, 1987.

Deleyto, Celestino. "Focalisation in Film Narrative." *Atlantis* 13.1–2 (1991): 159–177.

del Río, Elena. *Deleuze and the Cinemas of Performance: Powers of Affection*. Edinburgh: Edinburgh University Press, 2008.

Del Río, Joel. "Identidad gay en el cine latinoamericano reciente: Estrategias de omisión, circunloquio y lugares comunes." *Temas* 41–42 (2000): 61–70.

Downing, Lisa, and Libby Saxton. *Film and Ethics: Foreclosed Encounters*. New York: Routledge, 2010.

Edelman, Lee. *No Future: Queer Theory and the Death Drive*. Durham, NC: Duke University Press, 2004.

Elena, Alberto, and Marina Díaz López, eds. *The Cinema of Latin America*. London: Wallflower, 2003.

Epps, Brad. "Virtual Sexuality: Lesbianism, Loss, and Deliverance in Carme Riera's 'Te deix amor la mar com a penyora.'" *¿Entiendes?: Queer Readings, Hispanic Writings*. Ed. Paul Julian Smith and Emilie Bergmann, 317–345. Durham, NC: Duke University Press, 1995.

Féral, Josette. "Performance and Theatricality: The Subject Demystified." *Modern Drama* 25.1 (1982): 170–181.

Finnegan, Nuala. "'So What's Mexico Really Like?': Framing the Local, Negotiating the Global in Alfonso Cuarón's *Y tu mamá también*." *Contemporary Latin American Cinema: Breaking Into the Global Market*. Ed. Deborah Shaw, 29–50. Lanham, MD: Rowman and Littlefield, 2007.

Florida, Richard. *The Rise of the Creative Class: Revisited, Revised, and Expanded*. New York: Basic Books, 2012.

Foster, David William. *El ambiente nuestro: Chicano/Latino Homoerotic Writing*. Tempe, AZ: Bilingual Press, 2006.

———. *Ensayos sobre culturas homoeróticas latinoamericanas*. Ciudad Juárez, Mex.: Universidad Autónoma de Ciudad Juárez, 2009.

———. "Plan B." *Chasqui* 42.1 (2013): 256–257.

———. *Queer Issues in Contemporary Latin American Cinema*. Austin: University of Texas Press, 2003.

Foucault, Michel. "Questions on Geography." *Power/Knowledge: Selected Interviews and Other Writings, 1972–1977*. Ed. Colin Gordon, 63–77. New York: Pantheon, 1980.

Fuentes-León, Javier. "Interview with Javier Fuentes-León, Director of *Contracorriente*." *Latin America News Dispatch*, 8 February 2010; Web, 16 September 2012.

Fuguet, Alberto. *Mala onda*. Buenos Aires: Planeta, 1991.

———. "Presentación." *McOndo*. Ed. Alberto Fuguet and Sergio Gómez, 9–18. Barcelona: Grijalbo Mondadori, 1996.

Gallagher, David. *Latin American Studies: Critiques of Contemporary Cinema, Literatures, Politics and Revolution*. Palo Alto, CA: Academica, 2009.

Galt, Rosalind. "Default Cinema: Queering Economic Crisis in Argentina and Beyond." *Screen* 54.1 (2013): 62–81.

García Canclini, Néstor. *Consumers and Citizens: Globalization and Multicultural Conflicts*. Minneapolis: University of Minnesota Press, 2001.

Gil, José. *Metamorphoses of the Body*. Minneapolis: University of Minnesota Press, 1998.

González Espitia, Juan Carlos. *On the Dark Side of the Archive: Nation and Literature in Spanish America at the Turn of the Century*. Lewisburg, PA: Bucknell University Press, 2010.

Grønstad, Asbjørn. *Screening the Unwatchable: Spaces of Negation in Post-Millennial Art Cinema*. New York: Palgrave Macmillan, 2012.

Halberstam, Judith. *In a Queer Time and Place: Transgender Bodies, Subcultural Lives*. New York: New York University Press, 2005.

Irwin, Robert Mckee. *Mexican Masculinities*. Minneapolis: University of Minnesota Press, 2003.

Jeffrey, Sheila. *Unpacking Queer Politics*. Malden, UK: Polity, 2003.

Jones, Ward E., and Samantha Vice, eds. *Ethics at the Cinema*. New York: Oxford University Press, 2011.

Kapur, Jyotsna, and Keith B. Wagner, eds. *Neoliberalism and Global Cinema: Capital, Culture, and Marxist Critique*. New York: Routledge, 2011.

Lastra, James. *Sound Technology and the American Cinema: Perception, Representation, Modernity*. New York: Columbia University Press, 2000.

Lewis, Vek. *Crossing Sex and Gender in Latin America*. New York: Palgrave Macmillan, 2010.

Losson, Pierre. "De *No se lo digas a nadie* a *Contracorriente*: Representaciones de la homosexualidad en el cine peruano contemporáneo." *El Ojo Que Piensa* 5 (2012).

Lury, Karen. "The Child in Film and Television: Introduction." *Screen* 46.3 (2005): 307–315.

Manrique, Jaime. *Eminent Maricones: Arenas, Lorca, Puig, and Me*. Madison: University of Wisconsin Press, 1999.

Marks, Laura. *The Skin of the Film: Intercultural Cinema, Embodiment, and the Senses*. Durham, NC: Duke University Press, 2000.

———. "Video Haptics and Erotics." *Screen* 39.4 (1998): 331–348.

Martin, Deborah. "Growing Sideways in Argentine Cinema: Lucía Puenzo's XXY and Julia Solomonoff's *El último verano de la Boyita*." *Journal of Romance Studies* 13.1 (2013): 34–48.

Martin, Jean-Clet. "Of Images and Worlds: Towards a Geology of the Cinema." *The Brain Is the Screen: Deleuze and the Philosophy of Cinema*. Ed. Gregory Flaxman, 61–85. Minneapolis: University of Minnesota Press, 2000.

Martínez Expósito, Alfredo. "El cine gay mexicano y su impacto en la imagen nacional." *Amerika* 7 (2012).

Massumi, Brian. *Parables for the Virtual: Movement, Affect, Sensation*. Durham, NC: Duke University Press, 2002.

McLuhan, Marshall, and Eric McLuhan. *Laws of Media: The New Science*. Toronto: University of Toronto Press, 1988.

Molina, Eduardo. "Pantalla grande / *La otra familia*." *El Norte*, Web, 25 March 2011.

Moraña, Mabel. "Postscríptum: El afecto en la caja de herramientas." *El lenguaje de las emociones: Afecto y cultura en América Latina*. Ed. Mabel Moraña and Ignacio Sánchez Prado. Madrid: Iberoamericana Verveurt, 2012.

Mosse, George. *The Image of Man: The Creation of Modern Masculinity*. New York: Oxford University Press, 1996.

Nabal Aragón, Eduardo. *El marica, la bruja y el armario: Misoginia gay y homofobia femenina en el cine*. Barcelona/Madrid: Editorial Egales, 2007.

Nagib, Lúcia. *World Cinema and the Ethics of Realism*. New York: Continuum, 2011.

Nichols, Bill. *Representing Reality: Issues and Concepts in Documentary*. Bloomington: Indiana University Press, 1991.

Palencia, Leandro. *La pantalla visible: El cine queer en 33 películas*. Madrid: Editorial Popular, 2011.

Patton, Paul. *Deleuzian Concepts: Philosophy, Colonization, Politics*. Stanford: Stanford University Press, 2010.

Pedwell, Carolyn. *Affective Relations: The Transnational Politics of Empathy*. Basingstoke, UK: Palgrave Macmillan, 2014.

Peidro, Santiago. "Dos casos de intersexualidad en el cine argentino." *Sexualidad, Salud y Sociedad* 14 (2013): 66–90.

Pérez-Melgosa, Adrián. *Cinema and Inter-American Relations: Tracking Transnational Affect*. New York: Routledge, 2012.

Perriam, Christopher. *Spanish Queer Cinema*. Edinburgh: Edinburgh University Press, 2013.

Podalsky, Laura. *The Politics of Affect and Emotion in Contemporary Latin American Cinema: Argentina, Brazil, Cuba, and Mexico*. New York: Palgrave Macmillan, 2011.

Pratt, Mary Louise. "Arts of the Contact Zone." *Profession*, 33–40. New York: Modern Language Association, 1991.

Quiroga, José. "Homosexualities in the Tropic of Revolution." *Sex and Sexuality in Latin America*. Ed. Daniel Balderston and Donna J. Guy, 133–151. New York: New York University Press, 1997.

———. *Tropics of Desire: Interventions from Queer Latino America*. New York: New York University Press, 2000.

Raymond, Janice. *The Transsexual Empire: The Making of the She-Male*. Boston: Beacon, 1979.

Reber, Dierdra. "Headless Capitalism: Affect as Free-Market Episteme." *Differences* 23.1 (2012): 62–100.

———."La afectividad epistémica: El sentimiento como conocimiento en *El secreto de sus ojos* y *La mujer sin cabeza*." *El lenguaje de las emociones: Afecto y cultura en América Latina*. Ed. Mabel Moraña and Ignacio Sánchez Prado, 93–108. Madrid: Iberoamericana Verveurt, 2012.

Respighi, Emanuel. "Rodrigo de la Serna, actor ideal para papeles intensos." *Página 12*, Web, 12 November 2011.

Rich, Ruby. *New Queer Cinema: The Director's Cut*. Durham, NC: Duke University Press, 2013.

Rocha, Carolina, and Georgia Seminet, eds. *Representing History, Class and Gender in Latin America: Children and Adolescents in Film*. New York: Palgrave Macmillan, 2012.

Rodríguez, Antoine. "El joto decente se casa: Normas y margen en *Doña Herlinda y su hijo* de Jaime Humberto Hermosillo." *Razón y Palabra* 46 (2005).

Ross, Miriam. "Latin American Transnational Film: Divergent Practice in Ricardo de Montreuil's *La mujer de mi hermano* and *Máncora*." *Transnational Cinemas* 3.2 (2012): 193–209.

Ruffinelli, Jorge. "Dime tu sexo y te diré quién eres: La diversidad sexual en el cine latinoamericano." *Cinémas d'Amérique Latine* 18 (2010): 58–71.

Russo, Vito. *The Celluloid Closet: Homosexuality in the Movies*. New York: Harper & Row, 1987.

Sánchez Prado, Ignacio. "Innocence Interrupted: Neoliberalism and the End of Childhood in Recent Mexican Cinema." *Representing History, Class and Gender in Latin America: Children and Adolescents in Film*. Ed. Carolina Rocha and Georgia Seminet, 117–135. New York: Palgrave Macmillan, 2012.

———. "Regimes of Affect: Love and Class in Mexican Neoliberal Cinema." *Journal of Popular Romance Studies* 4.1 (2014).

———. *Screening Neoliberalism: Transforming Mexican Cinema, 1988–2012*. Nashville: Vanderbilt University Press, 2014.

Schroeder Rodríguez, Paul. "After New Latin American Cinema." *Cinema Journal* 51.2 (2012): 87–112.

Schuessler, Michael. "*Vestidas, Locas, Mayates* and *Machos*: History and Homosexuality in Mexican Cinema." *Chasqui* 34 (2005): 132–144.

Schulz-Cruz, Bernard. *Imágenes gay en el cine mexicano: Tres décadas de joterio 1970–1999*. Mexico City: Fontamara, 2008.

Shaviro, Steven. *The Cinematic Body*. Minneapolis: University of Minnesota Press, 1993.

———. *Post Cinematic Affect*. Winchester, UK: Zero, 2010.

Shaw, Deborah, ed. *Contemporary Latin American Cinema: Breaking into the Global Market*. Lanham, MD: Rowman & Littlefield, 2007.

———. "Sex, Texts and Money, Funding and Latin American Queer Cinema: The Cases of Martel's *La niña santa* and Puenzo's XXY." *Transnational Cinemas* 4.2 (2013): 165–184.

———. "(Trans)National Images and Cinematic Spaces: The Cases of Alfonso Cuarón's *Y tu mamá también* (2001) and Carlos Reygadas' *Japón* (2002)." *Iberoamericana* 11.44 (2011): 117–131.

Sifuentes-Jáuregui, Ben. *The Avowal of Difference: Queer Latino American Narratives*. Albany: State University of New York Press, 2014.

———. "Gender without Limits: Transvestism and Subjectivity in *El lugar sin límites*." *Sex and Sexuality in Latin America*. Ed. Daniel Balderston and Donna J. Guy, 44–61. New York: New York University Press, 1997.

Silverstein, Stephen. "Ragpickers of Modernity: Cristina Rivera Garza's *Nadie me verá llorar* and Walter Benjamin's *Theses on the Philosophy of History*." *Revista de Estudios Hispánicos* 47.3 (2013): 533–559.

Smith, Murray. *Engaging Characters*. Oxford: Clarendon, 1995.

Sobchack, Vivian. *Carnal Thoughts: Embodiment and Moving Image Culture*. Berkeley: University of California Press, 2004.

Soja, Edward W. *Postmetropolis: Critical Studies of Cities and Regions*. Oxford: Blackwell, 2000.

Straayer, Chris. *Deviant Eyes, Deviant Bodies: Sexual Re-Orientations in Film and Video*. New York: Columbia University Press, 1996.

Subero, Gustavo. "The Different *Caminos* of Latino Homosexuality in Francisco J. Lombardi's *No se lo digas a nadie*." *Hispanic Cinemas* 2–3 (2005): 189–204.

———. *Queer Masculinities in Latin American Cinema: Male Bodies and Narrative Representations*. London: I. B. Tauris, 2014.

Thrift, Nigel. *Non-Representational Theory: Space, Politics, Affect*. New York: Routledge, 2008.

Tierney, Dolores. "The Link between Funding and Text: Transnational Aesthetics in Lucrecia Martel's Films." *Mediático*, Web, 23 March 2014.

Tongson, Karen. *Relocations: Queer Suburban Imaginaries*. New York: New York University Press, 2011.

Vélez, Irma. "Género y 'performance' en las escenas de lectura de *El último verano de la Boyita* de Julia Solomonoff." *Lectures du Genre* 8 (2011): 11–27. Web.

Venkatesh, Vinodh. "Rewriting Mexican Masculinity: Stereotyping/Countertyping Men in Cristina Rivera Garza's *Nadie me verá llorar*." *Explicación de Textos Literarios* 36.1–2 (2008): 52–64.

———. "Androgyny, Football, and Pedophilia: Rearticulating Mexican Masculinities in the Works of Enrique Serna." *Revista de Literatura Mexicana Contemporánea* 49 (2011): 25–36.

———. "Challenging Global Masculinities in Jaime Bayly's *El cojo y el loco*." *Revista Canadiense de Estudios Hispánicos* 37.2 (2013): 279–296.

———. "Malaysia *Boleh*?: Carles Casajuana and the Demythification of Neoliberal Space." *Romance Notes* 54.1 (2014): 67–73.

Vieira, Patricia. *Seeing Politics Otherwise: Vision in Latin American and Iberian Fiction*. Toronto: University of Toronto Press, 2011.

Walkerdine, Valerie. "Communal Beingness and Affect: An Exploration of Trauma in an Ex-Industrial Community." *Body and Society* 16 (2010): 91–116.

Waugh, Thomas. *The Fruit Machine: Twenty Years of Writings on Queer Cinema*. Durham, NC: Duke University Press, 2000.

Wetherell, Margaret. *Affect and Emotion: A New Social Science Understanding*. London: SAGE, 2012.

Zambrano, Lourdes. "Crítica Iglesia a *La otra familia*." *El Norte*, Web, 27 March 2011.

Zamostny, Jeffrey. "Constructing Ethical Attention in Lucía Puenzo's XXY: Cinematic Strategy, Intersubjectivity, and Intersexuality." *Representing History, Class and Gender in Spain and Latin America: Children and Adolescents in Film*. Ed. Carolina Rocha and Georgia Seminet, 189–204. New York: Palgrave Macmillan, 2012.

Zapata, Luis. *Las aventuras, desventuras y sueños de Adonis García: El vampiro de la Colonia Roma*. Mexico City: Grijalbo, 1979.

Index

Lightning Source UK Ltd.
Milton Keynes UK
UKOW01n1332080916

282552UK00001B/44/P

9 781477 310144